Logistic Regression – Inside-Out

Logistic Regression – Inside-Out

© 2017, Jeffrey S. Strickland

ISBN 978-1-365-81915-5

Lulu

Printed in the United States of America

Acknowledgements

The author would like to thank colleague Paul Dalen for his challenging questions; and Cameron Warren for his desire to learn. Working with them over the past several years has validated the concepts presented herein.

A special thanks to Dr. Bob Simmonds, who mentored me as a senior operations research analyst.

Preface

I spend most of my days building logistic regression models and have been doing so for five years. It was once new to me, even though I had been building different kinds of models prior to this short era. Combat models, missile models, drone models, space launch models, and reliability models were my forte. But I became quite adept at building logistic regression models. I learned a few things along the way and I thought I would share them with you.

If you have a yes or no question, then you can probably answer it with a logistic regression model. I have used neural network models as well, but customers are not comfortable with them and they usually just confirm the validity of the logistic regression model. I will tell you all about them in the main body of the text. For now, I would like to suggest the best way to use the text.

First, I will start with the last. If you are reading this in grayscale, start with the index. There I have highlighted in bold-gray all the R programming libraries and functions beneath the headings R-Packages and R-Functions, respectively. I have done this with SAS Procedures as well. Definitions and Examples are listed in the same manner. In this manner, you can find and return to and example or command with ease.

Second, there are "call-outs" throughout the text with background information. There are also a few definitions and two theorems. These appear in the index as well.

Chapter 1 may seem trivial on the surface and you might be tempted to skip it. However, it defines and frames the "business case," "modeling objective," and "target variable definition." These are important processes in industry and without them you could build a very good model, which turns out to be the wrong model. Chapter 1 also introduces an example that is a "thread" throughout the text. Each chapter includes examples, but the thread appears as well.

Work through the R Studio and SAS Studio examples, as practice will make perfect. All the steps are here in living color and each one is designed to teach a certain aspect of our subject.

The chapter flow from Chapter 1 through Chapter 9 is sequential and would be best if treated that way. Chapters 10 through 12 are optional. Chapters 13 – 14 contain fully worked examples in SAS Studio and R Studio.

Though we review generalized linear models and multinomial logistic regression, we are in the world of binary responses. These are problems with only two choices, like "yes" or "no", "one" or "zero".

Data files and solutions can be downloaded from my website at http://www.humalytica.com/Downloads/. When I teach this material, I do not use PowerPoint slides. Instead I teach using R-Studio and SAS Studio, primarily. So, I do not produce and supply PPT decks. However, I do provide all the code used in the text.

There might be a typo are two. I do not pay an editor, which keeps the cost of my books down in the "affordable space." If you find an error, please send me a note so I can publish an errata.

I hope you have fun using the text and learning more about logistic regression.

jeff@humalytica.com

Table of Contents

x

1. Introduction

What is Logistic Regression?

I am often asked if logistic regression is a *machine learning algorithm*. I say that it is not, for I can formulate it mathematically and solve it using *matrix equations*, for example. Its solution is derived deterministically, and estimation is performed mathematically, through optimization methods.

The *logit link function*, which we will discuss thoroughly in later chapters, is the mathematical expression,

$$logit = e^{\beta_0 + \beta_1 x},$$

a nonlinear, exponential equation, and we transform it to a linear equation by applying the *natural logarithm*,

$$g(x) = \ln\frac{F(x)}{1 - F(x)} = \beta_0 + \beta_1 x,$$

which we'll also explain in detail later. It only "learns" what we tell it to learn!

This book is about mathematical probability and statistics. Machine learning has its place in our world of analytics, but not here. Here we find mathematical modeling, probability, and statistics. Here I will take you on a journey into the art and science of predictive modeling using logistic regression, inside-and-out.

When do we use Logistic Regression?

Logistic regression is most appropriate when the dependent variable (target variable) has two possible outcomes (binary). Will customers respond to an offer or unsubscribe, will the enemy fight or flee, will subjects respond to treatment or grow ill, will livestock live or die? Yes or no? One or zero?

I have applied logistic regression mostly in the financial services industry (FSI) and personal and casualty insurance industry (PCII). On a more limited scale, I have applied it in combat modeling. However, I have seen it applied in fields such as pharmaceutical research, medical research, sociological research, and more. Yes or no? Black or White? There are no shades of gray here, other than that which we call "modeler judgment". But the answer we derive is ultimately yes or no. If we want what lies between, there are other methods and other models.

There is an extension of logistic regression, used when the dependent variable is nominal with more than two levels. It is called multinomial logistic regression, but we will not cover it in the same detail we cover logistic regression. Yet, we will show an example using R later on.

An Application of Logistic Regression

Consider a bank analytics team that wants to predict product acquisition from a marketing campaign with external data they have available to them. The bank marketing team currently places customers on an outbound call list based on website visits. A larger percentage of these will not apply for a new credit card and the cost of calling them with an offer is constrained.

The analytics team has told the marketing team that a predictive model would help them focus their outbound calls on a select number of customers who will have a high propensity to apply for a credit card with an offer. The analytics team has selected data from the bank's customer database that might be predictive, and have identified the target variable as customers who will respond to an offer or not. The target variable, response (RESP) is binary (yes or no) and can be modeled using logistic regression. This dataset is publically available for research. The details are described in (Moro, Laureano, & Cortez, 2011). Please include this citation if you plan to use this database. I have two additional variables, married_people (yes/no) and manual_labor (yes/no).

The variables the team identified include:

- job (categorical)
- marital (categorical)
- education (categorical)
- age (numeric)

- balance (numeric, bank deposit balance)
- homeowner (1=yes or 0=no)
- loans (1=yes or 0=no)
- In_default (1=yes or 0=no)
- day (numeric, day of the month)
- contact month (ordinal, 1-12)
- duration (numeric)
- campaign (categorical)
- pdays (numeric – elapsed days since previous campaign)
- previous (1=yes or 0=no)
- poutcome (numeric – outcome of previous campaign
- married_people (1=yes or 0=no)
- manual_labor (1=yes or 0=no)

We will follow this example throughout the text as we apply different steps in the modeling process, from variable reduction, to variable transformation, to model fitting and predictor coefficient estimation, to goodness-of-fit, to model performance and stability, and model scoring. While traveling this path, we will unravel the key concepts of predictive modeling using logistic regression.

Although we will look at numerous examples, the bank credit card marketing model will be a thread to follow, and we begin with defining the problem.

The Business Case

The business case is a statement (or question) put forth by the business unit expressing the challenge and desired outcome (and hopefully one or more metrics). It does not contain the jargon of analytics, except perhaps the metric(s) by which to measure successful solution to the problem. Suppose the bank (perhaps with our help) poses the following.

Business Case: Outbound calling is an expensive venture with a insignificant return on the investment (ROI) due to customer response rate being low. The bank wants to identify customers to place on the outbound call list that are more likely to respond to a credit card offer, while minimizing the cost of a marketing campaign and maximizing the profit.

The Modeling Objective

The modeling objective is formulated by the analytics team, but is written in language that the business unit understands in order to assess whether or not it ties directly to the business case. Our analytics team poses the following objective:

Modeling Objecting: The team will construct a model that will predict which customers have a greater (or lesser) likelihood to accept a credit card offer upon receiving an outbound call, while minimizing the cost of calls and maximizing ROI.

Note that the business unit used the metric, profit, in stating its business case, while the analytics team used ROI. This difference would be reconciled, which might result in changing the business case or modeling objective, or a determination that the two are equivalent.

Target Variable Identification

This step may seem trivial (hopefully it is), but getting this incorrect will result in building the wrong model. The target variable is the dependent variable with a *desired outcome*, agreed upon by all the stakeholders. The analytics team poses the following.

Target Variable: The target variable, in this instance, is whether or not an individual customer will respond to a credit card offer, and the desired outcome is "yes", the customer will respond positively.

Technically speaking, the desired outcome is producing a call list that will result in a higher rate of credit card applications compared to calling all customers who visit the website. But the desired outcome for the target variable is "yes" versus "no," making this a binary (two) response model. Consequentially, the team chooses logistic regression for the predictive model, abbreviating the target variable as RESP as follows:

$$RESP = \begin{cases} 1, & \text{if a customer accepts the credit card offer} \\ 0, & \text{if the customer does not accept the offer} \end{cases}$$

This sets the stage for our more detail discussion of logistic regression.

Summary

In this chapter we have looked at logistic regression at a very high level, including the logit link function, which we will see at a deeper level in subsequent chapters. We have also looked at the kinds of situations that we my apply logistic regression to, which is comprised primarily of binary response problems, i.e. "Yes"/"No" problems. We have also looked at what constitutes a business case, modeling objective, target variable and desired outcome. We will use these concepts throughout the remainder of our study of logistic regression.

Exercises

1. Suppose the bank, presented in this chapter, decided to market deposit accounts rather than credit cards.
   a. Prepare a new business case.
   b. Draft a modeling objective that supports the business case.
   c. Determine that target variable and desired outcome.

2. SafeLife Insurance Company traditionally covers middle-class white collar working families but is beginning to lose market share. They now want to market a term life product to a new sector, which includes Millennials with families comprised of a spouse and at least one child, based on internal market analysis. They want the analytics team to develop a model that will help them determine the likelihood that members of the target audience will acquire the term life product. As the analytics team lead, you have been tasked to formulate a business case and associated model objective for a business unit review.
   a. Draft a business case statement.
   b. Would a logistic regression model support the business case? If so, write a modeling objective that support the business case.
   c. Identify the target variable and desired outcome.

2. Regression from the Inside-Out

What is Regression?
Regression is a statistical measure used in the financial services industry (FSI), healthcare and medical industry (HMI) and other industries that attempts to determine the strength of the relationship between one dependent variable (usually denoted by Y) and a series of other changing variables (known as independent variables).

In retail marketing, regression helps analysts to value the effectiveness of marketing campaigns on customers. For instance, the marketing analyst can explore the effect of sending multiple, frequent campaign email offers on customer churn (opt-out) rates. In the FSI, regression can aid financial and investment managers to price assets and understand the relationships between variables, such as commodity values and the stocks of companies dealing in those commodities.

There are several types of regression including Linear Regression, Log-Linear Regression, Multi-Linear (or Multiple-Linear) Regression, Ridge Regression, Logistic Regression (our subject), and others, including regression dependent methods, like regression trees.

What is Linear Regression?
Linear regression measures the liner relationship between a dependent variable (the outcome of interest) and one (simple) or more (multiple) independent (predictor) variables. Simple linear (or just linear) regression examines the relations shown below:

$$Y = a + bX + e \qquad (2.1)$$

But we usually use Greek letters for the lower-case factors, like

$$Y = \alpha + \beta X + \varepsilon \qquad (2.2)$$

Where Y is the dependent variable, α is the intercept, β is the slope of the line, X is the predictor (independent) variable and ε is the regression residual or noise.

Multiple linear regression uses the following expression

$$Y = \alpha + \beta_i X_i + \beta_i X_i + \cdots + \beta_i X_n + \varepsilon \qquad (2.3)$$

Where the β_i's are the coefficients of the independent X_i's or predictors.

What is the Least Squares Method?

The least squares method is a practice of using mathematical matrices in regression analysis to finds the line of best fit for a dataset. This form of analysis provides a graphical demonstration of the relationship between the data points, where each point represents the relationship between a known independent variable and an unknown dependent variable.

The least squares method relies on a particular matrix that must be invertible in order for a unique solution to exist. The matrix in question solves the matrix equation $Y = X\vec{\beta} + \vec{e}$ (in the simple linear regression it reduces to $Y = \alpha + \beta X + \varepsilon$). The solution to the problem depends on the matrix $(X^T X)^{-1}$, which represents the inverse of the matrix X multiplied by its transpose X^T. When the matrix inverse does not exist, we call this a singular matrix, $X^T X$. When it is singular, there is either no solution to our matrix equation or there are infinitely many (no unique solution). This is analogous to division by zero in arithmetic.

The possibility of a singular matrix $X^T X$ has resulted in other forms of regression analysis. In fact, linear regression solves very few real life problems!

What is Ridge Regression?

Ridge regression is an attempt to introduce a term in the matrix equation that allows $X^T X$ to be invertible for any situation. The term is denoted λ, the Greek letter "lambda." In this case, the matrix $(X^T X + \lambda I)$ is invertible (the value of λ is specifically selected through mathematical operations so that an inverse exists). When $\lambda = 0$, we are back to linear regression and $X^T X$, which is rarely invertible in practice.

What is Log-Linear Regression?

To avoid some confusion, we will not fully describe log-linear regression. Suffice it to say that it is different from logistic regression, which also involves logarithms. Although different, some log-linear models correspond to logit models (the link function of logistic regression. It is best used when there is no clear relationship between the dependent variable and its predictors.

What is Logistic Regression?

Some things in our world are black and white; other are shades of gray. At other times we may see black and white with shades of gray between. At any rate, when our outcome is either black or white, come or go, or yes or no, we say that our choice is binary. More formally the set of outcomes with only two possibilities is a binary set.

Whenever our outcome is binary, we use binary logistic regression. *Binary Logistic Regression* is a special type of regression where binary response variable is related to a set of explanatory variables. The explanatory variable can be discrete or continuous, interval or ordinal, numerical or categorical.

Some situations that might call for binary logistic regression appear in many industries. In the healthcare and medical industry (HMI) the effects of treatment with a new drug could be positive or negative. In the financial services industry (FSI) an investment may have an outcome of growth or decay. In the insurance industry a claim could be approved or disapproved. In marketing, a product add could lead to acquisition or not acquired. In retail, a product could be in inventory or not in inventory.

Flat or Air-up

One of my wife's cousins related the story of his teaching experience in an inner-city public school where he asked students to name two types of tires. One response he received was, "flat and aired-up." That would imply that the maintenance status of your tiers is a binary outcome also.

What is Different about Logistic Regression?

Recall in linear regression, the expected values $E[Y]$'s of the response variable are modeled based on combination of values taken by the predictors. In logistic regression Probability $P[Y]$'s or Odds of the response taking a particular value is modeled based on combination of values taken by the predictors. Like regression, we make a clear distinction between a response variable and one or more predictor or explanatory variables.

As an example, suppose we want a model for marketing a credit card product, denoted C, with two explanatory variables, bank deposit amount last month (D) and number of automobiles in a household (A). To show that log-linear models are not exactly the same as logit models, the log-linear models describe the joint distribution of all three variables, $p(C, D, A)$, whereas the logit models describe only the conditional distribution of A given D and S, $p(A|D)$ and $p(A|S)$.

Regression Example using SAS Studio

The *Lahman Baseball Database* (Lahman, 2015) is comprised of 24 tables containing detailed data on baseball from its inception to 2015. I have formed an additional table by using the Batting table and joining it with the Master table (for years in the league) and the Salaries table (to compute Log(salary)). The Lahman Baseball Database can be downloaded at http://www.baseball1.com. The modified file can be downloaded at http://www.humalytica.com/Downloads.

Suppose you want to investigate whether you can model the players' salaries for the 2015 season based on batting statistics for the previous season and lifetime batting performance.

Salary is a numeric (continuous) variable and we believe it is a linear combination of batting statistics like number of hits and bases on balls. Since the variation in salaries is much greater for higher salaries, it is appropriate to apply a log transformation for this analysis. The following SAS Studio code starts the analysis:

```
ODS graphics on;
PROC REG DATA=baseball;
   ID name team league;
```

```
MODEL logSalary = no_1b no_2b no_3b no_hits no_home no_runs
no_bb no_rbi years;
RUN;
```

Figures 3-1 to 3-4 show the default output produced by PROC REG. The number of observations table shows that 59 observations are excluded because they have missing values for at least one of the variables used in the analysis. The analysis of variance and parameter estimates tables provide details about the fitted model.

The REG Procedure

Model: BASEBALL MODEL

Dependent Variable: logSalary

Number of Observations Read	1054
Number of Observations Used	1053
Number of Observations with Missing Values	1

Figure 3-1. Model information

		Analysis of Variance			
Source	DF	Sum of Squares	Mean Square	F Value	Pr > F
Model	8	5.50958	0.68870	2.33	0.0176
Error	1044	308.47111	0.29547		
Corrected Total	1052	313.98069			

Figure 3-2. Analysis of Variance

Root MSE	0.54357	R-Square	0.0175
Dependent Mean	6.27130	Adj R-Sq	0.0100
Coeff Var	8.66761		

Figure 3-3. Fit Statistics

Recall the multiple linear regression model,

$$Y = \alpha + \beta_i X_i + \beta_i X_i + \cdots + \beta_i X_n + \varepsilon.$$

11

Our model will look like

$$\log(\text{Salary}) = \text{intercept} + \beta_i \text{no\_hits} + \beta_i \text{no\_rbis} + \cdots + \beta_i \text{years} + \text{error}$$

and the parameter estimates for the coefficients, $\beta_1, \beta_2, \cdots, \beta_n$, are shown in Figure 3-4.

Parameter Estimates					
Variable	DF	Parameter Estimate	Standard Error	t Value	Pr > |t|
Intercept	1	6.17306	0.03362	183.60	<.0001
no_1b	B	-0.01353	0.00728	-1.86	0.0634
no_2b	B	-0.01801	0.00987	-1.83	0.0683
no_3b	B	0.00329	0.01626	0.20	0.8396
no_hits	B	0.01668	0.00821	2.03	0.0425
no_home	0	0	.	.	.
no_runs	1	-0.00648	0.00411	-1.57	0.1156
no_bb	1	0.00282	0.00228	1.24	0.2157
no_rbi	1	-0.00517	0.00384	-1.35	0.1781
years	1	0.01264	0.00452	2.79	0.0053

Figure 3-4. Parameter estimates

Summary

In this chapter we have observed several different kinds of regression and learned when they are appropriate to use. We have also worked an example using SAS Studio.

Exercises

1. Apple is planning to release a new iPhone to a test area and want to determine if people in the test area will purchase a phone. Use the Catalog.csv to build a logistic regression model using SAS Studio.

a. Download catalog.csv from
   http://www.humalytica.com/downloads.html.
b. Upload catalog.csv to your SAS Studio directory
c. Double-click on the catalog.csv icon in SAS Studio and
   run the code it generates.

2. Using as SAS Studio and cadata.csv, build a generalized linear
   model that will predict future home values in this California
   district.
   a. What is the proper link function for this problem?
   b. What is the target variable for this model?
   c. What is the desired outcome?
   d. Which variable are significant?

3. Generalized Linear Models from the Inside- Out

The generalized linear model (GLIM or GLM)—not to be confused with general linear model or generalized least squares—is a flexible generalization of ordinary linear regression that allows for response variables that have error distribution models other than a normal distribution. The GLM generalizes the linear regression we looked at in Chapter 2 by allowing the linear model to be related to the response variable via a link function and by allowing the magnitude of the variance of each measurement to be a function of its predicted value.

GLMs were formulated by John Nelder and Robert Wedderburn as a way of unifying various other statistical models, including linear regression, logistic regression and Poisson regression (Nelder & Wedderburn, 1989). They proposed an iteratively reweighted least squares method for *maximum likelihood estimation* of the model parameters. Maximum-likelihood estimation remains popular and is the default method on many statistical computing packages. Other approaches, including Bayesian approaches and least squares fits to variance stabilized responses, have been developed.

In these models, the response variable y_i is assumed to follow an exponential family of distributions with mean μ_i, which is assumed to be some (often nonlinear) function of $x_i^T \beta$. Some would call these "nonlinear" because μ_i is often a nonlinear function of the covariates, but McCullagh and Nelder consider them to be linear, because the covariates affect the distribution of y_i only through the linear combination $x_i^T \beta$. (McCullagh & Nelder, 1989)   The first widely used software package for fitting these models was called GLIM. Because of this program, "GLIM" became a well-accepted abbreviation for generalized linear models, as opposed to "GLM" which often is used for general linear models. Today, GLIM's are fit by many packages, including SAS Studio Proc Genmod and R function glm().

The generalized linear models are a broad class of models that include linear regression, ANOVA, Poisson regression, log-linear models etc. The Table 3-1 provides a good summary of GLMs.

Table 3-1. GLM Class of Models

Model	Random	Link	Systematic
Linear Regression	Normal	Identity	Continuous
ANOVA	Normal	Identity	Categorical
ANCOVA	Normal	Identity	Mixed
Logistic Regression	Binomial	Logit	Mixed
Log-Linear	Poisson	Log	Categorical
Poisson Regression	Poisson	Log	Mixed
Multinomial response	Multinomial	Generalized Logit	Mixed

Intuition

Ordinary linear regression predicts the expected value of a given unknown quantity (the response variable, a random variable) as a linear combination of a set of observed values (predictors). This implies that a constant change in a predictor leads to a constant change in the response variable (i.e. a linear-response model). This is appropriate when the response variable has a normal distribution (intuitively, when a response variable can vary essentially indefinitely in either direction with no fixed "zero value", or more generally for any quantity that only varies by a relatively small amount, e.g. human heights).

However, these assumptions are inappropriate for many types of response variables. For example, in many cases when the response variable must be positive and can vary over a wide scale, constant input changes lead to geometrically varying rather than constantly varying output changes. As an example, a model that predicts that each decrease in 10 degrees Fahrenheit leads to 1,000 fewer people going to a given beach is unlikely to generalize well over both small beaches (e.g. those where the expected attendance was 50 at the lower temperature) and large beaches (e.g. those where the expected attendance was 10,000 at the lower temperature). An even worse problem is that, since the model also implies that a drop in 10 degrees leads 1,000 fewer people going to a given beach, a beach whose expected attendance was 50 at the higher temperature would now be predicted to have the impossible attendance value of -950. Logically, a more realistic model would instead predict a constant rate of increased beach attendance (e.g. an increase in 10 degrees leads to a doubling in beach attendance, and a drop in 10 degrees leads to a halving in attendance). Such a model is termed an exponential-response model (or log-linear model, since the logarithm of the response is predicted to vary linearly).

Similarly, a model that predicts a probability of making a yes/no choice (a Bernoulli variable) is even less suitable as a linear-response model, since probabilities are bounded on both ends (they must be between 0 and 1). Imagine, for example, a model that predicts the likelihood of a given person going to the beach as a function of temperature. A reasonable model might predict, for example, that a change in 10 degrees makes a person two times more or less likely to go to the beach. But what does "twice as likely" mean in terms of a probability? It cannot literally mean to double the probability value (e.g. 50% becomes 100%, 75% becomes 150%, etc.). Rather, it is the odds that are doubling: from 2:1 odds, to 4:1 odds, to 8:1 odds, etc. Such a model is a log-odds model.

Generalized linear models cover all these situations by allowing for response variables that have arbitrary distributions (rather than simply normal distributions), and for an arbitrary function of the response variable (the link function) to vary linearly with the predicted values (rather than assuming that the response itself must vary linearly). For example, the case above of predicted number of beach attendees would typically be modeled with a Poisson distribution and a log link, while the case of predicted probability of beach attendance would typically be modeled with a Bernoulli distribution (or binomial distribution, depending on exactly how the problem is phrased) and a log-odds (or logit) link function.

Overview

In a generalized linear model (GLM), each outcome of the dependent variables, Y, is assumed to be generated from a particular distribution in the exponential family, a large range of probability distributions that includes the normal, binomial, Poisson and gamma distributions, among others. The mean, μ, of the distribution depends on the independent variables, X, through:

$$E(Y) = \mu = g^{-1}(X\beta), \qquad (3.1)$$

where $E(Y)$ is the expected value of Y; $X\beta$ is the linear predictor, a linear combination of unknown parameters, β; and g is the link function.

In this framework, the variance is typically a function, V, of the mean:

$$\text{Var}(Y) = V(\mu) = V\big(g^{-1}(X\beta)\big). \qquad (3.2)$$

It is convenient if V follows from the exponential family distribution, but it may simply be that the variance is a function of the predicted value.

The unknown parameters, β, are typically estimated with maximum likelihood, maximum quasi-likelihood, or Bayesian techniques.

Model components
The GLM consists of three elements:

1. Random Component – A probability distribution (i.e., the binomial distribution for binary logistic regression) of the response variable (Y) from the exponential family.

2. Systematic Component - A linear predictor $\eta = X\beta$, specifies the explanatory variables $(X_1, X_2, \dots X_k)$ in the model, more specifically their linear combination in creating the so called linear predictor;

3. A link function η or $g(\mu)$ such that $E(Y) = \mu = g - 1(\eta)$, which specifies the link between random and systematic components. It says how the expected value of the response relates to the linear predictor of explanatory variables. For example, $\eta = logit(\pi)$ is used for logistic regression.

Probability distribution
The overdispersed exponential family of distributions is a generalization of the exponential family and exponential dispersion model of

distributions and includes those probability distributions, parameterized by $\boldsymbol{\theta}$ and τ, whose density functions f (or probability mass functions) can be expressed in the form

$$f_Y(\boldsymbol{y}|\boldsymbol{\theta}, \tau) = h(\boldsymbol{y}, \tau)\exp\left(\frac{\boldsymbol{b}(\boldsymbol{\theta})\boldsymbol{T}(\boldsymbol{y}) - A(\boldsymbol{\theta})}{d(\tau)}\right).$$

(3.3)

In Equation (3.3), we typically know τ, called the *dispersion parameter*, and it is usually related to the variance of the distribution. We also know the functions $h(\boldsymbol{y}, \tau)$, $\boldsymbol{b}(\boldsymbol{\theta})$, $\boldsymbol{T}(\boldsymbol{y})$, $A(\boldsymbol{\theta})$, and $d(\tau)$. Many common distributions are in this family.

For scalar Y and θ, this reduces to

$$f_Y(y|\theta, \tau) = h(y, \tau)\exp\left(\frac{b(\theta)T(y) - A(\theta)}{d(\tau)}\right).$$

(3.4)

In Equation (3.4), $\boldsymbol{\theta}$ is related to the mean of the distribution. If $\boldsymbol{b}(\boldsymbol{\theta})$ is the identity function, then we say the distribution is in *canonical form* (or natural form). Note that we can convert any distribution to canonical form by rewriting $\boldsymbol{\theta}$ as $\boldsymbol{\theta}'$ and then applying the transformation $\boldsymbol{\theta} = \boldsymbol{b}(\boldsymbol{\theta}')$. It is always possible to convert $A(\boldsymbol{\theta})$ in terms of the new parameterization, even if $\boldsymbol{b}(\boldsymbol{\theta}')$ is not a one-to-one function. If, in addition, $T(y)$ is the identity and τ is known, then we call $\boldsymbol{\theta}$ the canonical parameter (or natural parameter) and is related to the mean through

$$\mu = E(Y) = \nabla A(\boldsymbol{\theta}). \tag{3.5a}$$

For scalar Y and θ, this reduces to

$$\mu = E(Y) = A'^{(\theta)}. \tag{3.5b}$$

Under this scenario, the variance of the distribution can be shown to be (McCullagh & Nelder, 1989)

$$\text{Var}(\boldsymbol{Y}) = \nabla\nabla^T A(\boldsymbol{\theta})d(\tau). \tag{3.6a}$$

For scalar Y and θ, this reduces to

$$\text{Var}(Y) = A''(\theta)d(\tau). \qquad (3.6b)$$

Linear predictor

The linear predictor is the quantity which incorporates the information about the independent variables into the model. The symbol η (Greek "eta") denotes a linear predictor. It is related to the expected value of the data (thus, "predictor") through the link function.

We express η as linear combinations (thus, "linear") of unknown parameters $\boldsymbol{\beta}$ (a matrix of coefficients). We represent the coefficients of the linear combination as the matrix of independent variables, $\boldsymbol{X}$. Then, we can express η as

$$\eta = \boldsymbol{X\beta}. \qquad (3.7)$$

Link function

The *link function* provides the relationship between the linear predictor and the mean of the distribution function. There are many commonly used link functions, and their choice can be somewhat arbitrary. We should always try to match the domain of the link function to the range of the distribution function's mean.

When using a distribution function with a canonical parameter θ, the canonical link function is the function that expresses θ in terms of μ, i.e. $\theta = b(\mu)$. For the most common distributions, the mean μ is one of the parameters in the standard form of the distribution's density function. Then $b(\mu)$ is the function as defined above that maps the density function into its canonical form. When using the canonical link function, $b(\mu) = \theta = \boldsymbol{X\beta}$, which allows $\boldsymbol{X}^{\mathsf{T}}\boldsymbol{Y}$ to be a sufficient statistic for $\boldsymbol{\beta}$.

Table 3-2 shows several exponential-family distributions in common use and the data they are typically used for, along with the canonical link functions and their inverses (sometimes referred to as the mean function, as done here).

In the cases of the exponential and gamma distributions, the domain of the canonical link function is not the same as the permitted range of the mean. In particular, the linear predictor may be negative, which would give an impossible negative mean. When maximizing the likelihood, precautions must be taken to avoid this. An alternative is to use a noncanonical link function.

Table 3-2. Common distributions with typical uses and canonical link functions

Distribution	Support of distribution	Typical uses	Link name	Link function	Mean function
Normal	real: $(-\infty, \infty)$	Linear-response data	Identity	$X\beta = \mu$	$\mu = X\beta$
Exponential Gamma	real: $(0, \infty)$	Exponential-response data, scale parameters	Inverse	$X\beta = -\mu^{-1}$	$\mu = (-X\beta)^{-1}$
Inverse Gaussian	real: $(0, \infty)$		Inverse squared	$X\beta = -\mu^{-2}$	$\mu = (-X\beta)^{-1/2}$
Poisson	integer: $(0, \infty)$	count of occurrences in fixed amount of time/space	Log	$X\beta = \ln(\mu)$	$\mu = e^{X\beta}$
Bernoulli	integer: $[0,1]$	outcome of single yes/no occurrence	Logit	$X\beta = \ln\left(\dfrac{\mu}{1-\mu}\right)$	$\mu = \dfrac{1}{1 + e^{X\beta}}$
Binomial	integer: $[0, N]$	count of # of "yes" occurrences out of N yes/no occurrences			
Categorical	integer: $[0, K]$ K-vector of integer: $[0,1]$, where exactly one element in the vector has the value 1	outcome of single K-way occurrence			
Multinomial	K-vector of $[0, N]$	count of occurrences of different types (1 .. K) out of N total K-way occurrences			

Note also that in the case of the Bernoulli, binomial, categorical and multinomial distributions, the support of the distributions is not the same type of data as the parameter being predicted. In all of these cases, the predicted parameter is one or more probabilities, i.e. real numbers in the range [0,1]. The resulting model is known as logistic regression (or multinomial logistic regression in the case that K-way rather than binary values are being predicted).

For the Bernoulli and binomial distributions, the parameter is a single probability, indicating the likelihood of occurrence of a single event. The Bernoulli still satisfies the basic condition of the generalized linear model in that, even though a single outcome will always be either 0 or 1, the expected value will nonetheless be a real-valued probability, i.e. the probability of occurrence of a "yes" (or 1) outcome. Similarly, in a binomial distribution, the expected value is Np, i.e. the expected proportion of "yes" outcomes will be the probability to be predicted.

For categorical and multinomial distributions, the parameter to be predicted is a K-vector of probabilities, with the further restriction that all probabilities must add up to 1. Each probability indicates the likelihood of occurrence of one of the K possible values. For the multinomial distribution, and for the vector form of the categorical distribution, the expected values of the elements of the vector can be related to the predicted probabilities similarly to the binomial and Bernoulli distributions.

Assumptions:

- The data $Y_1, Y_2, \dots, Y_n$ are independently distributed, i.e., cases are independent.
- The dependent variable Y_i does NOT need to be normally distributed, but it typically assumes a distribution from an exponential family (e.g. binomial, Poisson, multinomial, normal,...)
- GLM does NOT assume a linear relationship between the dependent variable and the independent variables, but it does assume linear relationship between the transformed response in terms of the link function and the explanatory variables; e.g., for binary logistic regression $logit(\pi) = \beta_0 + \beta_X$.
- Independent (explanatory) variables can be even the power terms or some other nonlinear transformations of the original independent variables.
- The homogeneity of variance does NOT need to be satisfied. In fact, it is not even possible in many cases given the model structure, and overdispersion (when the observed variance is larger than what the model assumes) maybe present.
- Errors need to be independent but NOT normally distributed.
- It uses maximum likelihood estimation (MLE) rather than ordinary

least squares (OLS) to estimate the parameters, and thus relies on large-sample approximations.

Goodness-of-fit measures rely on sufficiently large samples, where a heuristic rule is that not more than 20% of the expected cells counts are less than 5.

GLM using R
We will use the *Longley* dataset, a macroeconomic data set which provides a well-known example for a *highly collinear regression*.

Viewing the Data
A data frame with seven economic variables, observed yearly from 1947 to 1962 (n=16).

- GNP.deflator: GNP implicit price deflator (1954=100)
- GNP: Gross National Product
- Unemployed: number of unemployed
- Armed.Forces: number of people in the armed forces
- Population: 'noninstitutionalized' population ≥ 14 years of age
- Year: the year (time)
- Employed: number of people employed

Figure 3-1 shows a matrix plot of the independent variables. We made the plot using:

```
require(stats)
require(graphics)
plot(longley)
```

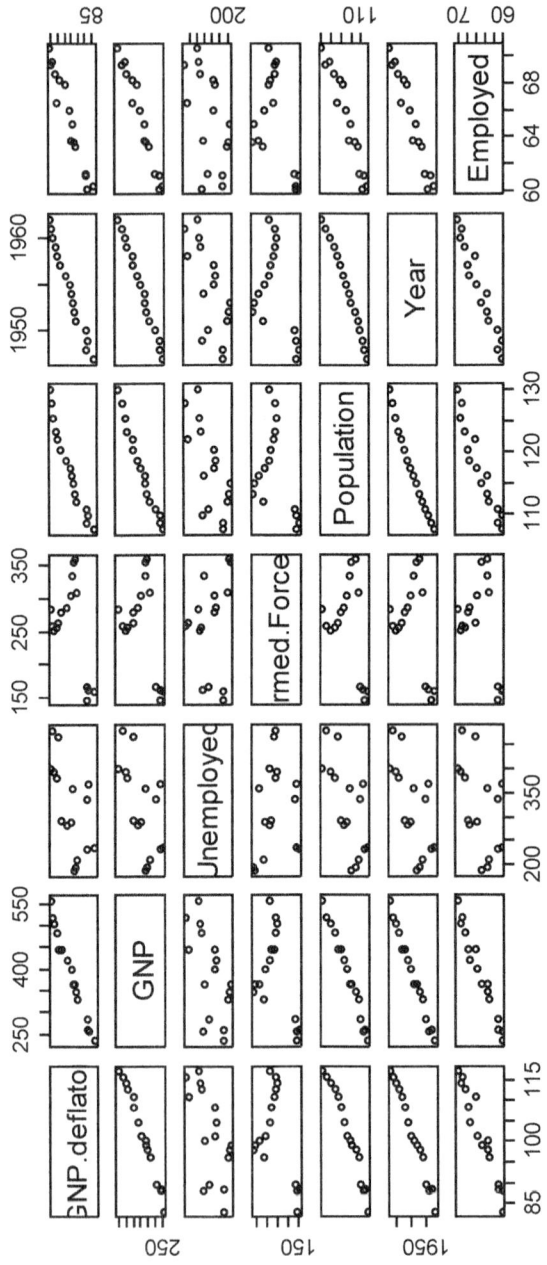

Figure 3-1. scatterplot matrix of the data

Here we will see the ability of R to discriminate between most appropriate function forms of the following models. We should expect, given the highly collinear nature of the regression `lm(Employed ~ .")` should be modeled with the Gaussian family.

- binomial(link = "logit")
- binomial(link = "probit")
- gaussian(link = "identity")
- poisson(link = "log")
- quasi(link = "identity", variance = "constant")

```
require(stats)
require(graphics)
longley.x <- data.matrix(longley[, 1:6])
summary(longley.x)
```

The summary function generates the following output, which shows us summary statics for each variable in the data set including the target variable, "Employed."

```
  GNP.deflator         GNP             Unemployed
Min.   : 83.00   Min.   :234.3   Min.   :187.0
1st Qu.: 94.53   1st Qu.:317.9   1st Qu.:234.8
Median :100.60   Median :381.4   Median :314.4
Mean   :101.68   Mean   :387.7   Mean   :319.3
3rd Qu.:111.25   3rd Qu.:454.1   3rd Qu.:384.2
Max.   :116.90   Max.   :554.9   Max.   :480.6
  Armed.Forces      Population         Year
Min.   :145.6    Min.   :107.6   Min.   :1947
1st Qu.:229.8    1st Qu.:111.8   1st Qu.:1951
Median :271.8    Median :116.8   Median :1954
Mean   :260.7    Mean   :117.4   Mean   :1954
3rd Qu.:306.1    3rd Qu.:122.3   3rd Qu.:1958
Max.   :359.4    Max.   :130.1   Max.   :1962
```

Now, we set up a generalized linear model (we will talk about this in more detail in the next chapter), with "Employed" as the dependent variable and all the other variables as explanatory model effects. The statement "Employed ~ ." takes care of this requirement, while "data=longley" designates the data set, and "family=Gaussian" makes this a liner regression model having normal residuals.

```
longley.y <- longley[, "Employed"]
pairs(longley, main = "longley data")
longley.mod1<-glm(Employed ~ .,data=longley,family=gaussian
    (identity))
summary(longley.mod1)
```

The "Call" statement merely shows us the GLM again. This is followed by output, including "Deviance Residuals," which are critically important in logistic regression as we will see in later chapters. Then the output shows the model effect (explanatory variables) with their coefficient estimates and suitability statistics. At the end of the output, the Null Deviance and Residual Deviance are important goodness-of-fit metrics.

```
Call:
glm(formula = Employed ~ ., family = gaussian(identity), da
ta = longley)

Deviance Residuals:
      Min        1Q    Median        3Q       Max
 -0.41011  -0.15767  -0.02816   0.10155   0.45539

Coefficients:
                Estimate Std. Error t value Pr(>|t|)
(Intercept)   -3.482e+03  8.904e+02  -3.911 0.003560
GNP.deflator   1.506e-02  8.492e-02   0.177 0.863141
GNP           -3.582e-02  3.349e-02  -1.070 0.312681
Unemployed    -2.020e-02  4.884e-03  -4.136 0.002535
Armed.Forces  -1.033e-02  2.143e-03  -4.822 0.000944
Population    -5.110e-02  2.261e-01  -0.226 0.826212
Year           1.829e+00  4.555e-01   4.016 0.003037

(Intercept)   **
GNP.deflator
GNP
Unemployed    **
Armed.Forces  ***
Population
Year          **
---
Signif. codes:
0 '***' 0.001 '**' 0.01 '*' 0.05 '.' 0.1 ' ' 1

(Dispersion parameter for gaussian family taken to be 0.092
93601)
```

```
Null deviance: 185.00883  on 15  degrees of freedom
Residual deviance:   0.83642  on  9  degrees of freedom
AIC: 14.187

Number of Fisher Scoring iterations: 2
```

The next section of R code gives use four GLM's with different link functions to compare: Gamma, Gaussian, Poisson, and Inverse Gaussian. When we run the code, we will get coefficient estimates for each model.

```
longley.mod1<-glm(formula = Employed ~ ., family = Gamma(in
    verse), data = longley)
longley.mod2<-glm(formula = Employed ~ ., family = gaussian
    (identity), data = longley)
longley.mod3<-glm(formula = Employed ~ ., family = poisson(
    log), data = longley)
longley.mod4<-glm(formula = Employed ~ ., family = inverse.
    gaussian, data = longley)
rbind(Gamma= longley.mod1$coef, gaussian= longley.mod2$coef
    , poisson=longley.mod3$coeff, inverse.gaussian=longley.m
    od4$coef)
```

```
                     (Intercept)  GNP.deflator
Gamma              9.216863e-01  -7.325451e-06
gaussian          -3.482259e+03   1.506187e-02
poisson           -5.262691e+01   3.570455e-04
inverse.gaussian   2.907252e-02  -2.786624e-07
                          GNP     Unemployed
Gamma              9.297934e-06   4.783348e-06
gaussian          -3.581918e-02  -2.020230e-02
poisson           -5.788587e-04  -3.111645e-04
inverse.gaussian   2.971755e-07   1.468006e-07
                  Armed.Forces    Population
Gamma              2.126791e-06   3.201065e-05
gaussian          -1.033227e-02  -5.110411e-02
poisson           -1.489846e-04  -1.444313e-03
inverse.gaussian   5.999068e-08   1.277048e-06
                         Year
Gamma             -4.681685e-04
gaussian           1.829151e+00
poisson            2.931733e-02
inverse.gaussian  -1.490691e-05
```

The rbind() function takes a sequence of vector, matrix or data-frame arguments and combine by rows (cbind() does the same for columns).

Here we want to look at a measure for model quality called AIC, or Akaike information criterion, for each of the four models. The $aic suffix after the model names does this for us. The lowest AIC value will indicate the best model.

```
rbind(Gamma= longley.mod1$aic, gaussian= longley.mod2$aic,
    poisson=longley.mod3$aic, inverse.gaussian=longley.mod4$
    aic)
```

```
                         [,1]
Gamma             15.42875
gaussian          14.18670
poisson                Inf
inverse.gaussian 16.66554
```

It should be readily apparent that the Gaussian family with the identity link function works best with this collinear regression, and it is not improved upon by other functional forms.

GLM using SAS Studio

For this example we use the bank credit card marketing example we framed in Chapter 1.

Model Code

```
PROC GENMOD DATA=WORK.BANKING descending plots = (all)
PLOTS=(predicted resraw(index)
            stdreschi(index) );
        CLASS job marital education / param=glm;
        MODEL RESP=age default balance homeowner loans
            contact length /
        DIST=binomial
        LINK=logit;
        SCORE OUT=bank_scores; CODE;
RUN;
```

The "Model Information" tables in Figures 3-2 through 3-8 summarize information about the model we fit, including the model functional form, variable information, and response profile. This information is default output for PROC GENMOD. Figure 3-6 shows the model fit statistics. We will go through the tables and look at what they contain, but will hold off on the interpretation until later chapters.

28

Model Information	
Data Set	WORK.BANKING
Distribution	Binomial
Link Function	Logit
Dependent Variable	RESP

Figure 3-2. Model Information

Number of Observations Read	45212
Number of Observations Used	45211
Number of Events	5289
Number of Trials	45211
Missing Values	1

Figure 3-3. Model Observation Information

Class Level Information		
Class	Levels	Values
job	12	admin. blue-collar entrepreneur housemaid management retired self-employed services student technician unemployed unknown
marital	3	divorced married single
education	4	primary secondary tertiary unknown

Figure 3-4. Model Class Level Information

Response Profile		
Ordered Value	RESP	Total Frequency
1	1	5289
2	0	39922

Figure 3-5. Model Response Profile

PROC GENMOD is modeling the probability that RESP='1'.

In Figure 3-6, AIC is the same Akaike Information Criterion we saw in the R example. There are other measures, including BIC or Bayesian Information Criterion (BIC), and the ever so important Log Likelihood, which we will decipher later.

Criteria For Assessing Goodness Of Fit			
Criterion	DF	Value	Value/DF
Log Likelihood		-12561.4817	
Full Log Likelihood		-12561.4817	
AIC (smaller is better)		25140.9634	
AICC (smaller is better)		25140.9674	
BIC (smaller is better)		25219.4352	

Algorithm converged.

Figure 3-6. Model Goodness of Fit Information

The "Analysis of Maximum Likelihood Parameter Estimates" table in Figure 3-7 summarizes maximum likelihood estimates of the model parameters. Figure 3-8 shows the diagnostic plots for the response variable.

Analysis Of Maximum Likelihood Parameter Estimates								
Parameter		DF	Estimate	Standard Error	Wald 95% Confidence Limits		Wald Chi-Square	Pr > ChiSq
Intercept		1	-4.0299	0.0887	-4.204	-3.856	2062.86	<.0001
age		1	-0.0009	0.0015	-0.004	0.002	0.40	0.5268
ln_default		1	-0.4380	0.1583	-0.748	-0.127	7.66	0.0056
balance		1	0.0000	0.0000	0.000	0.000	29.22	<.0001
homeowner		1	-0.8761	0.0356	-0.946	-0.806	605.10	<.0001
loans		1	-0.7676	0.0564	-0.878	-0.657	185.17	<.0001
contact	cellular	1	1.5181	0.0549	1.411	1.625	764.30	<.0001
contact	telepho	1	1.3689	0.0821	1.208	1.529	278.27	<.0001
contact	unknwn	0	0.0000	0.0000	0.000	0.000	.	.
duration		1	0.0039	0.0001	0.004	0.004	4215.90	<.0001
Scale		0	1.0000	0.0000	1.000	1.000		

Figure 3-7. Maximum Likelihood Parameter Estimates

Note: The scale parameter was held fixed.

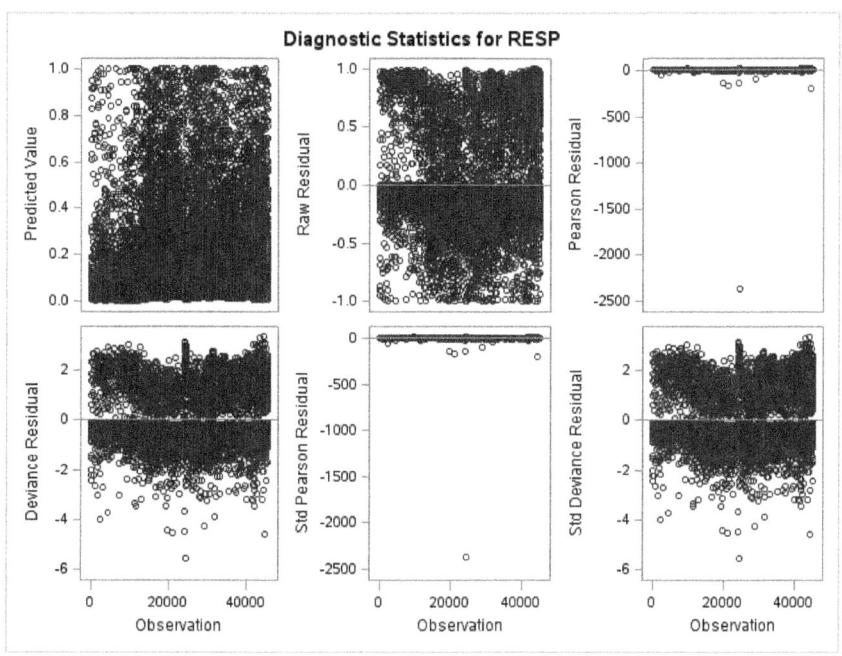

Figure 3-8. one of several response diagnostic plots

Summary

In this chapter we have examined generalized linear models using various link functions, and compared them for different modeling situations. We have also implemented GLMs in SAS and R, and examined the output we get from these functions and procedures.

Exercises

1. Implement the Bank modeling problem we looked at in the chapter using R. Compare your results to the SAS output in this chapter.
2. Using the Longley data from this chapter, perform a model comparison using SAS for Logit, Probit, and Identity link functions.

4. Logistic Regression from the Inside-Out

Logistic regression, or logit regression, is a type of probabilistic (also called stochastic), statistical model used for classifying categorical responses (Bishop, 2006). It is also used to predict a binary response from a binary predictor, and used for predicting the outcome of a categorical dependent variable (i.e., a class label like "yes" or "no"), based on one or more predictor variables (features). In other words, it is used in estimating the parameters of a qualitative response model. The probabilities describing the possible outcomes of a single trial are modeled, as a function of the explanatory (predictor) variables, using a logistic function. Frequently (and subsequently in this text) "logistic regression" is used to refer specifically to the problem in which the dependent variable is binary—that is, the number of available categories is two. Problems with more than two categories are referred to as *multinomial logistic regression* or, if the multiple categories are ordered, as *ordinal logistic regression*.

Formally, logistic regression measures the relationship between a categorical dependent variable Y and one or more independent variables X or X_i, with $i = 1,2,...,n$, which are usually (but not necessarily) continuous, by using *probability scores* as the predicted values of the dependent variable (Bhandari & Joensson, 2008). That is, we extract the probability of A given the probability of X, or $p(A|X)$, or the probability of A given the probabilities of the X_i's, with $i = 1,2,...,n$. These are also called the *posterior probabilities*, as we do not know there distribution beforehand. As such it treats the same set of problems as does *probit regression* using similar techniques.

Fields and examples of applications
Logistic regression was suggested in the 1940s as an alternative to Fisher's 1936 classification method, *linear discriminant analysis* (James, Witten, Hastie, & Tibshirani, 2013). It is used extensively in numerous disciplines, including the medical and social science fields. For example, the Trauma and Injury Severity Score (TRISS), which is widely used to predict mortality in injured patients, was originally developed by Boyd

et al. using logistic regression (Boyd, Tolson, & Copes, 1987). Logistic regression might be used to predict whether a patient has a given disease (e.g. diabetes), based on observed characteristics or behavior of the patient (age, gender, body mass index, exercise frequency, etc.). Another example, called a *propensity model*, might be to predict whether an American will acquire a mortgage, based on age, income, household role, credit card usage, state of residence, votes in general elections, etc. (Harrell, 2010). The technique can also be used in engineering, especially in *reliability engineering* for predicting the probability of failure of a given process, system or product (Strano & Colosimo, 2006) (Palei & Das, 2009). It is also used in political applications such as prediction of a citizen's propensity to vote along one party line or another. In economics, it can be used to predict the likelihood of a person's choosing to be in the labor force or not. *Conditional random fields*, an extension of logistic regression to sequential data, are used in *natural language processing*.

Basics

Recall that logistic regression can be *binomial* or *multinomial*. Binomial or *binary logistic regression* deals with situations in which the observed outcome for a dependent variable can have only two possible types (for example, "click-through" vs. "opt-out" in a email campaign). *Multinomial logistic regression* deals with situations where the outcome can have three or more possible types (e.g., "disease A" vs. "disease B" vs. "disease C"). In *binary logistic regression*, the outcome is usually coded as "0"or "1", as this leads to the most direct explanation of the outcomes (Hosmer & Lemeshow, 2000). If a particular observed outcome for the dependent variable is the notable possible outcome, (referred to as a "success" or a "case"), like "will purchase" in a product marketing campaign, it is usually coded as "1". The opposing outcome (referred to as a "failure" or a "noncase") is coded as "0", like "will not purchase." Logistic regression is used to predict the odds of being a *case* based on the values of the independent variables (predictors). The odds are defined as the probability that a particular outcome is a *case* divided by the probability that it is a *noncase*,

$$\frac{p(case)}{p(noncase)} \text{ or } \frac{odds(success)}{odds(failure)}.$$

These are referred to as the *odds ratios*. More cases than noncases results in an odds ratio greater than one, and more noncases than cases results in an odds ration less than one and greater than zero, i.e.

$$0 < \frac{p(case)}{p(noncase)} < 1.$$

Like other forms of regression analysis, logistic regression makes use of one or more predictor variables that may be either continuous or categorical data. Unlike conventional *linear regression*, however, logistic regression is used for predicting binary outcomes of the dependent variable (treating the dependent variable as the outcome of a Bernoulli trial) rather than continuous outcomes. Given this difference, it is necessary that logistic regression take the *natural logarithm* of the odds of the dependent variable being a case (referred to as the *logit* or *log-odds*) to create a continuous criterion as a transformed version of the dependent variable, for example

$$logit = \log_e \left(\frac{p(case)}{p(noncase)} \right)$$

(4.1)

lies between negative and positive infinity, $(-\infty < \log odds < +\infty)$. Hence, the *logit* transformation is referred to as the link function in logistic regression—although the dependent variable in logistic regression is binomial, the logit is the continuous criterion upon which linear regression is conducted (Hosmer & Lemeshow, 2000).

The logit of success is then fit to the predictors using linear regression analysis. The predicted value of the logit is converted back into predicted odds via the inverse of the natural logarithm, namely the exponential function. Equivalent to Equation (4.1), the logit can be represented as the exponentiation of the log-odds

$$logit = e^{\beta_0 + \beta_1 x}$$

(4.2a)

Or for multiple predictors

$$logit = e^{\beta_0 + \beta_1 x_1 + \beta_2 x_2 + \cdots + \beta + n\, x_n} \qquad (4.2b)$$

This exponential relationship provides an interpretation for β_1: the odds multiply buy e^{β_1} for every one-unit increase in the predictor variable,

$$\log_e e^{\beta_0 + \beta_1 x} = \beta_0 + \beta_1 x \qquad (4.3a)$$

with

$$\log_e \left(\frac{p}{1-p}\right) = \beta_0 + \beta_1 x_1 + \beta_2 x_2 + \cdots + \beta_n x_n \qquad (4.3b)$$

where $p = case$ and $1 - p = noncase$ for multiple predictors.

Therefore, although the observed dependent variable in logistic regression is a zero-or-one variable, the logistic regression estimates the odds, as a continuous variable, that the dependent variable is a success (a case). In some applications the odds are all that is needed. In others, a specific yes-or-no prediction is needed for whether the dependent variable is or is not a case; this categorical prediction can be based on the computed odds of a success, with predicted odds above some chosen cut-off value being translated into a prediction of a success.

Logistic function, odds ratio, and logit

An explanation of logistic regression begins with an explanation of the logistic function, which always takes on values between zero and one (Hosmer & Lemeshow, 2000):

$$F(t) = \frac{e^t}{e^t + 1} = \frac{1}{1 + e^{t}}, \qquad (4.4)$$

Observing t as a linear function of an explanatory variable x (or of a linear combination of explanatory variables), the logistic function can be written as:

$$F(x) = \frac{1}{1 + e^{-(\beta_0 + \beta_1 x)}}.$$

This will be interpreted as the probability of the dependent variable equaling a "success" or "case" rather than a failure or non-case. We also define the inverse of the logistic function, the *logit* (equivalent to (4.1)):

$$g(x) = \ln\frac{F(x)}{1 - F(x)} = \beta_0 + \beta_1 x$$

(4.5)

Equivalently:

$$\frac{F(x)}{1 - F(x)} = e^{(\beta_0 + \beta_1 x)}.$$

A graph of the logistic function is shown in Figure 4-1. The input is the value of and the output is $F(x)$. The logistic function is useful because it can take an input with any value from negative infinity to positive infinity, whereas the output is confined to values between 0 and 1 and hence is interpretable as a probability. In the above equations, *g(x)* refers to the logit function of some given linear combination of the predictors, ln denotes the natural logarithm, *F(x)* is the probability that the dependent variable equals a case, β_0 is the intercept from the linear regression equation (the value of the criterion when the predictor is equal to zero), β_1 is the regression coefficient multiplied by some value of the predictor x, and base e denotes the exponential function.

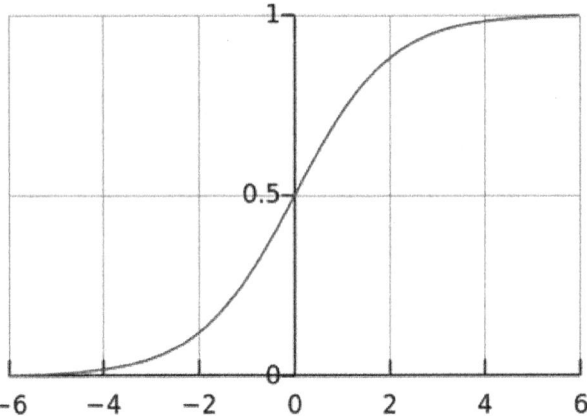

Figure 4-1. The logistic function, with $\beta_0 + \beta_1$ on the horizontal axis and $F(x)$ on the vertical axis

The formula for $F(x)$ illustrates that the probability of the dependent variable equaling a case is equal to the value of the logistic function of the linear regression expression. This is important in that it shows that the value of the linear regression expression can vary from negative to positive infinity and yet, after transformation, the resulting expression for the probability $F(x)$ ranges between 0 and 1. The equation for $g(x)$ illustrates that the logit (i.e., log-odds or natural logarithm of the odds) is equivalent to the linear regression expression. Likewise, the next equation illustrates that the odds of the dependent variable equaling a case is equivalent to the exponential function of the linear regression expression. This illustrates how the logit serves as a link function between the probability and the linear regression expression. Given that the logit ranges between negative infinity and positive infinity, it provides an adequate criterion upon which to conduct linear regression and the logit is easily converted back into the odds (Hosmer & Lemeshow, 2000).

Multiple explanatory variables

If there are multiple explanatory variables, then the above expression (4), $\beta_0 + \beta_1 x$, can be revised to $\beta_0 + \beta_1 x_1 + \beta_2 x_1 + \cdots + \beta_m x_m$. Then when this is used in the equation relating the logged odds of a success to the values of the predictors, the linear regression will be a multiple regression with m explanators; the parameters β_j for all $j = 0,1,2,\ldots,m$ are all estimated.

Formal mathematical specification

There are various equivalent specifications of logistic regression, which fit into different types of more general models. These different specifications allow for different sorts of useful generalizations.

Setup

The basic setup of logistic regression is the same as for standard linear regression.

We assume that we have a series of N observed data points. Each data point i consists of a set of m explanatory variables $x_{1,i}, \ldots, x_{m,i}$ (also called independent variables, predictor variables, input variables, features, or attributes), and an associated binary-valued outcome variable Y_i (also known as a dependent variable, response variable, output variable, outcome variable or class variable), i.e. it can assume only the two possible values 0 (often meaning "no" or "failure") or 1 (often meaning "yes" or "success"). The goal of logistic regression is to explain the relationship between the explanatory variables and the outcome, so that an outcome can be predicted for a new set of explanatory variables.

Some examples:

- The observed outcomes are the presence or absence of a given disease (e.g. diabetes) in a set of patients, and the explanatory variables might be characteristics of the patients thought to be pertinent (sex, race, age, blood pressure, body-mass index, etc.).
- The observed outcomes are the votes (e.g. Democratic or Republican) of a set of people in an election, and the explanatory variables are the demographic characteristics of each person (e.g. sex, race, age, income, etc.). In such a case, one of the two outcomes is arbitrarily coded as 1, and the other as 0.

As in linear regression, the outcome variables Y are assumed to depend on the explanatory variables $x_{1,i}, \ldots, x_{m,i}$.

Explanatory variables

As shown above in the above examples, the explanatory variables may be of any type: real-valued, binary, categorical, etc. The main distinction is between continuous variables (such as income, age and blood pressure) and discrete variables (such as sex or race). Discrete variables referring to more than two possible choices are typically coded using dummy variables (or indicator variables), that is, separate explanatory variables taking the value 0 or 1 are created for each possible value of the discrete variable, with a 1 meaning "variable does have the given value" and a 0 meaning "variable does not have that value". For example, a four-way discrete variable of blood type with the possible values "A, B, AB, O" can be converted to four separate two-way dummy variables, "is-A, is-B, is-AB, is-O", where only one of them has the value 1 and all the rest have the value 0. This allows for separate regression coefficients to be matched for each possible value of the discrete variable. (In a case like this, only three of the four dummy variables are independent of each other, in the sense that once the values of three of the variables are known, the fourth is automatically determined. Thus, it is only necessary to encode three of the four possibilities as dummy variables. This also means that when all four possibilities are encoded, the overall model is not identifiable in the absence of additional constraints such as a regularization constraint. Theoretically, this could cause problems, but in reality almost all logistic regression models are fit with regularization constraints.)

Outcome variables

Formally, the outcomes Y_i are described as being Bernoulli-distributed data, where each outcome is determined by an unobserved probability p_i that is specific to the outcome at hand, but related to the explanatory variables. This can be expressed in any of the following equivalent forms:

$$Y_i | x_{1,i}, \dots, x_{m,i} \sim \text{Bernoulli}(p_i) \tag{4.6a}$$

$$E[Y_i | x_{1,i}, \dots, x_{m,i}] = p_i \tag{4.6b}$$

$$\Pr(Y_i = y_i | x_{1,i}, \dots, x_{m,i}) = \begin{cases} p_i & \text{if } y_i = 1 \\ 1 - p_i & \text{if } y_i = 0 \end{cases} \tag{4.6c}$$

$$\Pr\left(Y_i = y_i \middle| x_{1,i}, \ldots, x_{m,i}\right) = p_i^{y_i}(1 - p_i)^{(1-y_i)} \qquad \text{(4.6d)}$$

The meanings of these four lines are:

1. Equation (4.6a) expresses the probability distribution of each Y_i: Conditioned on the explanatory variables, it follows a Bernoulli distribution with parameters p_i, the probability of the outcome of 1 for trial i. As noted above, each separate trial has its own probability of success, just as each trial has its own explanatory variables. The probability of success p_i is not observed, only the outcome of an individual Bernoulli trial using that probability.

2. Equation (4.6b) expresses the fact that the expected value of each Y_i is equal to the probability of success p_i, which is a general property of the Bernoulli distribution. In other words, if we run a large number of Bernoulli trials using the same probability of success p_i, then take the average of all the 1 and 0 outcomes, then the result would be close to p_i. This is because doing an average this way simply computes the proportion of successes seen, which we expect to converge to the underlying probability of success.

3. Equation (4.6c) writes out the probability mass function of the Bernoulli distribution, specifying the probability of seeing each of the two possible outcomes.

4. Equation (4.6d) is another way of writing the probability mass function, which avoids having to write separate cases and is more convenient for certain types of calculations. This relies on the fact that Y_i can take only the value 0 or 1. In each case, one of the exponents will be 1, "choosing" the value under it, while the other is 0, "canceling out" the value under it. Hence, the outcome is either p_i or $1 - p_i$, as in the previous line.

Linear predictor function

The basic idea of logistic regression is to use the mechanism already developed for linear regression by modeling the probability p_i using a linear predictor function, i.e. a linear combination of the explanatory variables and a set of regression coefficients that are specific to the model at hand but the same for all trials. The linear predictor function $f(i)$ for a particular data point i is written as:

$$f(i) = \beta_0 + \beta_1 x_{1,i} + \beta_2 x_{1,i} + \cdots + \beta_m x_{m,i}, \qquad (4.7)$$

where $\beta_0, \ldots, \beta_m$ are regression coefficients indicating the relative effect of a particular explanatory variable on the outcome.

The model is usually put into a more compact form as follows:

- The regression coefficients $\beta_0, \beta_1, \ldots, \beta_m$ β , β , ..., β are grouped into a single vector $\boldsymbol{\beta}$ of size $m + 1$.
- For each data point i, an additional explanatory pseudo-variable $x_{0,i}$ is added, with a fixed value of 1, corresponding to the intercept coefficient β_0 .
- The resulting explanatory variables $x_{0,i}, x_{1,i}, \ldots, x_{m,i}$ are then grouped into a single vector $\boldsymbol{X_i}$ of size $m + 1$.

This makes it possible to write the linear predictor function as follows:

$$f(i) = \boldsymbol{\beta} \cdot \boldsymbol{X_i}, \qquad (4.8)$$

using the notation for a dot product between two vectors.

Rare Outcome Events

Suppose you are building a logistic regression model in which percent of events (desired outcome) is very low (less than 1%). We need a method to make the model robust so that enough events would be used to train the model. Oversampling is one of the methods to deal rare-event problem.

Oversampling

Suppose we are working on a retail customer attrition (churn) problem for a telecommunications company. We started building a logistic regression model in which target (dependent) variable is defined as whether a customer is active or not. If a customer is NOT active, the target variable has a value of 1; otherwise it is 0. We calculated the attrition percentage (i.e. mean of the target variable) and found it is 1% of 10,000 customer base. That means there are 9900 active customers and 100 churners in 10k cases of our target variable. Since the distribution of the target variable is highly skewed, we need to oversample the event (churners). By oversampling, we mean decreasing the volume of non-events so that proportion of events and non-events becomes balanced or less skewed.

When should we perform Oversampling?

In logistic regression, we require a minimum of at least ten events per independent variable. Many people get confused about this rule-of-thumb as having minimum number of independent variables (predictors). It is commonly asked, "Does this rule apply before variable selection or after variable selection?" Suppose we have 30 events an you are running a stepwise selection method for variable selection (i.e. adding a variable one by one and checking the significance level of the previous variables at every addition). This rule would be applied on all the candidate variables in the stepwise algorithm but we should limit the algorithm to consider only three independent variables. Some researchers do not follow this rule strictly and do oversampling even if this rule is met. It is advisable to build two models (with or without oversampling) and test the model on the non-oversampling population and compare the accuracy of the models.

How to perform Oversampling with SAS

Method I : With PROC SURVEYSELECT

We typically use PROC SURVEYSELECT to perform random sampling, either by specifying a sample size or requiring a percentage of the set we are sampling. Here we use it to oversample.

```
PROC SORT DATA = full;
BY y;
RUN;
PROC SURVEYSELECT DATA = full
      OUT = SUB
      METHOD = SRS N = (100,100) SEED = 9876;
STRATA y;
RUN;
```

In the code above, we are performing stratified sampling. The option N= (number of 0s you want to keep, number of 1s you want to keep). Instead, you can use rate option – rate = (50,50). It means you want to retain 50% of 0s and 50% of 1s.

Method II : Without PROC SURVEYSELECT

```
DATA sub ;
SET full;
IF y = 1 OR (y = 0 AND RANUNI(75302) < 1/9) THEN OUTPUT;
RUN;
```

Note: 1/9 means 10% of events and 90% non-events in the original data (before sampling). After we run the above code, distribution of events and non-events would be 50:50.

Effect of oversampling

1. Oversampling does not effect the slopes (parameter estimates), but it does effect the intercept (making it too high). In other words, parameter estimates remain the same after sampling but the intercept increases significantly after sampling.
2. It affects predicted probabilities as they are calculated for both parameter estimates and intercept (an incorrect intercept as stated above). It increases after sampling as the intercept is overestimated.
3. Oversampling does not affect sensitivity or specificity measures but false positive and negative rates are affected.
4. The ROC curve is not affected by oversampling.
5. Oversampling does not affect rank ordering (sorting based on predicted probability) because adjusting after oversampling is just a linear transformation. Hence, it does not affect Gain and Lift charts if you score on an out-of-time sample or an non-sampled validation dataset. However, if you compare the lift of the non-sampled and sampled data of the training dataset, gain charts and lift charts are affected as proportion of events were changed. For example, the predicted probability score is 80% in one observation. After oversampling, the ratio is 50:50. The lift on the sampled data is 80%/50% = 1.6. After adjusting the probability, the adjusted

probability score is 30.8%. The lift on the original data is 3.08 (i.e., 30.8% / 10%).

Correcting Confusion Matrix

We will talk more about the confusion matrix in Chapter 8. A confusion matrix, like the one in Figure 4-2, is a table that is often used to describe the performance of a classification model (or "classifier") on a set of test data for which the true values are known. The confusion matrix itself is relatively simple to understand, but the related terminology can be confusing.

n=165	Predicted: NO	Predicted: YES	
Actual: NO	TN = 50	FP = 10	60
Actual: YES	FN = 5	TP = 100	105
	55	110	

Figure 4-2. An example of a confusion matrix

Suppose, π_0 is the proportion of *non-events* before sampling and π_1 is the proportion of *events* before sampling. Then, ρ_1 is the proportion of *events* after sampling and ρ_0 is the proportion of *non-events* after sampling.

True proportion of true positives = π_1 * sensitivity.

True proportion of true negatives = π_0 * specificity

True proportion of false positives = π_0 * (1 – specificity)

True proportion of false negatives = π_1 * (1 – sensitivity)

Note: When we correct for oversampling, you make the probabilities much, much smaller.

1. Correct the Intercept – *Offset Method*

p_1 is the population rate (before oversampling) – Let's say 1%.

r_1 is the sample rate (post oversampling - 10%)

α_1 is the intercept from oversampled data.

The intercept term for final model α when scoring non-sampled population is

$$\alpha = \alpha_1 + \log\left(\frac{p_1(1-r_1)}{1-p_1}r_1\right)$$

(4.9)

where log() represents the natural logarithm ($\log_e$ or ln).

2. Correct the probability – *Weight Method*

In the equation below, P_1 denotes the predicted probability for an event, P_0 denotes the predicted probability for non-event.

Step 1 :

$$A = \frac{P_1}{\dfrac{Oversampled\ \%\ of\ events}{Original\ \%\ of\ events}}$$

Step 2 :

$$B = \frac{P_0}{\dfrac{Oversampled\ \%\ of\ non-events}{Original\ \%\ of\ non-events}}$$

Step 3 :

$$Adj\ P_1 = \frac{A}{A+B}$$

Step 4 :

$$Adj\ P_0 = \frac{B}{A+B}$$

Solve the above equation :

$$Adj\ P_1 = \cfrac{1}{1 + \cfrac{\left(\frac{1}{original}\ \% \ of\ events\right) - 1}{\left(\frac{1}{oversampled}\ \% \ of\ events\right) - 1} * \left[\left(\frac{1}{P_1}\right) - 1\right]}$$

$$Adj\ P_0 = \cfrac{1}{1 + \cfrac{\left(\frac{1}{original}\ \% \ of\ non-events\right) - 1}{\left(\frac{1}{oversampled}\ \% \ of\ non-events\right) - 1} * \left[\left(\frac{1}{P_0}\right) - 1\right]}$$

Before Sampling: $1 - 5\%$ and $0 - 95\%$

Post Sampling: $1 - 50\%$ and $0 - 50\%$

$$Adj\ P_1 = \cfrac{1}{1 + \cfrac{\left(\frac{1}{0.05}\right) - 1}{\left(\frac{1}{0.5}\right) - 1} * \left(\left(\frac{1}{p_1}\right) - 1\right)}$$

$$Adj\ P_0 = \cfrac{1}{1 + \cfrac{\left(\frac{1}{0.95}\right) - 1}{\left(\frac{1}{0.5}\right) - 1} * \left(\left(\frac{1}{p_0}\right) - 1\right)}$$

Note: We do not need to adjust oversampling if our goal is to select the top 30% customers based on their high predicted probability. This is so, because oversampling is just a linear transformation and it does not affect rank ordering. We should perform it only when we need to know the "correct" probability of customer behavior.

I. Implementing Offset Method in SAS:

We can use the PRIOREVENT= option in the SCORE statement to specify the prior event probability.

```
PROC LOGISTIC DATA=training;
MODEL attrition(event='1')=Fees Balance Withdrawal Interest;
SCORE DATA=valid OUT=scored PRIOREVENT=0.05;
RUN;
```

Note: 0.05 means the 5% of the target event before sampling.

II. Implementing Sampling weights in SAS :

Sampling weights adjust the data so that it better represents the true population.

Sampling weight for events = (proportion of events before sampling / proportion of events after sampling)

Sampling weight for non-events = (proportion of non-events before sampling / proportion of non-events after sampling)

We can use the WEIGHT statement in PROC LOGISTIC to weight each observation in the input data set by the value of the WEIGHT variable.

```
%let priorprob = 0.05;
PROC SQL noprint;
SELECT MEAN(attrition) INTO:postprob FROM training;
QUIT;

DATA training1;
SET training;
sampwt=((1-&priorprob)/(1-
&postprob))*(attrition=0)+(&priorprob
/&postprob)*(attrition=1);
RUN;

PROC LOGISTIC DATA=training1;
WEIGHT sampwt;
MODEL attrition(event='1')=Fees Balance Withdrawal Interest;
SCORE DATA=valid OUT=scored;
RUN;
```

Note: priorprob is probability of an event before sampling and attrition is a dependent variable in this model.

We will have more to say about this topic in Chapter 8.

As a generalized linear model

The particular model used by logistic regression, which distinguishes it from standard linear regression and from other types of regression analysis used for binary-valued outcomes, is the way the probability of a particular outcome is linked to the linear predictor function:

$$\text{logit}\big(E\big[Y_i\big|x_{1,i}, \ldots, x_{m,i}\big]\big) = \text{logit}(p_i) = \ln\left(\frac{p_i}{1-p_i}\right) = \beta_1 x_{1,i} + \beta_2 x_{1,i} + \cdots + \beta_m x_{m,i}$$

Written using the more compact notation described above, this is:

$$\text{logit}(E[Y_i|X_i]) = \text{logit}(p_i) = \ln\left(\frac{p_i}{1-p_i}\right) = \boldsymbol{\beta} \cdot \boldsymbol{X}_i. \qquad (4.10)$$

This formulation expresses logistic regression as a type of generalized linear model, which predicts variables with various types of probability distributions by fitting a linear predictor function of the above form to some sort of arbitrary transformation of the expected value of the variable.

The intuition for transforming using the logit function (the natural log of the odds) was explained above. It also has the practical effect of converting the probability (which is bounded to be between 0 and 1) to a variable that ranges over $(-\infty, +\infty)$ — thereby matching the potential range of the linear prediction function on the right side of the equation.

Note that both the probabilities p_i and the regression coefficients are unobserved, and the means of determining them is not part of the model itself. They are typically determined by some sort of optimization procedure, e.g. maximum likelihood estimation, which finds values that best fit the observed data (i.e. that give the most accurate predictions for the data already observed), usually subject to regularization conditions that seek to exclude unlikely values, e.g. extremely large values for any of the regression coefficients. The use of a regularization condition is equivalent to doing maximum a posteriori (MAP) estimation, an extension of maximum likelihood. (Regularization is most commonly done using a squared regularizing function, which is equivalent to placing a zero-mean Gaussian prior distribution on the coefficients, but other regularizes are also possible.) Whether or not regularization is used, it is usually not possible to find a closed-form solution; instead, an iterative numerical method must be used, such as iteratively reweighted least squares (IRLS) or, more commonly these days, a quasi-Newton method such as the L-BFGS method.

The interpretation of the β_j parameter estimates is as the additive effect on the log of the odds for a unit change in the jth explanatory variable. In the case of a dichotomous explanatory variable, for instance gender, e^β is the estimate of the odds of having the outcome for, say, males compared with females.

An equivalent formula uses the inverse of the logit function, which is the logistic function, i.e.:

$$E[Y_i|X_i] = p_i = (\boldsymbol{\beta} \cdot X_i) = \frac{1}{1 + e^{-\boldsymbol{\beta} \cdot X_i}}.$$

(4.11)

The formula can also be written (somewhat awkwardly) as a probability distribution (specifically, using a probability mass function):

$$\Pr(Y_i = y_i|X_i) = p_i^{y_i}(1 - p_i)^{(1-y_i)}$$
$$= \left(\frac{1}{1 + e^{-\boldsymbol{\beta} \cdot X_i}}\right)^{y_i} \left(1 - \frac{1}{1 + e^{-\boldsymbol{\beta} \cdot X_i}}\right)^{1-y_i}.$$

(4.12)

As a latent-variable model

The above model has an equivalent formulation as a *latent-variable model*. This formulation is common in the theory of discrete choice models, and makes it easier to extend to certain more complicated models with multiple, correlated choices, as well as to compare logistic regression to the closely related probit model.

Imagine that, for each trial i, there is a continuous latent variable Y_i^* (i.e. an unobserved random variable) that is distributed as follows:

$$Y_i^* = \boldsymbol{\beta} \cdot X_i + \varepsilon,$$ (4.13)

Where

$$\varepsilon \sim \text{Logistic}(0,1),$$

i.e., the latent variable can be written directly in terms of the linear predictor function and an additive random error variable that is distributed according to a standard logistic distribution.

Then Y_i can be viewed as an indicator for whether this latent variable is positive:

$$Y_i = \begin{cases} 1 & \text{if } Y_i^* > 0, i.e. -\varepsilon < \boldsymbol{\beta} \cdot \boldsymbol{X}_i \\ 0 & \text{otherwise} \end{cases}. \tag{4.14}$$

The choice of modeling the error variable specifically with a standard logistic distribution, rather than a general logistic distribution with the location and scale set to arbitrary values, seems restrictive, but in fact it is not. It must be kept in mind that we can choose the regression coefficients ourselves, and very often can use them to offset changes in the parameters of the error variable's distribution. For example, a logistic error-variable distribution with a non-zero location parameter μ (which sets the mean) is equivalent to a distribution with a zero location parameter, where μ has been added to the intercept coefficient. Both situations produce the same value for Y_i^* regardless of settings of explanatory variables. Similarly, an arbitrary scale parameter s is equivalent to setting the scale parameter to 1 and then dividing all regression coefficients by s. In the latter case, the resulting value of Y_i^* will be smaller by a factor of s than in the former case, for all sets of explanatory variables — but critically, it will always remain on the same side of 0, and hence lead to the same Y_i choice.

(Note that this predicts that the irrelevancy of the scale parameter may not carry over into more complex models where more than two choices are available.)

It turns out that this formulation is exactly equivalent to the preceding one, phrased in terms of the generalized linear model and without any latent variables. This can be shown as follows, using the fact that the *cumulative distribution function* (CDF) of the standard logistic distribution is the logistic function, which is the inverse of the logit function, i.e.

$$Pr(\varepsilon < x) = (x). \tag{4.15}$$

Then:

$$
\begin{aligned}
\Pr(Y_i = 1|X_i) &= \Pr\big((Y_i^* > 0)\big|X_i\big) \\
&= \Pr(\boldsymbol{\beta} \cdot X_i + \varepsilon > 0) \\
&= \Pr(\varepsilon > -\boldsymbol{\beta} \cdot X_i) \\
&= \Pr(\varepsilon < \boldsymbol{\beta} \cdot X_i) \\
&= (\boldsymbol{\beta} \cdot X_i) \\
&= p_i.
\end{aligned}
$$

(4.16)

This formulation — which is standard in *discrete choice models* — makes clear the relationship between logistic regression (the "logit model") and the probit model, which uses an error variable distributed according to a standard normal distribution instead of a standard logistic distribution. Both the logistic and normal distributions are symmetric with a basic unimodal, "bell curve" shape. The only difference is that the logistic distribution has somewhat heavier tails, which means that it is less sensitive to outlying data (and hence somewhat more robust to model misspecifications or erroneous data).

Summary

In this chapter, we have explored setting up a logistic regression model and dealing with rare events. The former requires us to consider the outcome or target variable as well as the explanatory variables. The latter my require us to oversample, and thereby requiring us to correct the resulting confusion matrix. We also looked at formulating a logistic regression model as a GLM using the logit link function, and formulating a logistic regression model as a latent-variable model.

Exercises

1. Suppose we constructed a model with the following results:
   - There are 100 True Negatives
   - There are 150 True Positives
   - There are 15 False Negatives
   - There are 25 False Positives
   a. Complete the confusion matrix below

	Predicted: No	Predicted: Yes	
Actual: No			
Actual: Yes			

b. Calculate the Sensitivity of the model

c. Calculate the Specificity of the model

2. Given the confusion matrix below, calculate
    a. The model sensitivity
    b. The model specificity
    c. The model false positives
    d. The model false negatives

	Predicted: No	Predicted: Yes	
Actual: No	200	300	500
Actual: Yes	25	50	75
	225	350	

3. State three ways a logistic regression model differ from a linear regression model.

4. When should we over sample the target variable?

5. Use the data set "catalogs" to over sample for the target variable "purchase" using SAS Studio.
    a. Correct for the intercept
    b. Correct the confusion matrix

6. Formulate the model given in number 5 as a latent-variable model.

5. Variable Selection from the Inside-Out

In this day of *Big Data*, it is often the case that there exists a myriad of potential predictor (independent) variables. I often build models where there are 1000-plus potential predictors. However, good models have much fewer, often numbering less than 20. Even with modern software, stepping through 1000 variables is not an easy matrix manipulation. So, how do we down-select to achieve an achievable task?

It is common for analysts to perform exploratory data analysis and variable screening before modeling begins. Through this analysis you become very familiar with the data and begin to gain some intuition about what effects the data may have on the outcome. The following constitutes a few purposeful ways to perform this analysis.

Data Characterization and Missing Values

Data characterization is more than *descriptive statistics*. It includes determining measures of central tendency, like the mean, and measures of variation, like the standard deviation, but it also includes a holistic view of the data. Some other metrics include:

- Quartiles
- Inner quartile range
- Box plots
- Histograms
- Percent and number of missing values
- Information value (we will address this specifically later on)
- Effects of binning and re-binning the data
- Etc.

For an example (this was also introduced in Chapter 1), consider a bank analytics team that wants to predict product acquisition from a marketing campaign with data they have available as follows:

- job (categorical)
- marital (categorical)

- education (categorical)
- age (numeric)
- balance (numeric, bank deposit balance)
- homeowner (1=yes or 0=no)
- loans (1=yes or 0=no)
- ln_default (1=yes or 0=no)
- day (numeric, day of the month)
- contact month (ordinal, 1-12)
- duration (numeric)
- campaign (categorical)
- pdays (numeric – elapsed days since previous campaign)
- previous (1=yes or 0=no)
- poutcome (numeric – outcome of previous campaign
- married _people (1=yes or 0=no)
- manual_labor (1=yes or 0=no)

Modern software packages contain special functions to perform most of these analyses. Here I use SAS to explore some of the data.

SAS Code and Data Exploration I

```
/*** SAS Code ***/
/*** Analyze categorical variables ***/
title "Frequencies for Categorical Variables";
proc freq data=WORK.BANK;
        tables job marital education contact month poutcome /
plots=(freqplot);
run;
/*** Analyze numeric variables ***/
title "Descriptive Statistics for Numeric Variables";

proc means data=WORK.BANK n nmiss min mean median max std;
        var age balance homeowner loans lndefault day duration
        campaign pdays previous RESP;
run;
title;
proc univariate data=WORK.BANK noprint;
        histogram age balance homeowner loans lndefault day
        duration campaign pdays previous RESP;
run;
```

Partial SAS Output I

Table 5-1 contains our typical descriptive statistics for numerical data. One observation we can make is there are three binary variables, homeowner, Indefault, and loans. In a binary model like logistic regression, binary predictors are often the strongest. We can also see that age may approximately symmetric since the mean and median are nearly the same, but we do not know anything about skewness and kurtosis. The histogram in Figure 5-1 verifies that age is skewed to the right, which is also apparent from the boxplot in Figure 5-2. The boxplot also reveals some outliers in the top 25% or 4th quartile. The interquartile range is approximately twenty.

Table 5-1. Descriptive Statistics for Numeric Variables

Variable	N	Miss	Min	Mean	Median	Max	Std Dev
age	45211	0	18.00	40.9362	39.0000	95.000	10.6187
balance	45211	0	-8019.00	1362.27	448.0000	102127	3044.77
homeow	45211	0	0	0.5558	1.0000	1.000	0.4968
loans	45211	0	0	0.1602	16.0000	1.000	0.3668
Indefault	45211	0	0	0.0180	180.0000	1.000	0.1330
day	45211	0	1.00	15.8064	2.0000	31.000	8.3224
duration	45211	0	0	258.163	-1.0000	4918.00	257.527
campaig	45211	0	1.00	0		63.000	3.0980

Table 5-2 shows the results of correlation analysis for the variables age and homeowner. Based on the result, we probably do not have to be concerned about the correlation, since it is relatively small (-0.1876).

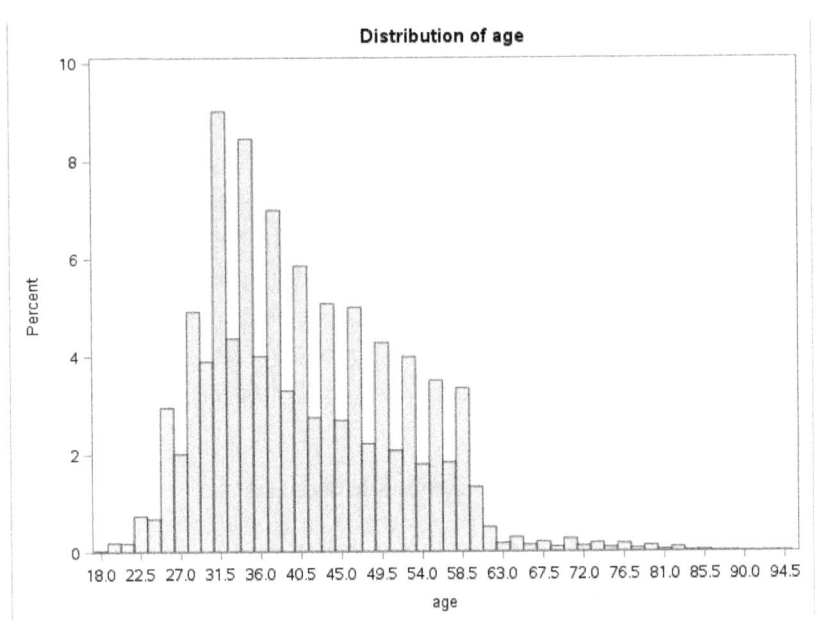

Figure 5-1. Histogram for age

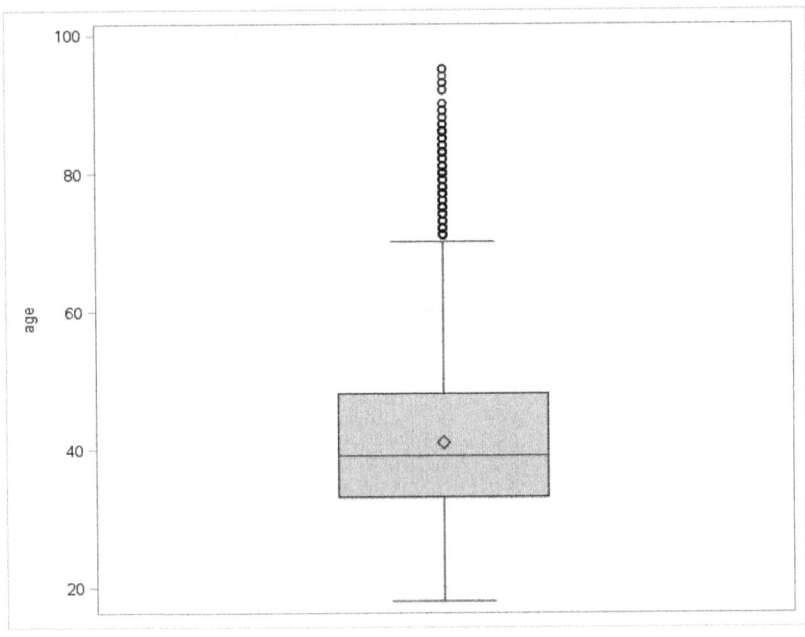

Figure 5-2. Box-plot for age showing the distribution of ages is skewed to the tight

Table 5-2. Pearson Correlation Statistics

Pearson Correlation Statistics (Fisher's z Transformation)						
Varia-ble	With Variable	N	Sample Correlation	Fisher's z	Bias Adjustment	Correlation Estimate
age	Home-owner	45211	-0.1855	-0.1876	-2.0517E-6	-0.1855

Next, we want to examine the distribution of age. The SAS code for performing this analysis follows.

SAS Code and Data Exploration II

```
ods noproctitle;
ods graphics / imagemap=on;

/*** Exploring Data ***/
proc univariate data=WORK.BANK;
        ods select Histogram;
        var age;
        histogram age / normal kernel;
        inset n / position=ne;
run;

proc univariate data=WORK.BANK normal;
        ods select Histogram GoodnessOfFit ProbPlot QQPlot;
        var age;

        /*** Checking for Normality ***/
        histogram age / normal(mu=est sigma=est);
        inset normaltest pnormal mean median std var skewness
            kurtosis n / position=ne;
        probplot age / normal(mu=est sigma=est);
        inset normaltest pnormal mean median std var skewness
            kurtosis n / position=nw;
        qqplot age / normal(mu=est sigma=est);
        inset normaltest pnormal mean median std var skewness
            kurtosis n / position=nw;
run;
```

Partial SAS Output II

We are reasonably certain age is not distributed normally based on the histogram in Figure 5-1. To check our conclusion we have also fit a normal distribution as shown in Figure 5-3. Viewing Figure 5-3 and the fit statistics in Table 5-3, the normal distribution fits the data reasonably well. However, the Q-Q plot in Figure 5-4 and the Probability plot in Figure 5-5 leads us to suspect the fit. So, we try a different fit.

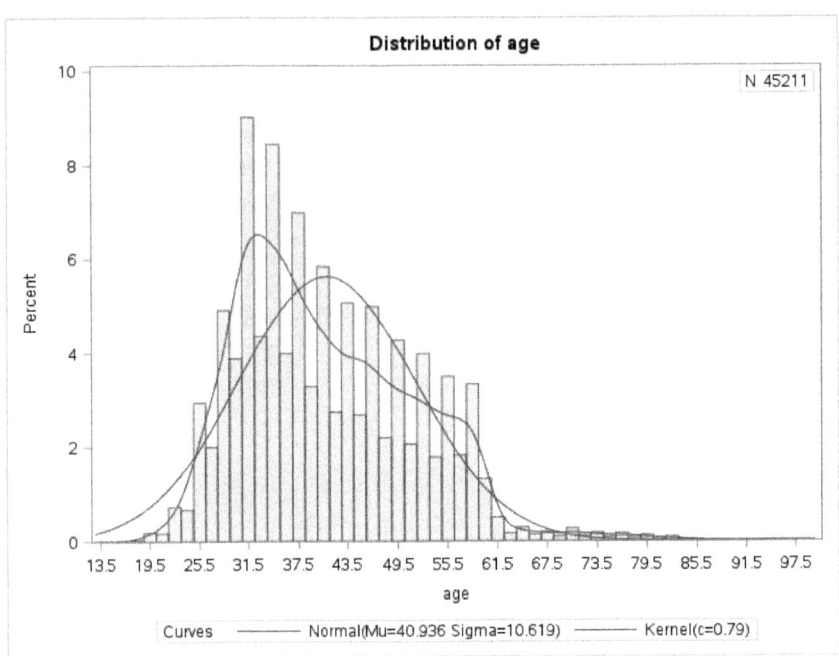

Figure 5-3. Age data histogram overlaid with normal distribution plot and normal kernel

Table 5-3. Fitted Normal Distribution for age

Goodness-of-Fit Tests for Normal Distribution				
Test	Statistic		p Value	
Kolmogorov-Smirnov	D	0.095980	Pr > D	<0.010
Cramer-von Mises	W-Sq	85.132552	Pr > W-Sq	<0.005
Anderson-Darling	A-Sq	496.088191	Pr > A-Sq	<0.005

Q-Q Plots

The quantile-quantile (Q-Q) plot is a graphical technique for determining if two data sets come from populations with a common distribution.

A q-q plot is a plot of the quantiles of the first data set against the quantiles of the second data set. By a quantile, we mean the fraction (or percent) of points below the given value. That is, the 0.3 (or 30%)

quantile is the point at which 30% percent of the data fall below and 70% fall above that value.

A 45-degree reference line is also plotted. If the two sets come from a population with the same distribution, the points should fall approximately along this reference line. The greater the departure from this reference line, the greater the evidence for the conclusion that the two data sets have come from populations with different distributions.

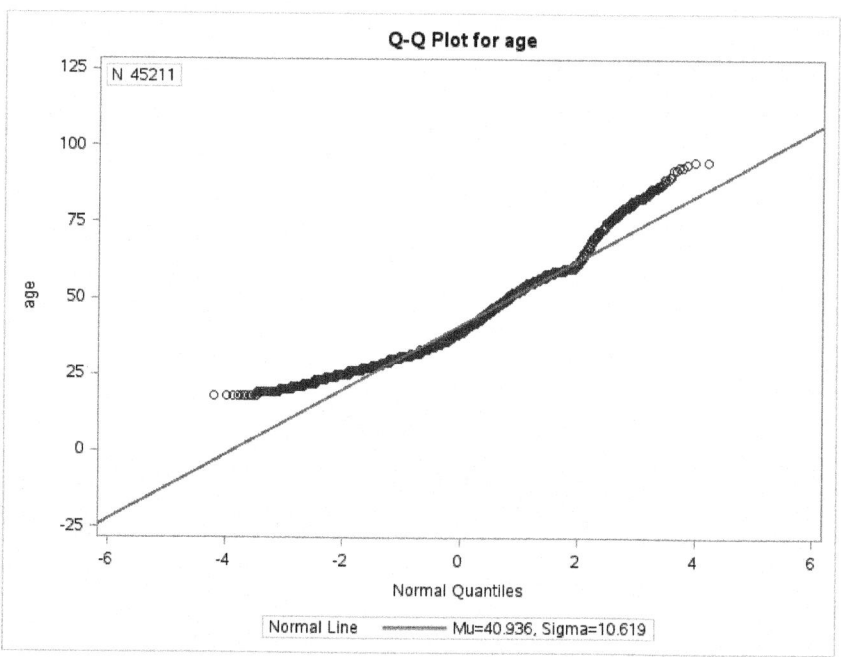

Figure 5-4. Q-Q Plot of the Age data fitted with a normal distribution

The Probability Plot

The probability plot (Chambers et al., 1983) is a graphical technique for assessing whether or not a data set follows a given distribution such as the normal or Weibull.

61

We plot the data against a theoretical distribution in such a way that the points should form approximately a straight line. Departures from this straight line indicate departures from the specified distribution.

As a measure of the goodness of the fit, we examine the correlation coefficient associated with the linear fit to the data in the probability plot. The intercept and slope provides estimates of the location and scale parameters of the distribution, respectively. We can generate probability plots for several competing distributions to see which provides the best fit. The probability plot generating the highest correlation coefficient is the best choice since it generates the straightest probability plot.

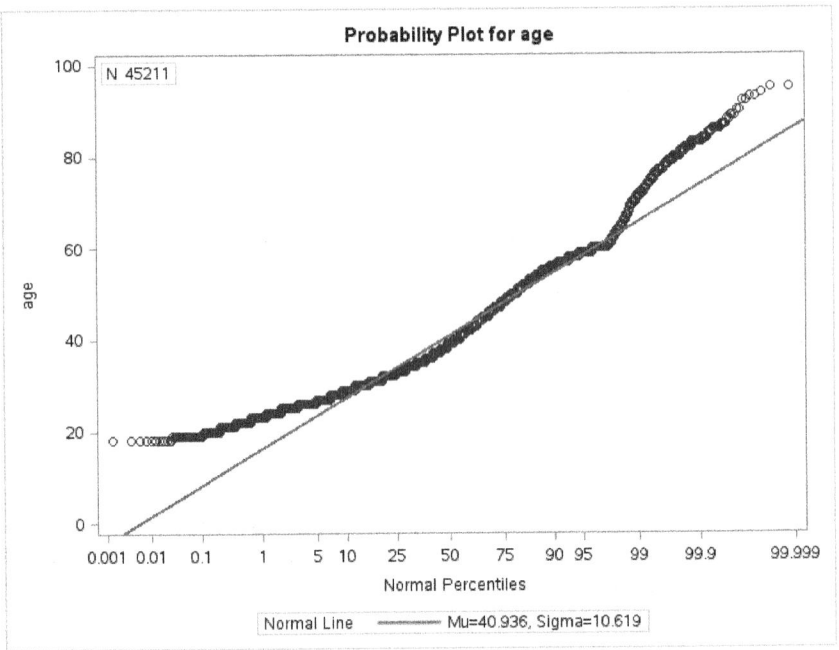

Figure 5-5. Probability Plot of the Age data fitted with a normal distribution

The next fit we try id the gamma distribution, since the gamma can "look" normal with a shape parameter over 25 (it is not the same distribution as a standard normal). The SAS code follows.

SAS Code and Data Exploration III

```
ods noproctitle;
ods graphics / imagemap=on;
/*** Exploring Data ***/
proc univariate data=WORK.BANK;
        ods select Histogram;
        var age;
        histogram age / normal kernel;
        inset n / position=ne;
run;
proc univariate data=WORK.BANK;
        ods select Histogram GoodnessOfFit ProbPlot QQPlot;
        var age;
        /*** Fitting Distributions ***/
        histogram age / gamma(alpha=est sigma=est theta=0);
        inset mean median std var n / position=ne;
        probplot age / gamma(alpha=est sigma=est theta=0);
        inset mean median std var n / position=nw;
        qqplot age / gamma(alpha=est sigma=est theta=0);
        inset mean median std var n / position=nw;
run;
```

Partial SAS Output III

Based on the plot shown in Figure 5-6, the *gamma distribution* with two parameters seems to fit the data. The fit statistics in Table 5-4 confirm this. Moreover the Q-Q plot in Figure 5-7 and the Probability plot in Figure 5-8 look much better than they did for the normal distribution. So, we conclude that the $gamma(\theta = 0, \alpha = 15.5, \gamma = 2.64)$ approximates the distribution of the age data.

Technically, we should pose a *null hypothesis* about the distribution of *age* like:

H_0 : The *age* data follows a gamma distribution with parameters theta, alpha and gamma, or in shorthand

$H_0: Age \sim \Gamma(\theta, \alpha, \gamma)$.

Alternatively,

H_a: *Age* does not follow a gamma distribution.

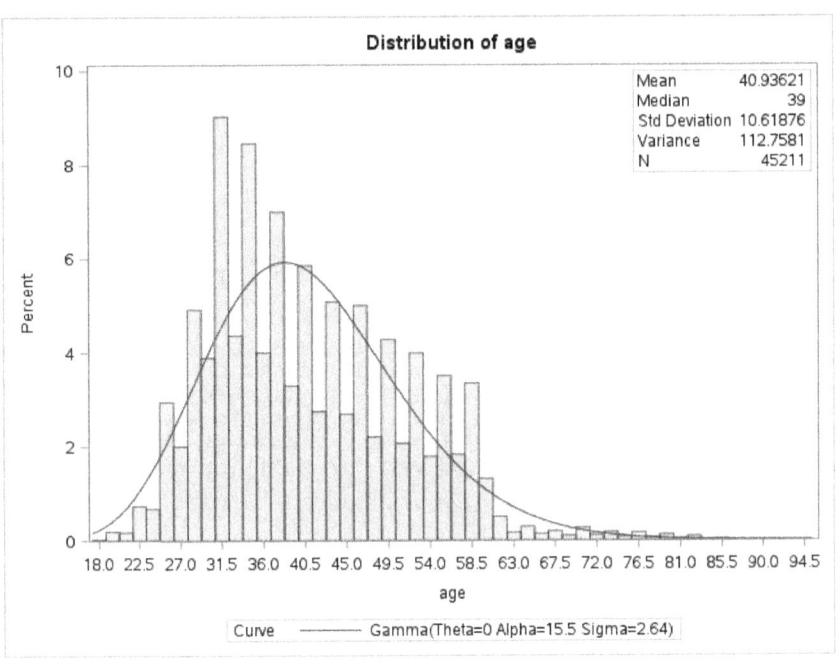

Figure 5-6. Age data histogram overlaid with a gamma distribution

Then, if the test statistic, i.e. *Kolmogorov-Smirnov test statistic*, is less than the *critical value*, then we fail to reject the null hypothesis, and conclude that we have no statistical cause to think otherwise.

Table 5-4. Goodness-of-Fit statistics for a gamma distribution

Goodness-of-Fit Tests for Gamma Distribution				
Test	Statistic		p Value	
Kolmogorov-Smirnov	D	0.072933	Pr > D	<0.001
Cramer-von Mises	W-Sq	42.921599	Pr > W-Sq	<0.001
Anderson-Darling	A-Sq	247.071735	Pr > A-Sq	<0.001

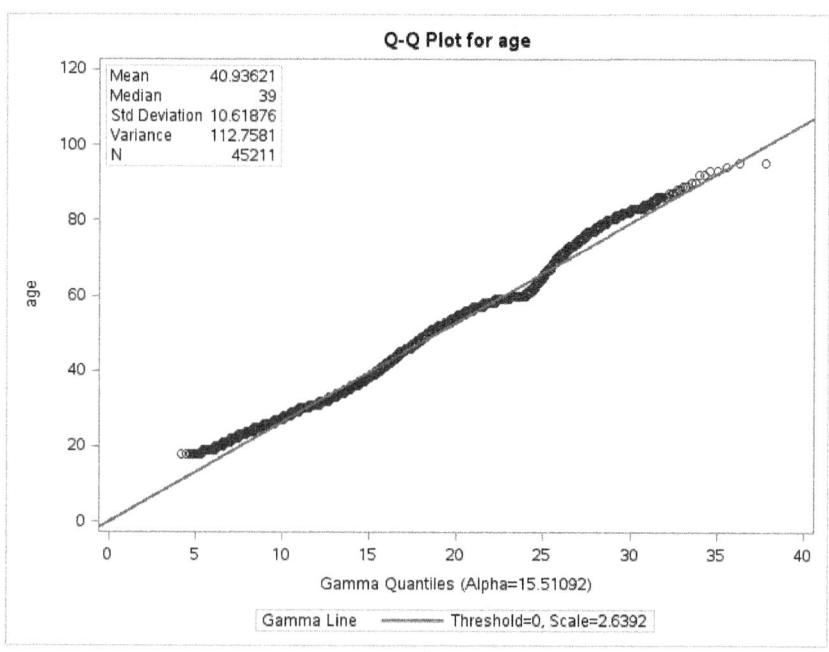

Figure 5-7. Q-Q Plot of the Age data fitted with a gamma distribution

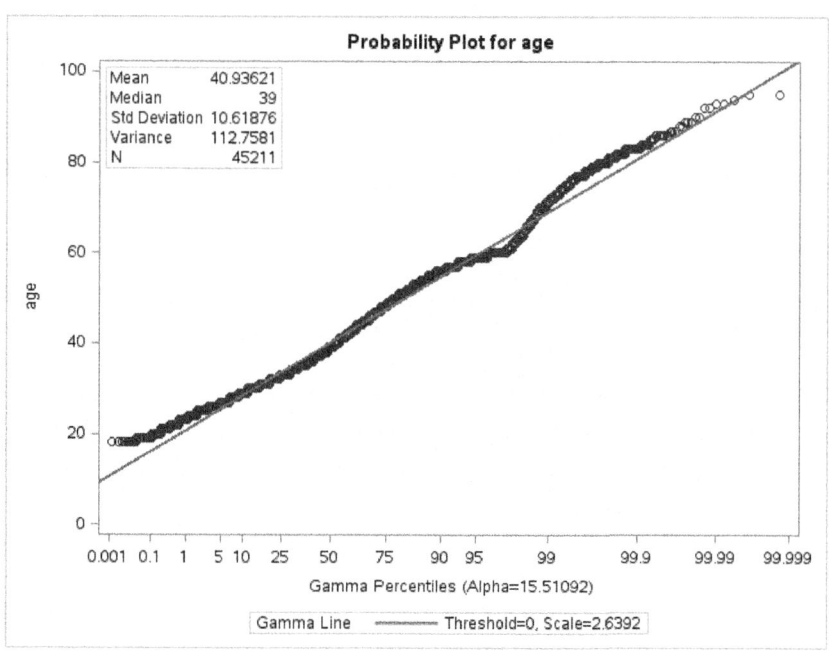

Figure 5-8. Probability Plot of the Age data fitted with a gamma distribution

With the analysis we just completed, we know more about the age data for this problem, but we still do not know if it will be a strong predictor. Therefore, we next examine a couple of useful metrics, *weight of evidence* and *information value*. Weight of Evidence (WOE) and Information Value (IV) have become important tools for analyzing and modeling binary outcomes such as acquire a product response to a marketing campaign.

Gamma Distributions

In probability theory and statistics, the gamma distribution is a two-parameter family of continuous probability distributions. The common exponential distribution and chi-squared distribution are special cases of the gamma distribution. There are three different parametrizations in common use (Park & Bera, 2009):

With a shape parameter k and a scale parameter θ.

With a shape parameter $\alpha = k$ and an inverse scale parameter $\beta = 1/\theta$, called a rate parameter.

With a shape parameter k and a mean parameter $\mu = k/\beta$.

In each of these three forms, both parameters are positive real numbers.

The parameterization with k and θ appears to be more common in econometrics and certain other applied fields, where e.g. the gamma distribution is frequently used to model waiting times. For instance, in life testing, the waiting time until death is a random variable that is frequently modeled with a gamma distribution (Hogg & Craig, 1978).

The parameterization with α and β is more common in Bayesian statistics, where the gamma distribution is used as a conjugate prior distribution for various types of inverse scale (aka rate) parameters, such as the λ of an exponential distribution or a Poisson distribution(Gopalan, Hofman, & Blei, 2014)– or for that matter, the β of the gamma distribution itself.

Weight of Evidence

Based on the information theory conceived in late 1940s and initially developed for scorecard development, Weight of Evidence (WOE) and Information Value (IV) have been gaining increasing attention in recent years for such uses as segmentation and variable reduction. As the calculation of WOE and IV requires the contrast between occurrence and non-occurrence (usually denoted by 1 and 0), they are highly suited for binary logistic regression. WOE and IV play two distinct roles when analyzing data:

- WOE describes the relationship between a predictive variable and a binary target variable.
- IV measures the strength of that relationship

Weight of Evidence (WOE) recodes the values of a variable into discrete categories and assigns to each category a unique WOE value for the purpose of producing the largest differences between the recoded categories. An important assumption here is that the dependent variable should be binary to denote occurrence and non-occurrence of an event. In the example of the bank marketing analysis, when a customer acquires a product (good) or does not (bad). In fact, WOE arose from the credit world to describe the separation of god and bad customers. (Bhalla, 2016).

Definition 5.1. WOE for any segment of customers is defined as the natural logarithm of the distribution of non-events over the distribution of events,

$$WOE = \left[ln \left(\frac{\% \text{ of non-events}}{\% \text{ of events}} \right) \right] \times 100,$$

$$(5.1)$$

and describes the relationship between a predictive variable and a binary response (target).

It is often calculated as $ln((\%Bad_i)/(\%Good_i))$, with Table 5-5a illustrating how it looks. Appendix A provides the SAS code used to produce the tables that follow, and was authored by Alec Zhixiao Lin

(PayPal Credit) and Tung-Ying Hsieh, (Dept. of Mathematics & Statistics, University of Maryland). (Lin & Hsieh, 2014)

For numerical variables, we can use WOE, Bin-Min and Bin-max to translate the variables for a subsequent logistic regression.

Table 5-5a. Extract from IV-WOE2 table showing numeric variables

tablevar	cnt	cnt_pct	dist_bad	woe	outcome-sum	Bin-min	Bin-max
homeowner	20081	0.4441	0.6341	-41.4428	0.16702	0	0
homeowner	25130	0.5558	0.3658	46.2531	0.07700	1	1
age	4088	0.0904	0.1431	-53.9634	0.18517	18	28
age	4938	0.1092	0.1123	-3.1626	0.12029	29	31
age	4057	0.0897	0.0814	10.8478	0.10623	32	33
age	5630	0.1245	0.1138	10.1221	0.10692	34	36
age	3162	0.0699	0.0593	18.3680	0.09930	37	38
age	5375	0.1188	0.0926	27.8220	0.09116	39	42
age	4688	0.1036	0.0794	29.7347	0.08959	43	46
age	4018	0.0888	0.0695	27.3101	0.09158	47	50
age	4355	0.0963	0.0769	25.0852	0.09345	51	55
age	4900	0.1083	0.1712	-53.7789	0.18489	56	95

For categorical variables (as in Table 5-6) and ordinal variables, we use the value from column Tier for variable transformation or for segmentation. Note that WOE is ordered alphabetically by classes shown in column Tier.

Table 5-6. Extract from IV-WOE2 table showing categorical variables

tablevar	cnt	cnt_pct	dist_bad	woe	outcomesum	tier
job	5171	0.11437	0.11930	-4.7921	0.122027	admin.
job	9732	0.21525	0.13386	52.3900	0.07275	blue-collar
job	1487	0.03289	0.02325	38.4694	0.082717	entrepreneur
job	1240	0.02742	0.02060	31.8211	0.087903	housemaid
job	9458	0.20919	0.24598	-18.5555	0.137556	management
job	2264	0.05007	0.09756	-80.1178	0.227915	retired

job	1579	0.03492	0.03535	-1.3910	0.118429	self-employed
job	4154	0.09188	0.06976	30.6706	0.08883	services
job	938	0.02074	0.05086	-111.023	0.28678	student
job	7597	0.16803	0.15882	6.3634	0.11057	technician
job	1303	0.02882	0.03819	-32.5592	0.155027	unemployed
job	288	0.00637	0.00642	-1.0324	0.118056	unknown

Due to space, I have not shown all of the table columns nor all the WOE tables produced. Table 5-7 shows a different look.

Table 5-7. Extract from IV-WOE2 table showing additional fields

table-var	tier	cnt	cnt-pct	sum-good	dist-good	sum-bad	dist-bad	woe
job	admin.	5171	0.1143	4540	0.1137	631	0.1193	-4.792
job	blue-collar	9732	0.2152	9024	0.2260	708	0.1338	52.390
job	entrepreneur	1487	0.0328	1364	0.0341	123	0.0232	38.469
job	housemaid	1240	0.0274	1131	0.0283	109	0.0206	31.821
job	management	9458	0.2092	8157	0.2043	1301	0.2459	-18.555
job	retired	2264	0.0500	1748	0.0437	516	0.0975	-80.117
job	self-employed	1579	0.0349	1392	0.0348	187	0.0353	-1.391
job	services	4154	0.0918	3785	0.0948	369	0.0697	30.670
job	student	938	0.0207	669	0.0167	269	0.0508	-111.02
job	technician	7597	0.1680	6757	0.1692	840	0.1588	6.363
job	unemployed	1303	0.0288	1101	0.0275	202	0.0381	-32.559
job	unknown	288	0.0063	254	0.0063	34	0.0064	-1.032

Here are some additional things you should know about WOE:

- Dist-Bad (%Bad) is not equivalent %Bad-Rate. Dist-Bad is the percentage of bad accounts in a score band over all bad counts. Same understanding applies to Dist-Good (%Good) in the example.
- It does not matter whether Dist-Good or Dist-Bad should be chosen as the numerator. If the two measures exchange their

positions in the division, the sign of WOE for each score band will reverse while the magnitude will remain unchanged. There is no impact on the subsequent calculation for IV.

- Multiplication by 100 is optional.

The WOE method consists of two steps:

1. We split (a continuous) variable into few categories or to group (a discrete) variable into few categories (and in both cases you assume that all observations in one category have "same" effect on dependent variable)
2. We calculate WOE value for each category (then the original x values are replaced by the WOE values)

The WOE transformation has (at least) three positive effects:

1. It can transform an independent variable so that it establishes monotonic relationship to the dependent variable. Actually it does more than this – to secure monotonic relationship it would be enough to "recode" it to any ordered measure (for example 1,2,3,4...) but the WOE transformation actually orders the categories on a *logistic scale* which is natural for logistic regression
2. For variables with too many (sparsely populated) discrete values, these can be grouped into categories (densely populated) and the WOE can be used to express information for the whole category
3. The (univariate) effect of each category on dependent variable can be simply compared across categories and across variables because WOE is standardized value (for example you can compare WOE of married people to WOE of manual workers)

The WOE transformation also has (at least) three drawbacks:

1. Loss of information (variation) due to binning to few categories
2. It is a "univariate" measure so it does not take into account correlation between independent variables

3. It is easy to manipulate (overfit) the effect of variables according to how categories are created

Conventionally, the betas (β) of the regression (where the x has been replaced by WOE) are not interpreted per se but they are multiplied with WOE to obtain a "score". For example, beta for variable "marital" (marital status) can be multiplied with WOE of "married people" group to see the score of married people; beta for variable "job" can be multiplied by WOE of "manual labor" to see the score of manual workers. Then if you are interested in the score of married manual workers, you sum up these two score and see how much is the effect on outcome. The higher the score is, the greater is probability of an outcome equal to 1.

WOE and Monotonic Relationships

I suppose we need a definition of monotonic before proceeding. A monotonic relationship is a relationship that does one of the following:

1. As the value of one variable increases, so does the value of the other variable
2. As the value of one variable increases, the other variable value decreases.

We can use the WOE values to transform non-monotonic variable into monotonic ones. If we take the values of the WOE values plotted against the outcomesum in Table 5-5 for homeowners, we can see the basic relationship, which will always be present with binary predictors, as seen in Figure 5-9.

Figure 5-9. Monotonic relationship of WOE and Outcome sum

Technically, If we take WOE with %Good in the denominator, we get exactly the one represented by Figure 5-9: As the value of the WOE variable decreases, the propensity for success increases, and we expect all the regression coefficients to be negative. Having %Good in the numerator presents the opposite effect.

It would be nice if monotonicity were the case for all numeric variables. Take age, for example, as shown in Figure 5-10.

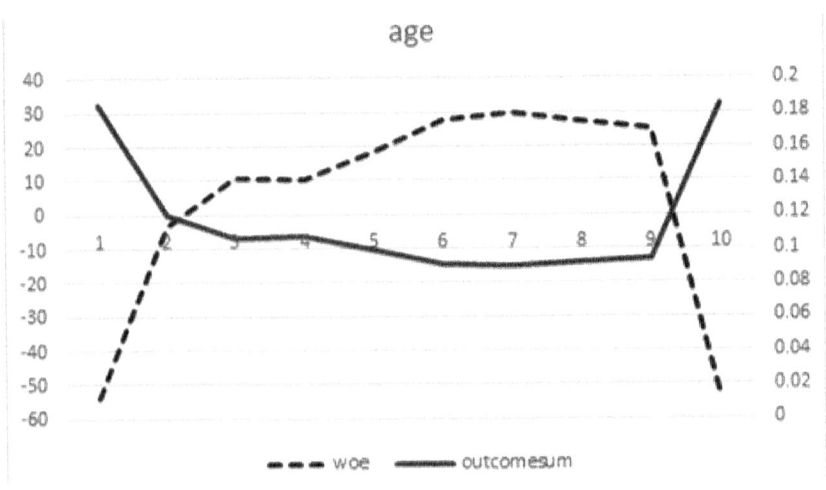

Figure 5-10. WOE values of Age plotted against the outcomesum

We can use the WOE values to re-bin Age so that it is monotonic. We want the Woe values to continue to increase, but the last value sends us along a negative slope. We can take the last four age categories and collapse to get Table 5-8.

Table 5-8. Re-binned WOE values for Age with 42-95 years collapsed

tablevar	cnt	cnt_pct	dist_bad	woe	outcome-sum	binmin	binmax
age	4088	0.09042	0.14312	-53.9634	0.185176	18	28
age	4938	0.10922	0.11230	-3.1626	0.120292	29	31
age	4057	0.08973	0.08149	10.8478	0.106236	32	33
age	5630	0.12452	0.11382	10.1221	0.106927	34	36
age	3162	0.06993	0.05936	18.3680	0.099304	37	38
age	5375	0.11888	0.09264	27.8220	0.091163	39	42
age	4900	0.10838	0.17129	28.3512	0.089736	42	95

Table 5-8 values produce the desired relationship we see in Figure 5-11.

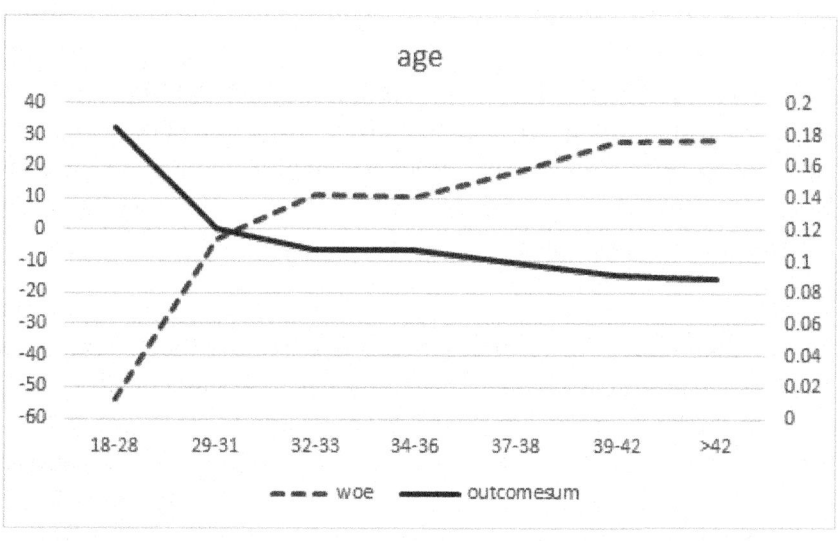

Figure 5-11. The re-binned WOE values for Age show a monotonic relationship

Dummy Variables

As I have mentioned, binary variables will always provide the desired outcome when applying the WOE transformation to those variables. We can often implement the effects of problematic numeric and categorical variables by using *dummy variables*, where 1 is a case and 0 is a noncase. For example, if bank balance is numeric but we cannot achieve monotonicity using WOE, we can use the dummy were the case is the presence of a balance and the noncase as the absence of a balance, such as:

$$D\_BALANCE = \begin{cases} 0 & \text{if no balance} \\ 1 & \text{if any balance} \end{cases}$$

The WOE-outcomesum plot would look similar to the one in Figure 5-9.

Information Value

In predictive modeling, we know there is a need to determine which variables are best in capturing a desired behavior out of a larger set of variables. For example, let's say we take our bank data and instead of using it as a marketing set, we look at a pool of customers have secured loans, and we want to determine who out of them are about to default (i.e. one of our fields is ln_default representing who refuses to pay up the balance of the loan). We need to then identify which of the attributes we have on the customer can potentially identify and alert us of such behavior. One of the popular ways in which this is done by analysts is by looking at something called *Information Value* (IV).

Definition

Information Value of x for measuring y is a number that attempts to quantify the predictive power of x in capturing y. Let's assume the target variable y which we are interested in being able to measure, is a 0-1 variable (or an indicator). Let's also further assume that it is the number of accounts who will go bad in the immediate future. Let's now divide our population in 10 equal parts (deciles) after sorting the entire pool by x, and create the deciles. Now we are all set to define Information Value:

Definition 5.2. The Information Value of an random variable x for measuring y is the value given by

$$IV_x = \sum_{x=1}^{10} (bad_i - good_i) ln \left(\frac{bad_i}{good_i} \right)$$

(5.2)

To quantify the predictive power of x in capturing y.

Note: In Equation 5.2 the presence of Equation 5.1, $ln \left(\frac{bad_i}{good_i} \right)$. So, IV is related to WOE mathematically.

Information Theory

Information theory kicked off when Claude Shannon (1948) wrote down an expression for the entropy of a probability distribution. Entropy is often described as the level of "disorder," but in the context of information theory it is better to think of it as one's level of uncertainty. High entropy means high uncertainty (you don't know what tomorrow holds) and low entropy mean low uncertainty (there will be no surprises tomorrow).

The code contained in Appendix A also produces the IV metrics we need in order to rank predictors. Table 5-9 shows an example of this with our Bank data.

Table 5-9. IV table for the Bank data

tablevar	type	iv	ivrank	pct_missing
homeowner	num	0.188681	1	0
job	char	0.155697	2	0
balance	num	0.107746	3	0
age	num	0.102996	4	0
loans	num	0.054859	5	0

As a rule of thumb, variables with higher IV values are better predictors as indicated in Table 5-10. Looking back at Table 5-9, we can conclude (for our example) there are no numeric variables with strong predictive power, based solely on IV. However, all but "loans" are still predictive to some degree.

Table 5-10. Rules-of-thumb for IV values

Strong predictive power	IV >0.3
Medium predictive power	0.1<IV<=0.3
Weak predictive power	0.02<IV<=0.1
No predictive power	IV<=0.02

The R Package – Information

The information package is designed to perform exploratory data analysis and variable ranking for binary logistic regression models using WOE and IV.

We will show an example using data contained in the information package. The data is from an historical marketing campaign from the insurance industry and is automatically downloaded when you install the Information package. The data is comprised of two files, one for the training dataset and one for the validation dataset. Each file has 68 predictive variables and 10,000 records.

If we want to see the first 20 variables we can enter:

```
library(Information)

### Loading the data
data(train, package="Information")
data(valid, package="Information")

### Exclude the control group
train <- subset(train, TREATMENT==1)
valid <- subset(valid, TREATMENT==1)
train[0,1:20]
```

```
[1]  TREATMENT                  M_SNC_MST_RCNT_ACT_OPN
[3]  TOT_HI_CRDT_CRDT_LMT        RATIO_BAL_TO_HI_CRDT
[5]  AGRGT_BAL_ALL_XCLD_MRTG     N_OF_SATISFY_FNC_REV_ACTS
[7]  AVG_BAL_ALL_FNC_REV_ACTS    N_BANK_INSTLACTS
[9]  M_SNCOLDST_BNKINSTL_ACTOPN  N_FNC_INSTLACTS
[11] N_SATISFY_INSTL_ACTS        M_SNC_MSTREC_INSTL_TRD_OPN
[13] TOT_INSTL_HI_CRDT_CRDT_LMT  M_SNC_OLDST_MRTG_ACT_OPN
[15] M_SNC_MSTRCNT_MRTG_ACT_UPD  M_SNC_MST_RCNT_MRTG_DEAL
[17] N30D_ORWRS_RTNG_MRTG_ACTS   N_OF_MRTG_ACTS_DLINQ_24M
[19] N_SATISFY_PRSNL_FNC_ACTS    RATIO_PRSNL_FNC_BAL2HICRDT
<0 rows> (or 0-length row.names)
```

The datasets contain two key indicators:

PURCHASE. This variable equals 1 if the client accepted the offer, and 0 otherwise

TREATMENT. This variable equals 1 if the client was in the test group (received the offer), and 0 otherwise.

Key Functions

`Information::create_infotables()` creates WOE tables and IVs for all variables in the input dataframe.

`Information::plot_infotables()` plots the WOE vector for one variable.

Ranking All Variables Using Adjusted IV

```
library(Information)
library(gridExtra)

options(scipen=10)

### Loading the data
data(train, package="Information")
data(valid, package="Information")

### Exclude the control group
train <- subset(train, TREATMENT==1)
valid <- subset(valid, TREATMENT==1)

### Ranking variables using penalized IV
```

```
IV <- Information::create_infotables(data=train,
        valid=valid,
        y="PURCHASE")

grid.table(head(IV$Summary), rows=NULL)
```

Partial Output

The output below is for two variables, created with the `Information::create_infotables()` function. Age is binned into categories of age ranges and the appropriate WOE , IV, and Penalty values are shown. Also not that the percentages of data, as well as N, are relatively the same and sum to 100%. The second variable is a dummy variable for debit cards, with 0 meaning no card and 1 meaning one or more cards.

```
$Tables$AGE
      AGE      N  Percent        WOE          IV      PENALTY
1   [21,28]  468 0.094127 -0.031251 0.000091077 0.000410123
2   [29,34]  478 0.096138  0.119702 0.001517485 0.001246391
3   [35,39]  479 0.096339  0.176212 0.004665078 0.003865117
4   [40,44]  547 0.110016 -0.134313 0.006571064 0.003927752
5   [45,48]  459 0.092316  0.147738 0.008674272 0.005761523
6   [49,53]  523 0.105189 -0.091538 0.009531825 0.006268676
7   [54,58]  457 0.091914 -0.157131 0.011696030 0.009208824
8   [59,66]  562 0.113032 -0.038861 0.011864774 0.009231145
9   [67,76]  469 0.094328  0.044692 0.012055680 0.009342350
10 [77,100]  530 0.106596 -0.035053 0.012185302 0.009578500

$Tables$D_DEPTCARD
  D_DEPTCARD    N   Percent        WOE       IV    PENALTY
1     [0,0] 3240 0.6516492 -0.2177474 0.028917 0.00232899
2     [1,1] 1732 0.3483508  0.3459560 0.074861 0.00628177
```

The `IV$Tables` object returned by Information is simply a list of dataframes that contains the WOE tables for all variables in the input dataset. Note that the penalty and IV columns are cumulative.

The `grid.table()` function produces the chart shown in Figure 5-12.

N_OPEN_REV_ACTS	N	Percent	WOE	IV	PENALTY
[0,0]	1469	0.29545455	-2.0465968	0.6401443	0.05703080
[1,2]	958	0.19267900	-0.5900120	0.6958705	0.06226262
[3,3]	310	0.06234916	0.2033085	0.6986029	0.06514553
[4,5]	583	0.11725664	0.4419768	0.7244762	0.06767437
[6,8]	632	0.12711183	0.6148243	0.7810611	0.07159274
[9,11]	453	0.09111022	0.8815772	0.8692672	0.07683238
[12,48]	567	0.11403862	0.9883818	1.0107695	0.08385690

Figure 5-12. IV/WOE Table produced by the grid.table() function

We can show the same information using:

```
print(IV$Tables$N_OPEN_REV_ACTS, row.names=FALSE)
```

```
N_OPEN_
REV_ACTS      N    Percent          WOE         IV     PENALTY
    [0,0] 1469 0.29545455  -2.0465968  0.6401443  0.05703080
    [1,2]  958 0.19267900  -0.5900120  0.6958705  0.06226262
    [3,3]  310 0.06234916   0.2033085  0.6986029  0.06514553
    [4,5]  583 0.11725664   0.4419768  0.7244762  0.06767437
    [6,8]  632 0.12711183   0.6148243  0.7810611  0.07159274
   [9,11]  453 0.09111022   0.8815772  0.8692672  0.07683238
  [12,48]  567 0.11403862   0.9883818  1.0107695  0.08385690
```

The table (in Figure 5-12) shows that the odds of PURCHASE=1 increases as N_OPEN_REV_ACTS increases, although the relationship is not linear.

If the variable under consideration is categorical, its distinct categories will show up as rows in the WOE table. Moreover, if the variable has missing values, the WOE table will contain a separate "NA" row which can be used to gauge the impact of missing values. Thus, the framework seamlessly handles missing values and categorical variables without any dummy-coding or imputation .

We can also plot this pattern for better visualization (see Figure 5-13):

```
Information::plot_infotables(IV, "N_OPEN_REV_ACTS")
```

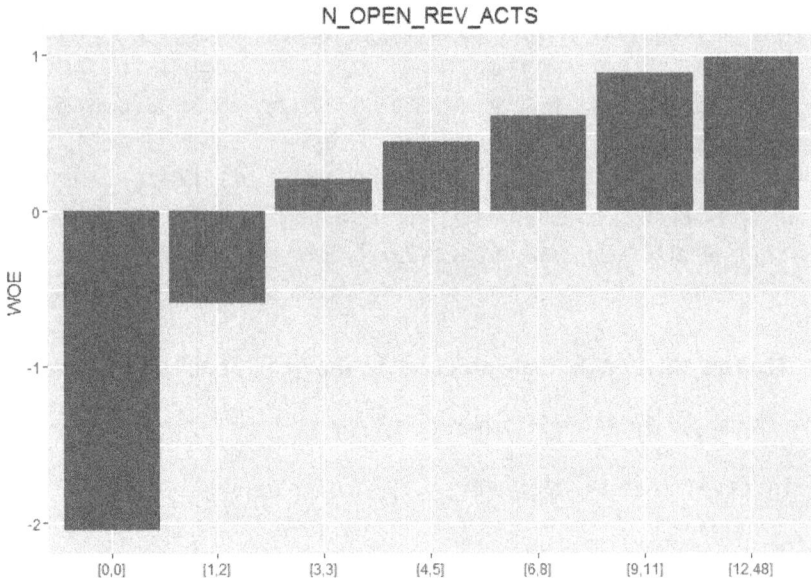

Figure 5-13. WOE plot for N_OPEN_REV_ACTS = number of open revolving accounts

If we want to plot all variables on separate pages, we can loop through all variables using:

```
names <- names(IV$Tables)
plots <- list()
for (i in 1:length(names)){
  plots[[i]] <- plot_infotables(IV, names[i])
}
# Showing the top 18 variables
plots[1:18]
```

For better visualization we can do a multiple plot to compare WOE patterns. Here we plot the first four variables on one page. Note that we can plot as many variables as we want; We can plot more and plot_infotables() will simply spread the plots over multiple pages (max of nine plots per page). The command is:

```
Information::plot_infotables(IV, IV$Summary$Variable[1:4],
          same_scale=TRUE)
```

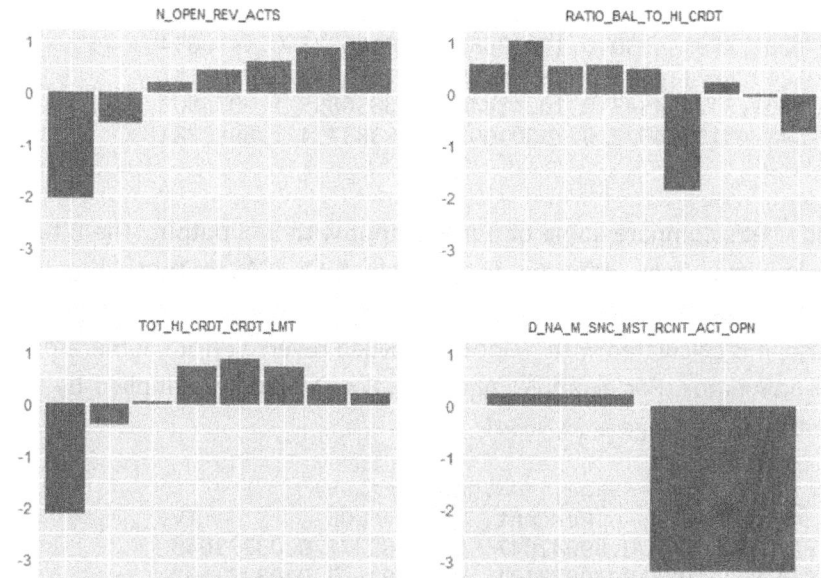

Figure 5-14. Multiple WOE plot showing four variables

```
bank <- read.csv("C:/Users/Strickland/Documents/Python Scri
pts/bank.csv", header=TRUE)

IV <- create_infotables(data=bank, y="RESP", ncore=2)
print(head(IV$Summary), row.names=FALSE)
```

```
  Variable        IV
  duration 1.6082281
  poutcome 0.5146091
     month 0.4361311
   contact 0.3003961
 homeowner 0.1886815
   mc_gold 0.1666374
```

```
print(IV$Tables$duration, row.names=FALSE)
```

```
 duration    N    Percent        WOE        IV
  [0,57]  4398 0.09727721 -4.1683338 0.4511710
 [58,88]  4530 0.10019685 -2.4740570 0.7054181
 [89,116] 4522 0.10001991 -1.4987072 0.8334604
[117,146] 4566 0.10099312 -1.0361483 0.9064864
[147,179] 4521 0.09999779 -0.5980215 0.9348989
```

```
[180,222]  4574 0.10117007 -0.2940997 0.9427131
[223,279]  4530 0.10019685  0.0586323 0.9430654
[280,367]  4505 0.09964389  0.1823939 0.9466187
[368,547]  4543 0.10048440  0.6856855 1.0074809
[548,4918] 4522 0.10001991  1.8385714 1.6082281
```

Now let's compare some of our R output with SAS output. The R table below may look different from Table 5-5b (SAS output), but it is equivalent. In Table 5-5b, the WOE is calculated and multiplied by 100. Also, it is calculated with %Good and %Bad reversed from numerator to denominator. For example, Ages 18-28 = 0.539634 multiplied by 100 with a sign change is 53.9634!

```
print(IV$Tables$age, row.names=FALSE)
    age    N    Percent        WOE          IV
 [18,28] 4088 0.09042047  0.53963377 0.03221049
 [29,31] 4938 0.10922121  0.03162682 0.03232107
 [32,33] 4057 0.08973480 -0.10847894 0.03333396
 [34,35] 3824 0.08458119 -0.10640671 0.03425329
 [36,38] 4968 0.10988476 -0.14893343 0.03655511
 [39,41] 4133 0.09141581 -0.27174265 0.04263540
 [42,45] 4755 0.10517352 -0.33134440 0.05279956
 [46,50] 5193 0.11486143 -0.24929906 0.05928534
 [51,55] 4355 0.09632612 -0.25085286 0.06478922
 [56,95] 4900 0.10838070  0.53778915 0.10310876
```

82

Table 5-5b. SAS extract from IV-WOE2 table showing the Age variables

tablevar	cnt	cnt_pct	dist_bad	woe	outcome-sum	Bin-min	Bin-max
age	4088	0.0904	0.1431	-53.9634	0.18517	18	28
age	4938	0.1092	0.1123	-3.1626	0.12029	29	31
age	4057	0.0897	0.0814	10.8478	0.10623	32	33
age	5630	0.1245	0.1138	10.1221	0.10692	34	36
age	3162	0.0699	0.0593	18.3680	0.09930	37	38
age	5375	0.1188	0.0926	27.8220	0.09116	39	42
age	4688	0.1036	0.0794	29.7347	0.08959	43	46
age	4018	0.0888	0.0695	27.3101	0.09158	47	50
age	4355	0.0963	0.0769	25.0852	0.09345	51	55
age	4900	0.1083	0.1712	-53.7789	0.18489	56	95

```
Information::plot_infotables(IV, "age")
```

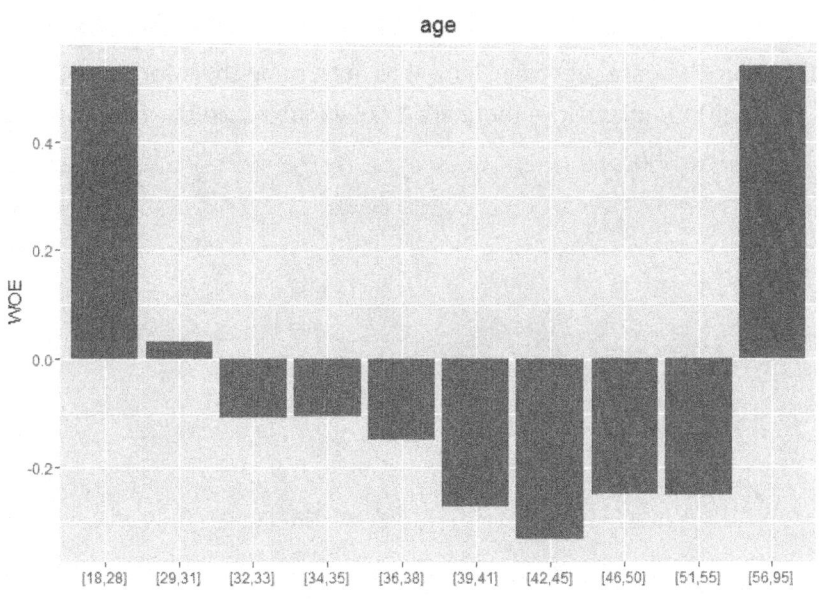

Figure 5-15. Woe plot for Age from the Bank data

83

Summary

In this chapter, we have looked at the concepts and methods of reducing a set of potential predictors to the most predictive variables. Exploring the data that may go into our model will ultimately provide us with a better model. WOE provides a method for binning data and imputing missing values that will assist in model development. IV give us a method of rank ordering variables and a metric by which to choose the best. We can calculate WOE and IV using SAS Studio and R's information package.

Exercises

1. Use the catalog data set using "purchase" as the target variable to perform the following tasks:
   a. Calculate the mean, median, variance, standard deviation, maximum, and minimum values for each variable.
   b. Find the information value for each explanatory variable and rank order them.
2. Using the catalog data set, construct WOE plots for each variable.
3. How does a WOE transformation affect a variable such as Age?
4. Using the data set "train," use R to determine the information value of the variables. Note there are 1776 variables . Record the variables and their IV.

6. Model fitting from the Inside-Out

Estimation

Maximum likelihood estimation

When we fit a regression model, the regression coefficients are usually estimated using *maximum likelihood estimation* (Menard, 2002). Unlike linear regression with normally distributed residuals, it is not possible to find a closed-form expression for the coefficient values that maximizes the likelihood function, so an iterative process must be used instead, for example *Newton's method*. This process begins with a tentative solution, revises it slightly to see if it can be improved, and repeats this revision until improvement is minute, at which point the process is said to have converged (Menard, 2002).

Two iterative maximum likelihood algorithms are available in PROC LOGISTIC (SAS). The default is the *Fisher scoring method*, which is equivalent to fitting by iteratively reweighted least squares. The alternative algorithm is the *Newton-Raphson method*. Both algorithms give the same parameter estimates. However, the estimated covariance matrix of the parameter estimators can differ slightly. This is due to the fact that Fisher scoring is based on the expected information matrix while the Newton-Raphson method is based on the observed information matrix. In the case of a binary logit model, the observed and expected information matrices are identical, resulting in identical estimated covariance matrices for both algorithms.

In some instances the model may not reach convergence. When a model does not converge this indicates that the coefficients are not meaningful because the iterative process was unable to find appropriate solutions. A failure to converge may occur for a number of reasons: having a large proportion of predictors to cases, multicollinearity, sparseness, or complete separation.

- Having a large proportion of variables to cases results in an overly conservative *Wald statistic* (discussed below) and can lead to nonconvergence.
- *Multicollinearity* refers to unacceptably high correlations between

predictors. As multicollinearity increases, coefficients remain unbiased but standard errors increase and the likelihood of model convergence decreases. To detect multicollinearity amongst the predictors, one can conduct a linear regression analysis with the predictors of interest for the sole purpose of examining the tolerance statistic used to assess whether multicollinearity is unacceptably high (Menard, 2002).

- *Sparseness* in the data refers to having a large proportion of empty cells (cells with zero counts). Zero cell counts are particularly problematic with categorical predictors. With continuous predictors, the model can infer values for the zero cell counts, but this is not the case with categorical predictors. The reason the model will not converge with zero cell counts for categorical predictors is because the natural logarithm of zero is an undefined value, so final solutions to the model cannot be reached. To remedy this problem, researchers may collapse categories in a theoretically meaningful way or may consider adding a constant to all cells (Menard, 2002).

- Another numerical problem that may lead to a lack of convergence is *complete separation*, which refers to the instance in which the predictors perfectly predict the criterion — all cases are accurately classified. In such instances, one should reexamine the data, as there is likely some kind of error (Hosmer & Lemeshow, 2000).

Although not a precise number, as a general rule of thumb, logistic regression models require a minimum of 10 events per explanatory variable (where event denotes the cases belonging to the less frequent category in the dependent variable) (Peduzzi, Concato, Kemper, Holford, & Feinstein, 1996).

Although the parameters of a regression model are usually estimated using the method of least squares, other methods which have been used include:

- Bayesian methods, e.g. Bayesian linear regression
- Percentage regression, for situations where reducing percentage errors is deemed more appropriate.[28]

- Least absolute deviations, which is more robust in the presence of outliers, leading to quantile regression
- Nonparametric regression, requires a large number of observations and is computationally intensive
- Distance metric learning, which is learned by the search of a meaningful distance metric in a given input space.[29]

History of Regression

The earliest form of regression was the method of least squares, which was published by Legendre in 1805, (Legendre, 1805) and by Gauss in 1809. (Gauss, 1809) Legendre and Gauss both applied the method to the problem of determining, from astronomical observations, the orbits of bodies about the Sun (mostly comets, but also later the then newly discovered minor planets). Gauss published a further development of the theory of least squares in 1821, (Gauss C. , 1823) including a version of the Gauss–Markov theorem.

The term "regression" was coined by Francis Galton in the nineteenth century to describe a biological phenomenon. The phenomenon was that the heights of descendants of tall ancestors tend to regress down towards a normal average (a phenomenon also known as regression toward the mean). (Mogull, 2004) (Galton, 1989) For Galton, regression had only this biological meaning, (Galton, Typical laws of heredity, 1877) (Galton, Presidential address, Section H, Anthropology, 1885) but his work was later extended by Udny Yule and Karl Pearson to a more general statistical context. (Yule, 1897) (Pearson, Yule, Blanchard, & Lee, 1903) In the work of Yule and Pearson, the joint distribution of the response and explanatory variables is assumed to be Gaussian. This assumption was weakened by R.A. Fisher in his works of 1922 and 1925. (Fisher, 1922) (Fisher R. A., 1954) (Aldrich, 2005) Fisher assumed that the conditional distribution of the response variable is Gaussian, but the joint distribution need not be. In this respect, Fisher's assumption is closer to Gauss's formulation of 1821.

In the 1950s and 1960s, economists used electromechanical desk calculators to calculate regressions. Before 1970, it sometimes took up to 24 hours to receive the result from one regression. (Ramcharan, 2006)

Regression methods continue to be an area of active research. In recent decades, new methods have been developed for robust regression, regression involving correlated responses such as time series and growth curves, regression in which the predictor (independent variable) or response variables are curves, images, graphs, or other complex data objects, regression methods accommodating various types of missing data, nonparametric regression, Bayesian methods for regression, regression in which the predictor variables are measured with error, regression with more predictor variables than observations, and causal inference with regression.

Selection

Selection allows for the construction of an optimal regression equation along with investigation into specific predictor variables. The aim of selection is to reduce the set of predictor variables to those that are necessary and account for nearly as much of the variance as is accounted for by the total set. In principle, selection helps to determine the level of importance of each predictor variable. It also assists in assessing the effects once the other predictor variables are statistically eliminated. The circumstances of the study, along with the nature of the research questions guide the selection of predictor variables.

Four selection procedures are used to yield the most appropriate regression equation: forward selection, backward elimination, stepwise selection, and block-wise selection. The first three of these four procedures are considered statistical regression methods. Many times researchers use sequential regression (hierarchical or block-wise) entry methods that do not rely upon statistical results for selecting predictors. Sequential entry allows the researcher greater control of the regression process. Items are entered in a given order based on theory, logic or practicality, and are appropriate when the researcher has an idea as to which predictors may impact the dependent variable.

Forward Selection

Forward selection begins with an empty equation. Predictors are added one at a time beginning with the predictor with the highest correlation with the dependent variable. Variables of greater theoretical importance are entered first. Once in the equation, the variable remains there.

Backward Selection

Backward elimination (or backward deletion) is the reverse process. All the independent variables are entered into the equation first and each one is deleted one at a time if they do not contribute to the regression equation.

Stepwise Regression

Stepwise selection is considered a variation of the previous two methods and is most widely used. Stepwise selection involves analysis at each step to determine the contribution of the predictor variable entered previously in the equation. In this way it is possible to understand the contribution of the previous variables now that another variable has been added. Variables can be retained or deleted based on their statistical contribution.

Stepwise selection is a semi-automated process of building a model by successively adding or removing variables based on the *Chi-Square* (χ^2) statistics of their estimated coefficients. I say it is "semi-automated" because it requires modeler input for selecting the maximum likelihood estimator and other parameters. Also, the modeler should use judgment to remove or replace variables that result in multicollinearity or correlation issues.

As the logistic regression steps through its analysis of each variable, it evaluates its χ^2 for entering the model, the Score χ^2, and continues to evaluate its χ^2 for removal from the model, the Wald χ^2, at a specified level of significance. The *Summary of Stepwise Selection* will show these steps as depicted in Table 1 for the bank marketing model we started in Chapter 3. Note one effect (default on loan) was removed and, therefore, has Wald Chi-Square value recorded in Table 6-1.

Table 6-1. Summary of stepwise regression for the bank model with no removed effects

	Summary of Stepwise Selection						
	Effect				Score	Wald	
				Number	Chi-	Chi-	
Step	Entered	Removed	DF	In	Square	Square	Pr > ChiSq
1	duration		1	1	7036.9489		<.0001
2	homeowner		1	2	1095.2015		<.0001
3	pdays		1	3	952.6370		<.0001
4	job		11	4	481.4613		<.0001
5	campaign		1	5	167.8769		<.0001
6	ln_default		1	6	145.4532		<.0001
7	loans		1	7	142.8996		<.0001
8	education		3	8	93.0279		<.0001
9	previous		1	9	80.9068		<.0001
10		ln_default	1			2.2341	0.4549
11	marital		2	10	54.7581		<.0001
12	balance		1	11	19.6743		<.0001

Block-wise Selection

Block-wise selection is a version of forward selection that is achieved in blocks or sets. The predictors are grouped into blocks based on psychometric consideration or theoretical reasons and a stepwise selection is applied. Each block is applied separately while the other predictor variables are ignored. Variables can be removed when they do not contribute to the prediction. In general, the predictors included in the blocks will be inter-correlated. Also, the order of entry has an impact on which variables will be selected; those that are entered in the earlier stages have a better chance of being retained than those entered at later stages.

Estimators and Odds

Table 6-2 shows the Analysis of Maximum Likelihood Estimates for the numerical effects in our model. We will now walk through each column heading and examine the meaning and derivation of each element.

First notice that SAS Studio calls the model effects "parameters." You might also see them as "effect", "variable", "vars", "tablevars", or other descriptors, but they are merely the predictors selected by the stepwise regression. We will discuss the "intercept" later in this chapter.

The first column, not including the parameter, is the estimate that was obtained through the maximum likelihood estimation procedure during the stepwise regression. You will often find the model effects (parameters) list by order if predictive strength, like the IV list. Here, they are listed alphabetically and "balance", which had the smallest χ^2 value is at the top of the list. So, how are these estimates obtained?

Table 6-2. Analysis of Maximum Likelihood Estimates of the numerical effects for the bank marketing model

Analysis of Maximum Likelihood Estimates					
Parameter	DF	Estimate	Standard Error	Wald Chi-Square	Pr > ChiSq
Intercept	1	-2.7301	0.2135	163.5866	<.0001
balance	1	0.000020	4.535E-6	19.2682	<.0001
homeowner	1	-1.0802	0.0372	841.5377	<.0001
loans	1	-0.6393	0.0567	127.3472	<.0001
duration	1	0.00394	0.000060	4243.3232	<.0001
campaign	1	-0.1276	0.00977	170.5185	<.0001
pdays	1	0.00290	0.000165	308.6231	<.0001
previous	1	0.0773	0.00779	98.4841	<.0001

The method of *maximum likelihood estimation* assumes that the random sample or observations in our model can be parameterized; that is, they come from an assumed probability distribution with an unknown parameter, theta (θ). Now, It seems reasonable that a good estimate of the unknown parameter θ would be the value of θ that maximizes the probability or likelihood of getting the data we observed. So, we will *maximize* the *estimate* that yields the best *likelihood*! We call this the *maximum likelihood estimator* or **mle**.

Suppose we have a random sample $X_1, X_2, ..., X_n$ for which the probability density function of each X_i is $f(x\_i, \theta)$. Then the joint probability density function of $X_1, X_2, ..., X_n$ is:

$$L = P(X_1 = x_1, X_2 = x_2, ..., X_n = x_n) = f(x_1; \theta) \cdot f(x_2; \theta) \cdots f(x_n; \theta)$$

$$= \prod_{i=1}^{n} f(x_i; \theta)$$

(6.1)

The first equality is of course just the definition of the joint probability mass function. The second equality comes from that fact that we have a random sample, which implies by definition that the X_i are independent. And, the last equality just uses the shorthand mathematical notation of a product of indexed terms. Now, in light of the basic idea of maximum likelihood estimation, one reasonable way to proceed is to treat the "likelihood function" $L(\theta)$ as a function of θ, and find the value of θ that maximizes it.

History of MLE

Maximum likelihood estimation was recommended, analyzed (with fruitless attempts at proofs) and widely popularized by Ronald Fisher between 1912 and 1922 (although it had been used earlier by Carl Friedrich Gauss, Pierre-Simon Laplace, Thorvald N. Thiele, and Francis Ysidro Edgeworth). (Edgeworth, 1908)

Maximum likelihood estimation finally transcended heuristic justification in a proof published by Samuel S. Wilks in 1938, now called "Wilks' theorem". (Wilks, The Large-Sample Distribution of the Likelihood Ratio for Testing Composite Hypotheses, 1938) The theorem shows that the error in the logarithm of likelihood values for estimates from multiple independent samples is χ^2 distributed, which enables determination of a confidence region around any one estimate of the parameters. Ironically, the only difficult part of the proof depends on the expected value of the Fisher information matrix, which is provided by a theorem by Fisher. (Owen, 2001) Wilks continued to improve on the generality of the theorem throughout his life, with his most general proof published in 1962. (Wilks, Mathematical Statistics, 1962)

Example

Suppose we have a random sample $X_1, X_2, \ldots, X_n$ where:

X_i = 0 if a randomly selected member does not own a credit card

X_i = 1 if a randomly selected member does own a credit card

Assuming that the X_i are independent Bernoulli random variables with unknown parameter p, find the maximum likelihood estimator of p, the proportion of members who own a credit card.

Solution. If the X_i are independent Bernoulli random variables with unknown parameter p, then the probability mass function of each X_i is:

$$f(x_i; p) = p^{x_i}(1-p)^{1-x_i}$$

for $x_i = 0$ or 1 and $0 < p < 1$. Therefore, the likelihood function $L(p)$ is:

$$L(p) = \prod_{i=1}^{n} f(x_i; p)$$
$$= p^{x_1}(1-p)^{1-x_1} \times p^{x_2}(1-p)^{1-x_2} \times \cdots$$
$$\times p^{x_n}(1-p)^{1-x_n}$$

for $0 < p < 1$. Simplifying, by summing up the exponents, we get the definition of $L(p)$.

Definition 6.1. The likelihood function $L(p)$ is defined as:

$$L(p) = p^{\sum x_i}(1-p)^{n-\sum x_i} \tag{6.2}$$

Now, in order to implement the method of maximum likelihood, we need to find the p that maximizes the likelihood $L(p)$. We need to put on our calculus hats now, since in order to maximize the function, we are going to need to differentiate the likelihood function with respect to p. In doing so, we'll use a "trick" that often makes the differentiation a

93

bit easier. Note, from Figure 6-1, the natural logarithm is an increasing function of x:

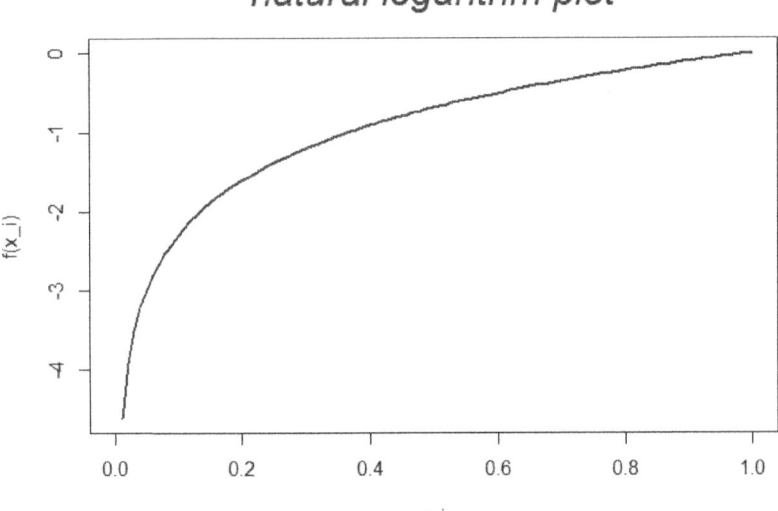

Figure 6-1. Plot of the natural logarithm function

That is, if $x_1 < x_2$, then $f(x_1) < f(x_2)$ (see Figure 6-1). That means that the value of p that maximizes the natural logarithm of the likelihood function $ln(L(p))$ is also the value of p that maximizes the likelihood function $L(p)$. So, the "trick" is to take the derivative of $ln(L(p))$ (with respect to p) rather than taking the derivative of $L(p)$. Again, doing so often makes the differentiation much easier.

In this case, the natural logarithm of the likelihood function is:

$$logL(p) = (\textstyle\sum x_i)\log(p) + (n - \textstyle\sum x_i)\log(1 - p)$$

Now, taking the derivative of the log likelihood, and setting to 0, we get:

$$\frac{\partial \log L(p)}{\partial p} = \frac{\sum x_i}{p} - \frac{(n - \sum x_i)}{1 - p} = 0$$

Now, multiplying through by $p(1 - p)$, we get:

$$(\textstyle\sum x_i)(1 - p) - (n - \textstyle\sum x_i)p = 0$$

94

Upon distributing, we see that two of the resulting terms cancel each other out:

leaving us with:

$$\sum x_i - np = 0 \sum x_i - np = 0$$

Now, all we have to do is solve for p. In doing so, you'll want to make sure that you always put a hat ("^") on the parameter, in this case p, to indicate it is an estimate:

$$\hat{p} = \frac{\sum_{i=1}^{n} x_i}{n}$$

(6.3a)

or, alternatively, an estimator:

$$\hat{p} = \frac{\sum_{i=1}^{n} X_i}{n}$$

(6.3b)

Oh, that looks like a *mean value*!

We should technically verify that we indeed did obtain a maximum. We can do that by verifying that the second derivative of the log likelihood with respect to p is negative. It is, but you might want to do the work to convince yourself!

Now, suppose out of 65 members, 20 members have a credit card and 45 members do not. Then the **mle** is

$$\frac{20(1) + 45(0)}{65} = \frac{20}{65} = 0.307692.$$

Suppose, instead, we have 100 member and 50 have credit cards and 50 do not. What is the **mle**? Is the likelihood 50:50. Is that 0.5 or 50%?

$$\frac{50(1) + 50(0)}{50} = \frac{50}{100} = 0.5.$$

Of course the **mle** depends on the *probability density function*, so the **mle** is not always equal to the average value we just derived. For a Poisson distribution the **mle** is λ and for the normal distribution there are two parameters, so we need the **mle** of μ and σ. The gamma distribution's **mle** results in an equation that has no closed form solution, so an iterative process must be used, like Fisher's Scoring method (the default in SAS Studio as shown in Figure 6-2).

```
proc logistic data=WORK.BANK plots
    (unpack)=all;
    class job marital education poutcome / param=glm;
    model RESP(event='1')=manual_labor age balance homeowner
        duration campaign pdays previous married job marital
        link=logit
        selection=stepwise
        slentry=0.05
        slstay=0.05 |
        technique=fisher;
run;
```

Figure 6-2. Proc Logistic using Fisher's Scoring as the optimization technique.

Odds Ratio and Log Odds

An odds ratio (OR) is a measure of association between an exposure and an outcome. The OR represents the odds that an outcome will occur given a particular exposure/treatment, compared to the odds of the outcome occurring in the absence of that exposure/treatment.

Odds and probability are two different ways to describe the chance of an even occurring. Odds expresses chance as a ratio of success to failure, the number of desired outcomes to the number of undesired outcomes. Probability expresses chance as a ratio of the number of desired outcomes to the total number of possible outcomes.

For example, the probability of getting heads when flipping a fair coin is 1/2 or 0.5. There is one desired event (heads) and two events total (heads and tails). Probability is read "x out of z," where x is the number of successes and z is the total number of possible outcomes. The odds of getting heads is 1:1 because there is one way to get heads and one way to not get heads, i.e. getting tails. Odds are read "x to y." where x is the number of successes and y is the number of failures.

In Table 6-3, we list a few probabilities along with their associated odds ratios and log odds. We calculate the odds ration from the probability by dividing the probability by its complement, such as

$$\frac{0.2}{1.0 - 0.2} = \frac{0.2}{0.8} = 0.25$$

We calculate the log odds from odds ratio by taking the natural log of the odds ratio, such as

$$ln(0.25) = -1.386294361$$

Table 6-3. Relationship of probability, odds, and log odds

p	odds	log odds
0.001	0.001001	-6.90675
0.01	0.010101	-4.59512
0.15	0.176471	-1.7346
0.2	0.25	-1.38629
0.25	0.333333	-1.09861
0.3	0.428571	-0.8473
0.35	0.538462	-0.61904
0.4	0.666667	-0.40547
0.45	0.818182	-0.20067
0.5	1	0
0.55	1.222222	0.200671
0.6	1.5	0.405465
0.65	1.857143	0.619039
0.7	2.333333	0.847298
0.75	3	1.098612
0.8	4	1.386294
0.85	5.666667	1.734601
0.9	9	2.197225
0.999	999	6.906755
0.9999	9999	9.21024

Figure 6-3 shows the graph of the relationship between the odds and probability, and Figure 6-4 shows the relationship between the odds and the log odds. Not surprisingly, the former appears to be an exponential distribution and the latter a natural logarithm.

When we calculate a logistic regression, the regression coefficient (β_1) is the estimated increase in the log odds of the outcome per unit increase in the value of the exposure/treatment.

Definition 6.2. The exponential function of the regression coefficient $\left(e^{\beta_1}\right)$ *is the odds ratio associated with a one-unit increase in the exposure.*

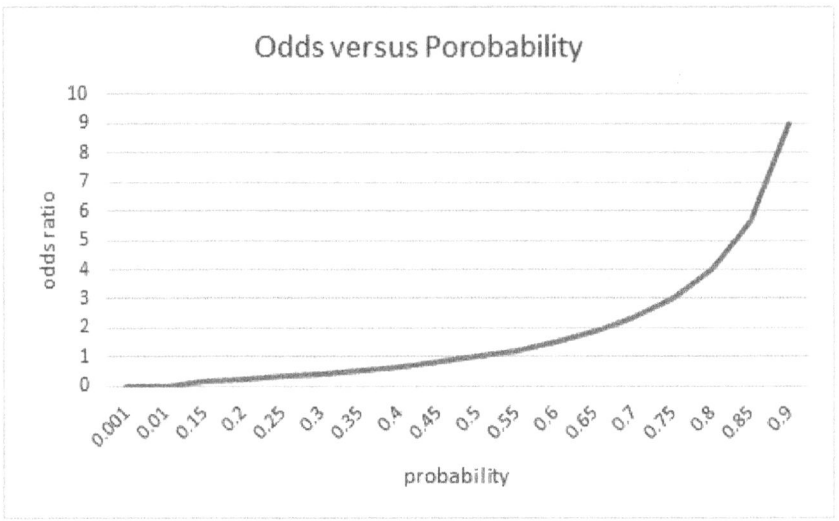

Figure 6.3. Relationship of odds ratio to probability

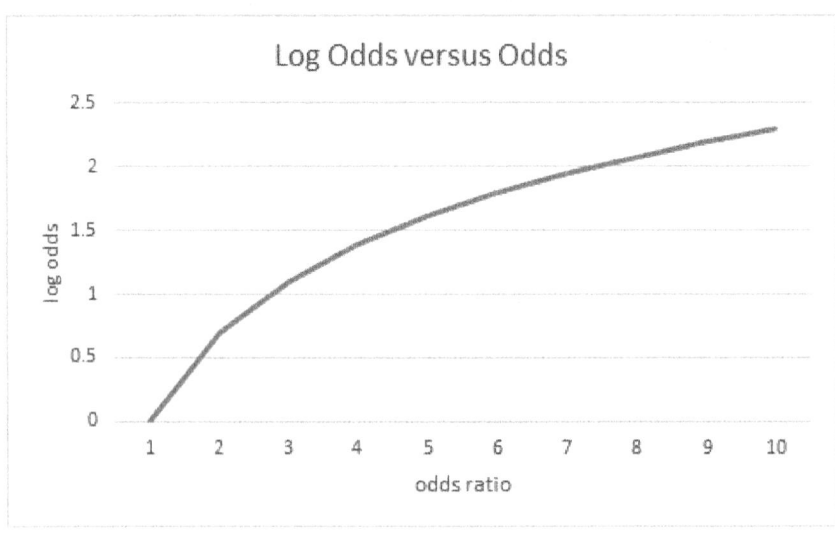

98

Figure 6-4. Relationship of log odds to odds ratio

We use odds ratios to compare the relative odds of the occurrence of the outcome of interest (e.g. disease or disorder or treatment), given exposure to the variable of interest (e.g. health characteristic, aspect of medical history, marketing characteristic). We can also use the odds ratio to determine whether a particular exposure is a risk factor for a particular outcome, and to compare the magnitude of various risk factors for that outcome.

OR=1: Exposure does not affect odds of outcome

OR>1: Exposure associated with higher odds of outcome

OR<1: Exposure associated with lower odds of outcome

We use a 95% confidence interval (CI) to estimate the precision of the OR. A large CI indicates a low level of precision of the OR, whereas a small CI indicates a higher precision of the OR. It is important to note, however, that unlike the p value, the 95% CI does not report a measure's statistical significance. In practice, we often use the 95% CI as a proxy for the presence of statistical significance if it does not overlap the null value (e.g. OR=1). Nevertheless, it would be inappropriate to interpret an OR with 95% CI that spans the null value as indicating evidence for lack of association between the exposure and outcome.

Confounding

When we observe a non-casual association between a given exposure and outcome is as a result of the influence of a third variable, designated *confounding*, with the third variable called a *confounding variable*. A confounding variable is causally associated with the outcome of interest, and non-causally or causally associated with the exposure, but is not an intermediate variable in the causal pathway between exposure and outcome (Szklo & Nieto, 2997). We use stratification and multiple regression techniques as methods to address confounding, and produce "adjusted" ORs.

Example

We will use data from an article published in the *Journal of the Canadian Association of Child and Adolescent Psychiatry* in November 2008 to illustrate how ORs (A) and 95% CIs (B) are calculated. In their article, Greenfield and his colleagues looked at previous suicidal adolescents (n=263) and used logistic regression to analyze the associations between baseline variables such as age, sex, previous hospitalizations, presence of psychiatric disorder, and drug and alcohol use, with suicidal behavior at six-month follow-up (Greenfield B, et al., 2008).

A. Calculating Odds Ratios

We will calculate odds ratios (OR) using a two-by-two frequency table.

		Outcome Status	
		+	−
Exposure Status	+	a	b
	−	c	d

Where

a = Number of exposed cases

b = Number of exposed non-cases

c = Number of unexposed cases

d = Number of unexposed non-cases

$$OR = \frac{\frac{a}{c}}{\frac{b}{d}} = \frac{ad}{bc}$$

$$OR = \frac{\frac{(n)\text{exposed cases}}{(n)\text{unexposed cases}}}{\frac{(n)\text{exposed non-cases}}{(n)\text{unexposed non-cases}}}$$

$$= \frac{(n)\text{exposed cases} \times (n)\text{unexposed non-cases}}{(n)\text{exposed non-cases} \times (n)\text{unexposed cases}}$$

In the study, 186 of the 263 adolescents previously judged as having experienced a suicidal behavior requiring immediate psychiatric consultation did not exhibit suicidal behavior (non-suicidal, NS) at six months follow-up. Of this group, 86 young people had been assessed as having depression at baseline. Of the 77 young people with persistent suicidal behavior at follow-up (suicidal behavior, SB), 45 had been assessed as having depression at baseline.

What is the OR of suicidal behavior at six months follow-up given presence of depression at baseline?

First we determine the numbers to use for (a), (b), (c), (d)

  a: Number of exposed cases (+ +) = ?

  b: Number of exposed non-cases (+ –) = ?

  c: Number of unexposed cases (– +) = ?

  d: Number of unexposed non-cases (– –) = ?

Question 1: Who are the exposed cases (++ = a)?

Answer 1: Youth with persistent SB assessed as having depression at baseline, a=45

Question 2: Who are the exposed non-cases (+ – = b)?

Answer 2: Youth with no SB at follow-up assessed as having depression at baseline, b=86

Question 3: Who are the unexposed cases (– + = c)?

Answer 3: Youth with persistent SB not assessed as having depression at baseline; c: 77(SB) – 45(depression) = 32

Question 4: Who are the unexposed non-cases (– – = d)?

Answer 4: Youth with no SB at follow-up not assessed as having depression at baseline; d: 186(NS) –86(depression) = 100

Then we substitute the values into the formula

  a: Number of exposed cases (++) = 45

  b: Number of exposed non-cases (+ –) = 86

  c: Number of unexposed cases (– +) = 32

  d: Number of unexposed non-cases (– –) = 100

$$OR = \frac{\frac{a}{c}}{\frac{b}{d}} = \frac{ad}{bc} = \frac{\frac{45}{32}}{\frac{86}{100}} = 1.63$$

Thus, the odds of persistent suicidal behavior is 1.63 higher given baseline depression diagnosis compared to no baseline depression.

B. Calculating 95% confidence intervals

What are the confidence intervals for the OR calculated above?

Confidence intervals are calculated using the formula shown below

$$Upper\ 95\%\ CI = e^{\left[\ln(OR)+1.96\sqrt{\left(\frac{1}{a}+\frac{1}{b}+\frac{1}{c}+\frac{1}{d}\right)}\right]}$$

$$Lower\ 95\%\ CI = e^{\left[\ln(OR)-1.96\sqrt{\left(\frac{1}{a}+\frac{1}{b}+\frac{1}{c}+\frac{1}{d}\right)}\right]}$$

Plugging in the numbers from the table above, we get:

$$Upper\ 95\%\ CI = e^{\left[\ln(OR)+1.96\sqrt{\left(\frac{1}{45}+\frac{1}{86}+\frac{1}{32}+\frac{1}{100}\right)}\right]} = 2.80$$

$$Lower\ 95\%\ CI = e^{\left[\ln(OR)-1.96\sqrt{\left(\frac{1}{45}+\frac{1}{86}+\frac{1}{32}+\frac{1}{100}\right)}\right]} = 0.96$$

Since the 95% CI of 0.96 to 2.80 spans 1.0, the increased odds (OR 1.63) of persistent suicidal behavior among adolescents with depression at baseline does not reach statistical significance. In fact, this is indicated in Table 1 of the reference article (Figure 6-5 below), which shows a p value of 0.07.

Interestingly, the odds of persistent suicidal behavior in this group given presence of borderline personality disorder at baseline was twice that of depression (OR 3.8, 95% CI:1.6–8.7), and was statistically significant (p 0.002)

This example illustrates a few important points. First, presence of a positive OR for an outcome given a particular exposure does not necessarily indicate that this association is *statistically significant*. One must consider the confidence intervals and p value (where provided) to determine significance. Second, while the psychiatric literature shows that overall, depression is strongly linked to suicide and suicide attempt (Kutcher & Szumilas, 2009), in a particular sample, with a particular size and composition, and in the presence of other variables, the association may not be significant.

Table 1. Clinical characteristics of the suicidal adolescents at baseline and between-group differences

Characteristic	Suicidal (S) (n=77) % or mean±SD	Non-Suicidal (NS) (n=186) % or mean±SD	Odds Ratio) (S/NS)	p-value	95% C.I.
Age	14.7 ± 1.4	14.5 ± 1.6	1.1	0.34	0.9 – 1.3
Sex (female)	79.2	64	2.2	0.02	1.2 – 4.0
IFR score	46.1 ± 23.8	42.4 ± 24.7	1	0.27	1.0 – 1.0
Depression	58.4	46.2	1.6	0.07	1.0 – 2.8
Conduct disorder	32.5	19.8	2	0.03	1.1 – 3.6
Life events	11.7 ± 7.0	10.2 ± 6.6	1	0.1	1.0 – 1.1
Number of previous hospitalization	0.5 ± 0.7	0.3 ± 0.5	1.6	0.03	1.1 – 2.5
Borderline personality disorder	90.9	72.6	3.8	0.002	1.6 – 8.7
Previous suicide attempt(s)	89.6	71.6	3.4	0.02	1.2 – 9.6

Drug use	71.4	45.9	3	0.001	1.7 – 5.2
Alcohol use	63.3	48.8	1.8	0.09	0.9 – 3.6
CGAS score	38.6 ± 11.5	40.0 ± 11.0	1	0.37	1.0 – 1.0
Parent previous suicide attempt(s)	87.5	78.7	1.9	0.37	0.5 – 7.7
Parental psychopathology	40.3	38.7	1.1	0.82	0.6 – 1.8
Living arrangement (group home)	5.4	4	1.4	0.63	0.4 – 4.8
Compliance to treatment	28.6	37.6	0.7	0.16	0.8 – 1.2

Figure 6-5. Table 1 from the original study: Clinical characteristics of the suicidal adolescents at baseline and between-group differences

More Log Odds

Log odds are an alternate way of expressing probabilities, which simplifies the process of updating them with new evidence. Unfortunately, it is difficult to convert between probability and log odds.

> **Definition 6.3.** The log odds is the log of the odds ratio. Hence, we can calculate the log odds of probability q as
>
> $$\log \text{odds of } q = \ln\left(\frac{q}{1-q}\right).$$
>
> (6.4)

Let's return to our bank marketing example. Recall that one of our predictors are homeowner, which is binary, yes or no (1 or 0). If we want to convert the log odds, Equation 6.4, to a probability. To do so, we must use exponential function, which is the invers of the natural logarithm function.

> **Definition 6.4.** To convert log odds to a probability, p, in logistic regression we use the exponential function as follows:
>
> $$p = \frac{e^q}{e^q + 1}$$
>
> (6.5)

Using Excel, we can make a spreadsheet that does the calculations for us, as shown in Table 6-6. (Note the intercept is the constant term.)

Table 6-6. Spreadsheet calculations for converting log odds to probabilities and determining percent differences as the value of the variables change

Variable	Coefficients	Yes	No
Intercept	-2.7301	1	1
homeowner	-1.0802	1	0
$q = ln(q/(1-q))$		-3.8103	-2.7301
$p = exp(q)/(exp(q)+1)$		0.021662	0.06122
Percent Difference			0.039559

Note the probability of responding to a campaign offer is higher if you are not a homeowner (6.12%) versus being a homeowner (2.17%), and that a non-homeowner is about 4% (0.039559) more likely to respond.

Now, suppose we add the variable "balance" and treat it as binary. That is, the value of balance is one if an individual has a balance and zero otherwise. Lets' see how this affects the outcome. The calculations are shown in Table 6-7.

Table 6-7. Spreadsheet calculations for converting log odds to probabilities and determining percent differences as the value of the variables change

Variable	Coefficients	Yes	No	No	Yes
Intercept	-2.7301	1	1	1	1
homeowner	-1.0802	1	0	0	1
balance	0.00002	1	1	0	0
$q = ln(q/(1-q))$		-3.81028	-2.73008	-2.7301	-3.8103
$p = exp(q)/(exp(q)+1)$		0.021662	0.061222	0.06122	0.02166
Percent Difference			0.039559	0.00000	-0.03956

Note, as we add "balance", the small coefficient and that there is no percent change as we go from non-homeowner with (6.12%) or without a balance (6.12%). Also, there is no percent change as we go from

105

homeowner with (2.17%) or without a balance (2.17%). This may be an indication that we could drop "balance" from the model. Moreover, the basic conclusion did not change: the non-homeowner is about 4% more likely to respond to a campaign offer, when both variables (homeowner and balance) are included.

Hence, we have a way for converting coefficients in a logistic regression to probabilities, and *vice versa*.

Minimum chi-squared estimator for grouped data

While individual data will have a dependent variable with a value of zero or one for every observation, with grouped data one observation is on a group of people who all share the same characteristics (e.g., demographic characteristics). For this event, we observe the proportion of people in the group for whom the response variable falls into one category or the other. If this proportion is neither zero nor one for any group, the minimum χ^2 estimator involves using *weighted least squares* to estimate a linear model in which the dependent variable is the logit of the proportion. That is, the log of the ratio of the fraction in one group to the fraction in the other group (Greene, 2011). We should probably define the χ^2 distribution before proceeding further.

Definition 6.5. Let X follow a gamma distribution with $\theta = 2$ and $\alpha = r/2$, where r is a positive integer. Then the probability density function of X is:

$$f(x) = \frac{1}{\Gamma\left(\frac{r}{2}\right) 2^{\frac{r}{2}}} x^{\frac{r}{2}-1} e^{-\frac{x}{2}}$$

(6.6)

for $x > 0$. We say that X follows a chi-square distribution with r degrees of freedom, denoted $\chi^2(r)$.

In certain chi-square tests, one rejects a null hypothesis about a population distribution if a specified test statistic is too large, when that statistic would have approximately a chi-square distribution if the null hypothesis is true. In minimum chi-square estimation, one finds the values of parameters that make that test statistic as small as possible.

Theorem 6.1. Let X be a chi-square random variable with r degrees of freedom. Then, the mean of X is:

$$\mu = E(X) = r\mu = E(X) = r \qquad (6.7)$$

That is, the mean of X is the number of degrees of freedom.

Proof. Since the $\chi^2(r)$ random variable is a special case of the gamma distribution, we take the mean of a gamma random variable $\mu = E(X) = \alpha\theta$ and substitute 2 for θ and $r/2$ for α.

Theorem 6.2. Let X be a chi-square random variable with r degrees of freedom. Then, the variance of X is:

$$\sigma^2 = Var(X) = 2r \qquad (6.8)$$

That is, the variance of X is the number of degrees of freedom.

Proof. The variance of a gamma random variable is:

$$\sigma^2 = Var(X) = \alpha\theta^2$$

The proof is again straightforward by substituting 2 in for θ and $r/2$ in for α.

Definition 6.6. The *Chi-Square test statistic* is a random variable defined by

$$\sum \frac{(O - E)^2}{E}$$

$$(6.9)$$

where O is the observed vales and E is the expected values.

Among the consequences of its use is that the test statistic actually does have approximately a chi-square distribution when the sample size is large. Generally, one reduces by 1 the number of degrees of freedom, r, for each parameter estimated by this method.

Illustration via an example

Suppose a certain random variable takes values in the set of non-negative integers 1, 2, 3, ... A simple random sample of size 20 is taken, yielding the following data set.

It is desired to test the null hypothesis that the population from which this sample was taken follows a *Poisson distribution*.

Definition 6.7. If X is a Poisson random variable, then the probability mass function is:

$$f(x) = \frac{e^{-\lambda}\lambda^x}{x!}$$

(6.10)

for $x = 0, 1, 2, \dots$ and $\lambda > 0$, where λ will be shown later to be both the mean and the variance of X.

The maximum likelihood estimate of the population average is 3.3. The value 3.3 came from the data, not from the null hypothesis. Since the null hypothesis did not specify that it was that particular Poisson distribution, but only that it is some Poisson distribution (see Table 6-8), we needed to calculate the estimate from the data.

A rule of thumb says that when a parameter is estimated, one reduces the number of degrees of freedom by 1, in this case from 9 (since there are 10 cells) to 8. One might hope that the resulting test statistic would have approximately a chi-square distribution when the null hypothesis is true. However, that is not in general the case when maximum-likelihood estimation is used. It is however true asymptotically when minimum chi-square estimation is used.

Table 6-8. Excel's showing the data and expected value

Category	Observed	Row Sum	E	(O -E)	(O - E)^2	(O - E)^2/E
0	1	0	3.300	-2.300	5.290	1.603
1	2	2	3.300	-1.300	1.690	0.512
2	4	8	3.300	0.700	0.490	0.148
3	5	15	3.300	1.700	2.890	0.876

4	3	12	3.300	-0.300	0.090	0.027
5	3	15	3.300	-0.300	0.090	0.027
6	1	6	3.300	-2.300	5.290	1.603
7	0	0	3.300	-3.300	10.890	3.300
8	1	8	3.300	-2.300	5.290	1.603
	20		Seek		T.S.=	9.7000
lambda =	3.3		3.3		C.V.=	10.4455
					Do not reject H0	

Finding the minimum chi-square estimate

The minimum chi-square estimate of the population mean λ is the number that minimizes the chi-square statistic from Equation (6.9).

Minimize:

$$\sum \frac{(observed - expected)^2}{expected}$$

$$= \sum_{k=0}^{8} \frac{\left((count\ in\ cell\ k) - 20\left(\frac{\lambda^k e^{-\lambda}}{k!}\right)\right)^2}{20\left(\frac{\lambda^k e^{-\lambda}}{k!}\right)} + \frac{(0-a)^2}{a}$$

Subject to:

$$a \neq 0.$$

where a is the estimated expected number in the ">=8" cell, and "20" appears because it is the sample size. The value of a is 20 times the probability that a Poisson-distributed random variable exceeds 9, and it is easily calculated as 1 minus the sum of the probabilities corresponding to 0 through 8. By trivial algebra, the last term reduces simply to a. Numerical computation shows the value of λ that minimizes the chi-square statistic is about 3.5242, which is the minimum chi-square estimate of λ (I found it using Excel's Solver – see Table 6-9). For $\lambda = 3.5242$, the chi-square statistic is about 10.4455.

Table 6-9. Excel's Solver add-in showing the data an minimum chi-square estimator achieved

109

Category	Observed	Row Sum	E	(O -E)	(O - E)^2	(O - E)^2/E
0	1	0	3.524	-2.524	6.372	1.808
1	2	2	3.524	-1.524	2.323	0.659
2	4	8	3.524	0.476	0.226	0.064
3	5	15	3.524	1.476	2.178	0.618
4	3	12	3.524	-0.524	0.275	0.078
5	3	15	3.524	-0.524	0.275	0.078
6	1	6	3.524	-2.524	6.372	1.808
7	0	0	3.524	-3.524	12.420	3.524
8	1	8	3.524	-2.524	6.372	1.808
	20		Seek		T.S.=	10.4455
	lambda =	3.3	3.52421		C.V.=	10.4455
					Do not Reject H0	

If the null hypothesis had specified a single distribution, rather than requiring λ to be estimated, then the null distribution of the test statistic would be a chi-square distribution with $10 - 1 = 9$ degrees of freedom, since there are 10 cells. Since λ had to be estimated, one additional degree of freedom is lost. The expected value of a chi-square random variable with 8 degrees of freedom is $E(X) = r = 8$ (by Theorem 6.1). Hence, the observed value, 3.062764, is not assertive, and the null hypothesis is not rejected.

Summary

Exercises
1. Why does logistic regression use MLE instead of ordinary least squares?
2. Given the odds ratios below,
   a. calculate the log odds

c. calculate the coefficients

Odds Ratio Estimates		
Effect	Point Estimate	95% Wald Confidence Limits
Age	0.577	0.418	0.796
Gender	0.371	0.249	0.554
OwnHome	2.515	1.641	3.856
Married	6.804	4.168	11.107
Close	3.912	2.511	6.095
Catalogs	1.274	1.228	1.321
log_Salary	41.059	12.814	131.564

3. Provided the following partial table, calculated the empty columns and Chi-Square test statistic. Define the if the null hypothesis and determine if it should be accepted or rejected.

Category	Observed	Row Sum	E	(O -E)	(O - E)^2	(O - E)^2/E
0	2	1				
1	2	2				
2	4	8				
3	5	15				
4	3	16				
5	3	14				
6	2	6				
7	3	5				
8	2	8				
	20		Seek		T.S.=	
	lambda =	3.5			C.V.=	10.4455
					Do not reject H0	

111

7. Evaluating goodness of fit

Once we have a model and are satisfied with its estimates of predictors, as we saw in the previous chapter, we need to check to see that it actually fits the data. While this is something we need to do for our modeling sample (training and testing), we also need to do it Out-of-Time (OOT). Goodness of fit in linear regression models is generally measured using the R^2. Since this has no direct analog in logistic regression, various methods (Greene, 2011) including the following can be used instead.

Deviance and likelihood ratio tests

In linear regression analysis, one is concerned with partitioning variance via the sum of squares calculations – variance in the criterion is essentially divided into variance accounted for by the predictors and residual variance. In logistic regression analysis, deviance is used in lieu of sum of squares calculations (Cohen, Cohen, West, & Aiken, 2002). Deviance is analogous to the sum of squares calculations in linear regression (Hosmer & Lemeshow, 2000) and is a measure of the lack of fit to the data in a logistic regression model (Cohen, Cohen, West, & Aiken, 2002). Deviance is calculated by comparing a given model with the *saturated model*—a model with a theoretically perfect fit. This computation is called the likelihood-ratio test (Hosmer & Lemeshow, 2000).

Definition 7.1. A saturated model is one with a theoretically perfect fit.

Definition 7.2. A measure of discrepancy between observed and fitted values is the *deviance statistic,* which is given by

$$D = -2\ln\lambda(y_i) = -2\ln\frac{\text{likelihood of the fitted model}}{\text{likelihood of the saturated model}}$$

(7.2)

where y_i is the ith observed value and the saturated model is one that has a theoretically perfect fit.

In the above equation D represents the deviance and ln represents the natural logarithm, and $\Lambda = \lambda(y_i)$. The log of the likelihood ratio (the ratio of the fitted model to the saturated model) will produce a negative value, so the product is multiplied by negative two times its natural logarithm to produce a value with an approximate χ^2-squared distribution (Hosmer & Lemeshow, 2000). Smaller values indicate better fit as the fitted model deviates less from the saturated model (see Table 7-1). When assessed upon a chi-square distribution, nonsignificant chi-square values indicate very little unexplained variance and thus, good model fit. Conversely, a significant chi-square value indicates that a significant amount of the variance is unexplained.

Table 7-1. SAS output for Model Fit $(-2LogL = -2ln(\Lambda))$

Model Fit Statistics		
Criterion	Intercept Only	Intercept and Covariates
AIC	32632.96	24574.42
SC	32641.67	24783.68
-2 Log L	32630.955	24526.42

Two measures of deviance are particularly important in logistic regression: *null deviance* and *model deviance*. The null deviance represents the difference between a model with only the intercept (which means "no predictors") and the saturated model (Cohen, Cohen, West, & Aiken, 2002). And, the model deviance represents the difference between a model with at least one predictor and the saturated model. In this respect, the null model provides a baseline upon which to compare predictive models. Given that deviance is a measure of the difference between a given model and the saturated model, smaller values indicate better fit. Therefore, to assess the contribution of a predictor or set of predictors, one can subtract the model (fitted) deviance from the null deviance and assess the difference on a χ^2_{s-p} chi-square distribution with degree of freedom (Hosmer & Lemeshow, 2000) equal to the difference in the number of parameters estimated.

Let

$$D_{null} = -2\ln \frac{\text{likelihood of the null model}}{\text{likelihood of the saturated model}}$$

$$D_{fitted} = -2\ln \frac{\text{likelihood of the fitted model}}{\text{likelihood of the saturated model}}$$

Then

$$D_{fitted} - D_{null}$$

$$= \left(-2\ln \frac{\text{likelihood of the fitted model}}{\text{likelihood of the saturated model}}\right)$$
$$- \left(2\ln \frac{\text{likelihood of the null model}}{\text{likelihood of the saturated model}}\right)$$
$$= -2\left(\ln \frac{\text{likelihood of the fitted model}}{\text{likelihood of the saturated model}}\right.$$
$$\left. - \ln \frac{\text{likelihood of the null model}}{\text{likelihood of the saturated model}}\right)$$
$$= -2\ln \frac{\frac{\text{likelihood of the fitted model}}{\text{likelihood of the saturated model}}}{\frac{\text{likelihood of the null model}}{\text{likelihood of the saturated model}}}$$
$$= -2\ln \frac{\text{likelihood of the fitted model}}{\text{likelihood of the null model}}.$$

Definition 7.3. The deviance between the fitted deviance and the null deviance, given by

$$D_{fitted} - D_{null} = -2\ln \frac{\text{likelihood of the fitted model}}{\text{likelihood of the null model}},$$

(7.3)

can be used to assess the contribution of a predictor or set of predictors by assessing the difference on a χ^2_{s-p} chi-square distribution with degree of freedom equal to the difference in the number of parameters estimated. We can abbreviate the notation as $D_0^2 = \ln(L/L_0)$, where L is the Likelihood of the fitted model and L_0 is the likelihood of the null model. This is often denoted by ΔG^2, using G for goodness-of-fit.

If the model deviance is significantly smaller than the null deviance then one can conclude that the predictor or set of predictors significantly improved model fit. This is analogous to the F-test used in linear regression analysis to assess the significance of prediction (Cohen, Cohen, West, & Aiken, 2002). A convenient result, attributed to Samuel S. Wilks, says that as the sample size n approaches ∞, the test statistic $-2\ln(\Lambda)$ for a nested model will be asymptotically χ^2-distributed with degrees of freedom equal to the difference in dimensionality of the saturated model and null model (Wilks, 1938). This means that for a great variety of hypotheses, a modeler can compute the likelihood ratio Λ for the data and compare $-2\ln(\Lambda)$ to the χ^2 value corresponding to a desired statistical significance as an approximate statistical test. This is often referred to a Wilks' Theorem.

> **Wilks' Theorem.** as the sample size n approaches ∞, the test statistic $-2\log(\Lambda)$ for a nested model will be asymptotically chi-squared distributed (χ^2) with degrees of freedom equal to the difference in dimensionality of fitted model and the null model, when H_0 holds true.

Example

Suppose $Y_i \underset{iid}{\sim} Poisson(\lambda)$ and consider testing $H_0: \lambda = \lambda_0$ against $H_a: \lambda \neq \lambda_0$.

Solution. We have

$$L(\lambda|y) = \frac{\lambda^{\sum_{i=1}^n y_i} e^{-n\lambda}}{\prod_{i=1}^n y_i!}$$

The maximum likelihood estimate of λ is $\hat{\lambda} = \bar{y}$ and the restricted maximum likelihood estimate of λ under H_0 is $\hat{\lambda}_0 = \lambda_0$. Thus, the generalized likelihood ratio is

$$L(\lambda|\boldsymbol{y}) = \frac{L(\lambda_0|\boldsymbol{y})}{L(\hat{\lambda}|\boldsymbol{y})} = \frac{\lambda^{\sum_{i=1}^n y_i} e^{-n\lambda}}{\prod_{i=1}^n y_i!} \frac{\prod_{i=1}^n y_i!}{\bar{y}^{\sum_{i=1}^n y_i} e^{-n\bar{y}}} = \left(\frac{\lambda_0}{\bar{y}}\right)^{\prod_{i=1}^n y_i} e^{n(\bar{y}-\lambda_0)}.$$

It follows that

$$-2\log\{\lambda(\bar{y})\} = -2\left\{n\bar{y}\ln\left(\frac{\lambda_0}{\bar{y}}\right) + n(\bar{y} - \lambda_0)\right\}$$

$$= 2n\left\{\bar{y}\ln\left(\frac{\bar{y}}{\lambda_0}\right) + \lambda_0 - \bar{y}\right\}$$

Here, $p = 1$ and $p_0 = 0$, and so $v = 1$. Therefore, by Wilks' theorem, when H_0 is true and n is large,

$$2n\left\{\bar{Y}\ln\left(\frac{\bar{Y}}{\lambda_0}\right) + \lambda_0 - \bar{Y}\right\} \sim \chi_1^2.$$

Hence, for a test with approximate significance level α, we reject H_0 if and only if

$$2n\left\{\bar{y}\ln\left(\frac{\bar{y}}{\lambda_0}\right) + \lambda_0 - \bar{y}\right\} \geq \chi_{1,\alpha}^2.$$

Pseudo-R^2s

In linear regression the squared multiple correlation, R^2 is used to assess goodness-of-fit as it represents the proportion of variance in the criterion that is explained by the predictors (Cohen, Cohen, West, & Aiken, 2002). In logistic regression analysis, there is no agreed upon analogous measure, but there are several competing measures each with limitations. Three of the most commonly used indices are examined in this section beginning with the likelihood ratio R^2, R_L^2 (Cohen, Cohen, West, & Aiken, 2002).

Definition 7.4. The Likelihood Ratio R-Squared is given by the ration between D_0^2 and the Null Deviance as follows

$$R_L^2 = \frac{D_{null} - D_{model}}{D_{null}}.$$

(7.4)

This is the most analogous index to the squared multiple correlation in linear regression (Menard, 2002). It represents the proportional reduction in the deviance, wherein the deviance is treated as a measure of variation analogous but not identical to the variance in linear regression analysis (Menard, 2002). One limitation of the likelihood ratio

R^2 is that it is not monotonically related to the odds ratio (Cohen, Cohen, West, & Aiken, 2002), meaning that it does not necessarily increase as the odds ratio increases, and does not necessarily decrease as the odds ratio decreases.

The Cox and Snell R^2 is an alternative index of goodness-of-fit related to the R^2 value from linear regression. The Cox and Snell index is problematic as its maximum value is 0.75, when the variance is at its maximum (0.25). The Nagelkerke R^2 provides a correction to the Cox and Snell R^2 so that the maximum value is equal to one. Nevertheless, the Cox and Snell and likelihood ratio R^2s show greater agreement with each other than either does with the Nagelkerke R^2 (Cohen, Cohen, West, & Aiken, 2002). Of course, this might not be the case for values exceeding 0.75 as the Cox and Snell index is capped at this value. The likelihood ratio R^2 is often preferred to the alternatives as it is most analogous to R^2 in linear regression, is independent of the base rate (both Cox and Snell and Nagelkerke R^2s increase as the proportion of cases increase from 0 to 0.5) and varies between 0 and 1.

A word of caution is in order when interpreting pseudo-R^2 statistics. The reason these indices of fit are referred to as pseudo R^2 is because they do not represent the proportionate reduction in error as the R^2 in linear regression does (Cohen, Cohen, West, & Aiken, 2002). Linear regression assumes *homoscedasticity*, that the error variance is the same for all values of the criterion. Logistic regression will always be *heteroscedastic* – the error variances differ for each value of the predicted score. For each value of the predicted score there would be a different value of the proportionate reduction in error. Therefore, it is inappropriate to think of R^2 as a proportionate reduction in error in a universal sense in logistic regression (Cohen, Cohen, West, & Aiken, 2002).

Hosmer–Lemeshow test

The *Hosmer–Lemeshow test* uses a test statistic that asymptotically follows a χ^2 distribution to assess whether or not the observed event rates match expected event rates in subgroups of the model population (Hosmer & Lemeshow, 2000).

The test is rather complicated to formulate and is beyond the scope of this text, so I give you the R code for it instead. First we will simulate some data from a logistic regression model with one covariate x, and then fit the correct logistic regression model. This means our model is correctly specified, and we should hopefully not detect evidence of poor fit.

```
library(ResourceSelection)
set.seed(43657)
n <- 100
x <- rnorm(n)
xb <- x
pr <- exp(xb)/(1+exp(xb))
y <- 1*(runif(n) < pr)
mod <- glm(y~x, family=binomial)
```

Next we pass the outcome y and model fitted probabilities to the hoslem.test function, choosing g=10 groups:

```
hl <- hoslem.test(mod$y, fitted(mod), g=10)
hl
```

```
        Hosmer and Lemeshow goodness of fit (GOF) test

data:  mod$y, fitted(mod)
X-squared = 7.4866, df = 8, p-value = 0.4851
```

Evaluating binary classification performance

If we use the estimated probabilities to classify each observation of independent variable values as predicting the category that the dependent variable is found in, then we can use the various methods below for judging the model's suitability in out-of-time forecasting on the data that were used for estimation—accuracy, precision (also called positive predictive value), recall (also called sensitivity), specificity and negative predictive value. In each of these evaluative methods, an aspect of the model's effectiveness in assigning instances to the correct categories is measured. We used *SAS Studio* PROC LOGISTIC output to demonstrate the tests.

Definition 7.5. Akaike Information Criterion (AIC): Suppose we have a logistic regression model M and L is the maximum likelihood function for the model, with k as the number of levels of the dependent variable in M and s is the number of predictors in M, then

$$AIC = -2 \, Log \, L + 2((k-1) + s) \qquad (7.5)$$

AIC is used for the comparison of non-nested models on the same sample. Ultimately, the model with the smallest AIC is considered the best, although the AIC value itself is not meaningful (see Table 7-2).

Table 7-2. SAS output for Model Fit $(-2LogL = -2ln(\Lambda))$

Model Fit Statistics		
Criterion	Intercept Only	Intercept and Covariates
AIC	32632.96	24574.42
SC	32641.67	24783.68
-2 Log L	32630.955	24526.42

Columns of Table 7-2

- **Intercept Only** – This column refers to the respective criterion statistics with no predictors in the model, i.e., just the response variable.
- **Intercept and Covariates** – This column corresponds to the respective criterion statistics for the fitted model. A fitted model includes all independent variables and the intercept. We can compare the values in this column with the criteria corresponding Intercept Only value to assess model fit/significance.

Schwarz Criterion (SC) – the Bayesian information criterion (BIC) or Schwarz criterion (also SBC, SBIC) is a criterion for model selection among a finite set of models; the model with the lowest BIC is preferred. It is based, in part, on the likelihood function and it is closely related to the Akaike information criterion (AIC). It is defined as follows:

> **Definition 7.6. Bayesian Information Criterion** is given by
>
> $$-2Log\ L + \big((k-1)+s\big)*\log(\Sigma y_i), \qquad (7.6)$$
>
> where y_i's are the frequency values of the ith observation, and k and s were defined previously in Definition 7.5.

Like AIC, Schwarz Criterion penalizes for the number of predictors in the model and the smallest SC is most desirable and the value itself is not meaningful (see Table 7-2).

Test – These are three asymptotically equivalent Chi-Square tests. They test against the null hypothesis that at least one of the predictors' regression coefficient is not equal to zero in the model. The difference between them are where on the log-likelihood function they are evaluated (see Table 7-3). For further discussion, see *Categorical Data Analysis*, Third Edition, by Alan Agresti (pages 11-13).

Table 7-3. Model fit statistics for test the null hypothesis that all the $\beta_i = 0$

Testing Global Null Hypothesis: BETA=0			
Test	Chi-Square	DF	Pr > ChiSq
Likelihood Ratio	8104.535	23	<.0001
Score	9452.884	23	<.0001
Wald	5461.848	23	<.0001

Likelihood Ratio – This is the Likelihood Ratio (LR) Chi-Square test that at least one of the predictors' regression coefficient is not equal to zero in the model. The LR Chi-Square statistic can be calculated by -2 Log L(null model) - 2 Log L(fitted model) = 231.289-160.236 = 71.05, where L(null model) refers to the Intercept Only model and L(fitted model) refers to the Intercept and Covariates model.

Score – This is the Score Chi-Square Test that at least one of the predictors' regression coefficient is not equal to zero in the model.

Wald – This is the Wald Chi-Square Test that at least one of the predictors' regression coefficient is not equal to zero in the model.

Chi-Square, **DF** and **Pr > ChiSq** – These are the Chi-Square test statistic, Degrees of Freedom (DF) and associated p-value (PR>ChiSq) corresponding to the specific test that all of the predictors are simultaneously equal to zero (see Table 7-4).

Table 7-4. Residual Chi-Square test output from PROC LOGISTIC

Residual Chi-Square Test		
Chi-Square	DF	Pr > ChiSq
8.5081	3	0.0366

We are testing the probability (PR>ChiSq) of observing a Chi-Square statistic as extreme as, or more so, than the observed one under the null hypothesis; the null hypothesis is that all of the regression coefficients in the model are equal to zero. The degrees of freedom defines the distribution of the Chi-Square test statistics and is defined by the number of predictors in the model. Typically, PR>ChiSq is compared to a specified alpha level, our willingness to accept a type I error, which is often set at 0.05 or 0.01. The small p-value from the all three tests would lead us to conclude that at least one of the regression coefficients in the model is not equal to zero.

Percent Concordant – A pair of observations with different observed responses is said to be concordant if the observation with the lower ordered response value (RESP = 0) has a lower predicted mean score than the observation with the higher ordered response value (RESP = 1). See Pairs (below) for what defines a pair (see Table 7-5).

Table 7-5. Test statistics for Association of Predicted Probabilities and Observed Responses

Association of Predicted Probabilities and Observed Responses			
Percent Concordant	86.7	Somers' D	0.733
Percent Discordant	13.3	Gamma	0.733
Percent Tied	0	Tau-a	0.152
Pairs	2.11E+08	c	0.867

Percent Discordant – If the observation with the lower ordered response value has a higher predicted mean score than the observation with the higher ordered response value, then the pair is discordant (see Table 7-5).

Percent Tied – If a pair of observations with different responses is neither concordant nor discordant, it is a tie (see Table 7-5).

Pairs – This is the total number of distinct pairs in which one case has an observed outcome different from the other member of the pair. In the Response Profile table in the Model Information section above, we see that there are 5,289 observations with RESP=1 and 39,922 observations with RESP=0 (see Table 7-6). Thus the total number of pairs with different outcomes is 5289*39922=211,147,458 or 2.11E+08 (see Table 7-5).

Table 7-6. Model information regarding the response variable profile

Response Profile		
Ordered Value	RESP	Total Frequency
1	0	39922
2	1	5289

Somers' D statistic – Somers' D is used to determine the strength and direction of relation between pairs of variables. Its values range from -1.0 (all pairs disagree) to 1.0 (all pairs agree). It is defined as $(nc - nd)/t$ where nc is the number of pairs that are concordant, and the number of pairs that are discordant, and t is the number of total number of pairs with different responses. In our example, it equals the difference between the percent concordant and the percent discordant divided by 100: (86.7-13.3)/100 = 0.733 (see Table 7-5).

Gamma statistic – The *Goodman-Kruskal Gamma* method does not penalize for ties on either variable. Its values range from -1.0 (no association) to 1.0 (perfect association). Because it does not penalize for ties, its value will generally be greater than the values for Somers' D (see Table 7-5).

Tau-a statistic – *Kendall's Tau-a* is a modification of Somers' D that takes into the account the difference between the number of possible paired observations and the number of paired observations with a different response. It is defined to be the ratio of the difference between the number of concordant pairs and the number of discordant pairs to the number of possible pairs $(2(nc - nd)/(N(N - 1))$. Usually Tau-a is much smaller than Somers' D since there would be many paired observations with the same response (see Table 7-5).

c statistic – c is equivalent to the well known measure ROC. The values of c range from 0.5 to 1, where 0.5 corresponds to the model randomly predicting the response, and a 1 corresponds to the model perfectly discriminating the response (see Table 7-5).

We will discuss additional test for goodness of fit when we talk about model scoring and performance. However, we need to first take a detailed look at predictors (model effects or independent variables).

Example Using R

In veterinary epidemiology, often the outcome is dichotomous (yes/no), representing the presence or absence of disease or mortality. We code 1 for the presence of the outcome and 0 for its absence. This way, the mean of the outcome represents the proportion of subjects with the event, and its expectation π_i represents the probability for the event to occur. By definition, the expectation must lie in the range 0 to 1. We can't use a linear regression to analyze these data because:

- the error terms (ε) from this model will not be normally distributed. They can only take two values,
- the probability of the outcome occurring $\pi = p(Y = 1)$, , follows a binomial distribution and depends on the value of the predictor variables, X. Since the variance of a binomial distribution is a function of the probability, the error variance will also vary with the level of X and as such the assumption of homoscedasticity will be violated,

- the mean responses are constrained to lie within 0 and 1. With a linear regression model, the predicted values might fall outside of this range.

One way of getting around the problems described above is to use a suitable transformation, the logistic or logit function of π and model this as a linear function of a set of predictor variables. This leads to the model (4.3b from Chapter 4):

$$logit(\pi) = ln\left(\frac{p}{1-p}\right) = \beta_0 + \beta_1 x_1 + \beta_2 x_2 + \cdots + \beta_n x_n$$

Figure 7-1 show the function $ln(x/(1-x))$, generated in R-Studio with:

```
curve(log(x / (1 - x)), 0, 1)
```

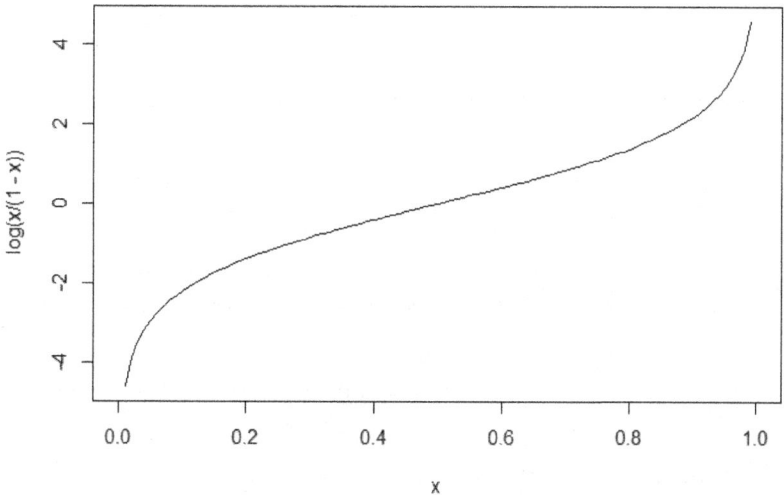

Figure 7-1. Plot of the function $ln(x/(1-x))$

The logit transform is $\ln\left(\frac{p}{1-p}\right)$. The logit of a probability is the log of the odds of the response taking the value 1. Then the above equation can be rewritten as

125

$$\pi(x_1 + x_2 + \cdots + x_n) = \left(\frac{\exp(\beta_0 + \beta_1 x_1 + \beta_2 x_2 + \cdots + \beta_n x_n)}{1 + \exp(\beta_0 + \beta_1 x_1 + \beta_2 x_2 + \cdots + \beta_n x_n)} \right)$$

While the logit function can take any real value, the associated probability always lie within the bounds of 0 and 1. Within a logistic regression model, the parameter β_i associated with the explanatory variable x_i is such that $\exp(\beta_i)$ is the odds that the response variable takes the value 1 when x_i increases by 1, conditional on the other explanatory variables remaining constant.

As with the linear regression, the logistic regression model involves a linear combination of explanatory variables, even if the binary response is not modelled directly but through a logistic transformation. The expression of predictors on the response from a linear combination of predictors can be extended to models for other types of response than continuous or binary and define the wider class of generalized linear models described by Nelder and Wedderburn. (Generalized Linear Models & Wedderburn, 1972) GLMs have 3 main features:

- an error distribution giving the distribution of the response around its mean. For ANOVA and linear regression it is the normal, for logistic regression it is the binomial. These distributions come from the same exponential family of probability distributions,
- a link function: how the linear function of the explanatory variables is related to the expected value of the response. For logistic regression it is the logit function (but can also be probit $\Phi^{-1}(p)$ where Φ^{-1} is the inverse normal cumulative distribution function) or complementary $\log - \log(\ln(-\ln(1-p)))$or analysis of variance and regression it is the identity function,
- the variance function: how the variance of the response variable depends on the mean.

The first example is from the Nocardia dataset: a case-control study of Nocardia spp. mastitis, from 54 case herds and 54 control herds, with the predictors related to the management of the cows during the dry period.

```
temp <- tempfile()
download.file(
"http://ic.upei.ca/ver/sites/ic.upei.ca.ver/files/ver2_data
_R.zip",
temp)
load(unz(temp, "ver2_data_R/nocardia.rdata"))
unlink(temp)

library(Hmisc)
```

Alternatively, we can manually download the Excel file nocaria.xls and save it as .CSV format. Then we enter:

```
file = "C:/Users/Strickland/Documents/Logistic Regression/n
ocardia.csv"
read.csv(file) -> nocardia
summary(nocardia)

library(Hmisc)
```

Then we update nocardia with:

```
nocardia <- upData(nocardia,
        labels = c(id = 'Herd identification number',
casecont = 'Case/control status of herd',
        prod = 'Average milk production of the herd',
        bscc = 'Average bulk tank SCC over the first 6 mon
ths of 1988',
        dbarn = 'Type of barn dry cows kept in',
        dout = 'Type of outdoor area used for dry cows',
        dcprep = 'Method of teat end preparation prior to d
ry cow therapy administration',
        dcpct = 'Percent of dry cows treated with dry-cow t
herapy',
        dneo = 'Dry-cow product containing neomycin used o
n farm in last year',
        dclox = 'Dry cow product containing cloxacillin us
ed on farm in last year',
        doth = 'Other dry cow products used on farm in las
t year'),
            levels = list(casecont = list('Control' =
0, 'Case' = 1),
            dbarn = list('freestall' = 1, 'tiestall' =
2, 'other' = 3),
        dout = list('pasture' = 1, 'yard/drylot' = 2, 'non
e' = 3, 'other' = 4),
```

```
         dcprep = list('no prep.' = 1, 'washed only' = 2, '
washed and disinfected' = 3, 'dry cow therapy not used' = 4
),
                 dneo = list('No' = 0, 'Yes' = 1),
                 dclox = list('No' = 0, 'Yes' = 1)),
                 units = c(prod = "kg/cow/day",
                           bscc = "'000s of cells/ml
",
                 dcpct = "%"))
```

We now formulate a logistic regression with three predictor variables. We can first have a look at a conditional density plot (Figure 7-2) of the response variable given the proportion of dry cows treated with dry cow therapy.

```
cdplot(as.factor(casecont) ~ dcpct, data = nocardia)
```

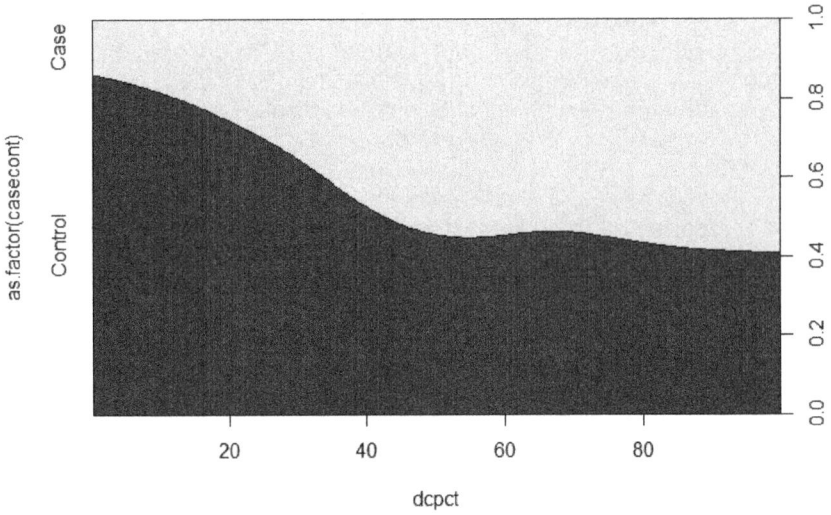

Figure 7-2. Plot of the response variable given the proportion of dry cows treated with dry cow therapy

The logistic regression model is:

```
mod1 <- glm(casecont ~ dcpct + dneo + dclox,
            family = binomial("logit"),
```

```
                data = nocardia) # "logit" can be omitted as it i
s the default

(mod1.sum <- summary(mod1))
```

```
Call:
glm(formula = casecont ~ dcpct + dneo + dclox, family = bin
omial("logit"),
    data = nocardia)

Deviance Residuals:
    Min       1Q   Median       3Q      Max
-1.8425  -0.8915   0.1610   0.6361   2.3745

Coefficients:
              Estimate Std. Error z value Pr(>|z|)
(Intercept) -2.984272   0.772196  -3.865 0.000111 ***
dcpct        0.022668   0.007187   3.154 0.001610 **
dneoYes      2.212564   0.578012   3.828 0.000129 ***
dcloxYes    -1.412516   0.557197  -2.535 0.011243 *
---
Signif. codes:  0 '***' 0.001 '**' 0.01 '*' 0.05 '.' 0.1 '
' 1

(Dispersion parameter for binomial family taken to be 1)

    Null deviance: 149.72  on 107  degrees of freedom
Residual deviance: 107.99  on 104  degrees of freedom
AIC: 115.99

Number of Fisher Scoring iterations: 4
```

The following R code will give us a 95% confidence interval for "dcpct."

```
confint.default(mod1, parm = "dcpct")
```

```
            2.5 %      97.5 %
dcpct 0.00858227 0.03675422
```

All variables are significant at the 5% level. An increase of one unit in the proportion of cows receiving dry cow therapy increases the log-odds to be a case herd by 0.02. The confidence interval can be constructed using normal approximation for the parameter estimate: $\hat{\beta}_i \pm z^{\alpha/2} SE(\hat{\beta}_i)$. The 95% confidence interval is $(0.009, 0.037)$. But it is better to construct a profile likelihood-based confidence interval (from MASS package):

```
confint(mod1, parm = "dcpct")
```

```
Waiting for profiling to be done...
      2.5 %      97.5 %
0.009211164 0.037694948
```

We can get the odds by exponentiating the estimates:

```
> cbind(exp(coef(mod1)), exp(confint(mod1)))
```

```
Waiting for profiling to be done...
                          2.5 %       97.5 %
(Intercept) 0.05057629 0.009587881  0.2007101
dcpct       1.02292712 1.009253717  1.0384144
dneoYes     9.13911806 3.139924972 31.3596110
dcloxYes    0.24352979 0.078283239  0.7094844
```

Again, the statistic to determine the overall significance of a logistic model is the likelihood ratio test. The likelihood ratio test statistic is: $D_0^2 = -2\ln\frac{L}{L_0}$ where L is the likelihood of the full model and L_0 is the likelihood of the null model. The likelihood ratio test statistic ($D_0^2 = 41.73$) can be compared to a χ^2 distribution with 3 degrees of freedom. The predictor variables are significant predictors of case-control status.

```
mod1.null <- glm(casecont ~ 1, family = binomial, data = no
cardia)
lr.mod1 <- -(deviance(mod1) / 2)
lr.mod1.null <- -(deviance(mod1.null) / 2)
(lr <- 2 * (lr.mod1 - lr.mod1.null))
```

```
[1] 41.73248
```

```
1 - pchisq(lr, 2)
```

```
[1] 8.667767e-10
```

We can also compare the likelihood of the model under investigation to the likelihood of a fully saturated model (one in which there would be one parameter fit for each data point):

```
pchisq(deviance(mod1), df.residual(mod1), lower = FALSE)
```

```
[1] 0.3748198
```

The p-value is over 0.05 and we can conclude this model fits sufficiently well.

Finally we can evaluate a single coefficient with a Wald test. If we add barn type to the model below, we can test for an overall effect of barn type (b gives the coefficient, Sigma the variance-covariance matrix of the error terms, and Terms indicates which terms in the model to test (in the order they appear in the table of coefficients). The overall effect of barn is significant. We can also test for other barn against tie-stall barn.

```
mod1b <- glm(casecont ~ dcpct + dneo + dclox + as.factor(db
    arn), family = binomial, data = nocardia)
summary(mod1b)
```

```
Call:
glm(formula = casecont ~ dcpct + dneo + dclox + as.factor(d
barn), family = binomial, data = nocardia)

Deviance Residuals:
    Min       1Q    Median       3Q      Max
-1.6949   -0.7853    0.1021    0.7692    2.6801

Coefficients:
                        Estimate   Std. Error  z value  Pr(>|z|)
(Intercept)            -2.445696     0.854328   -2.863   0.00420  **
dcpct                   0.021604     0.007657    2.821   0.00478  **
dneoYes                 2.685280     0.677273    3.965   7.34e-05 ***
dcloxYes               -1.235266     0.580976   -2.126   0.03349  *
as.factor(dbarn)       -1.333732     0.631925   -2.111   0.03481  *
tiestall
as.factor(dbarn)       -0.218350     1.154293   -0.189   0.84
other
```

```
---
Signif.codes: 0 '***' 0.001 '**' 0.01 '*' 0.05 '.' 0.1 ' ' 1

(Dispersion parameter for binomial family taken to be 1)

    Null deviance: 149.72  on 107  degrees of freedom
Residual deviance: 102.32  on 102  degrees of freedom
AIC: 114.32

Number of Fisher Scoring iterations: 5
```

We can now perform a Wald Chi-Square Test to evaluate the significance of terms 4 (as.factor(dbarn)tiestall) and 5 (as.factor(dbarn)other).

```
library(aod)
wald.test(b=coef(mod1b), Sigma = vcov(mod1b), Terms = 4:5)
```

```
Wald test:
----------

Chi-squared test:
X2 = 10.2, df = 2, P(> X2) = 0.0062
```

Alternatively, we can use the cbind function to assign the terms we wish to evaluate.

```
comp <- cbind(0, 0, 0, 0, 1, -1)
wald.test(b = coef(mod1b), Sigma = vcov(mod1b), L = comp)
```

```
Wald test:
----------

Chi-squared test:
X2 = 1.1, df = 1, P(> X2) = 0.29
```

Summary

In this chapter, we examined several goodness-of-fit metric, including the deviance statistic, likelihood ratio, and D_0^2. We also looked at the pseudo R^2 measure, as well as the Hosmer-Lemeshow test. We also studied the output of a SAS Studio program that included AIC, BIC, Wald Chi-Square, and other test results.

Exercises

1. Use you rank ordered variables from Chapter 5, problem 4, to build a logistic regression model in R, with "Activity" as the dependent variable. Evaluate the model's goodness-of-fit.

2. Repeat Exercise 1 but do it in SAS Studio using Appendix 1.sas, Appendix 2a.sas and Appendix 2b.sas. These files are located in the book download folder and are ready to run once they are imported to SAS Studio (except you must change the user name to your own). The data set, train, is included as well.

   a. What are the 10 most important variables?

   b. Export WOE_ALL, generated by Appendix 1.sas, and open it with Excel. Create plots for each of he 10 most important variables using "woe" and "outcomesum" on the same plot with different scales. Record your observations.

   c. Use the variables to build a logistic regression model in SAS Studio, with "Activity" as the target variable. Export the results to an html file.

   d. Discuss the results of the goodness-of-fit tests.

8. Evaluating Variable Contribution

Introduction

Thus far we have covered some of the concepts that will help us develop good logistic regression models. We will cover some additional measures in this chapter and set the stage for scoring the model, which follows this chapter.

Coefficients

After fitting the model, it is likely that researchers will want to examine the contribution of individual predictors. To do so, they will want to examine the regression coefficients. In linear regression, the regression coefficients represent the change in the criterion for each unit change in the predictor (Cohen, Cohen, West, & Aiken, 2002). In logistic regression, however, the regression coefficients represent the change in the logit for each unit change in the predictor. Given that the logit is not intuitive, researchers are likely to focus on a predictor's effect on the exponential function of the regression coefficient – the odds ratio from Chapter 6 (see Definition 6.1).

Here is the mathematical reason for not using the coefficients for interpretation, a mistake many modelers and analysts make. Recall that in linear regression, the regression equation is

$$Y = B_0 + B_1X_1 + B_2X_2 + \cdots + B_nX_n,$$

which expresses a linear relationship. That is for every unit change in a predictor's coefficient, there is a corresponding unit change in the dependent variable when all other predictors are held constant.

Now, here is our logistic regression equation (Equation 4.2) is

$$y = logit = e^{\beta_0 + \beta_1 x} \tag{8.1}$$

which is nonlinear. We make it linear by using the natural logarithm as follows (Equation 4.3):

$$\log_e e^{\beta_0 + \beta_1 x} = \beta_0 + \beta_1 x. \tag{8.2}$$

But, $\log_e e^{\beta_0 + \beta_1 x}$ is no longer y! So, we really do not know what is changing when we try to use the predictor coefficients for interpretation. Thus, we need to convert the coefficients to log odds and then to odds ratios or probabilities to make sense of them, as we did in Chapter 6.

Tests for Significance

In linear regression, the significance of a regression coefficient is assessed by computing a t-test. In logistic regression, there are several different tests designed to assess the significance of an individual predictor, most notably the likelihood ratio test and the Wald statistic.

Likelihood ratio test

The likelihood-ratio test discussed above to assess model fit is also the recommended procedure to assess the contribution of individual "predictors" to a given model (Cohen, Cohen, West, & Aiken, 2002) (Hosmer & Lemeshow, 2000) (Menard, 2002). In the case of a single predictive model, one simply compares the deviance of the predictive model with that of the null model on a chi-square distribution with a single degree of freedom. If the predictive model has a significantly smaller deviance (c.f. chi-square using the difference in degrees of freedom of the two models), then one can conclude that there is a significant association between the "predictor" and the outcome. Although some common statistical packages (e.g. SPSS) do provide likelihood ratio test statistics, without this computationally intensive test it would be more difficult to assess the contribution of individual predictors in the multiple logistic regression case. To assess the contribution of individual predictors one can enter the predictors hierarchically, comparing each new model with the previous to determine the contribution of each predictor (Cohen, Cohen, West, & Aiken, 2002). (There is considerable debate among statisticians regarding the appropriateness of so-called "stepwise" procedures. They do not preserve the nominal statistical properties and can be very misleading (Harrell, 2010).

Wald statistic

Alternatively, when assessing the contribution of individual predictors in a given model, one may examine the significance of the Wald statistic. The Wald statistic, analogous to the t-test in linear regression, is used to assess the significance of coefficients. The Wald statistic is the ratio of the square of the regression coefficient to the square of the standard error of the coefficient and is asymptotically distributed as a chi-square distribution (Menard, 2002).

$$W_j = \frac{B_j^2}{SE_{B_j}^2}.$$

(8.3)

Although several statistical packages (e.g., SPSS, SAS) report the Wald statistic to assess the contribution of individual predictors, the Wald statistic has limitations. When the regression coefficient is large, the standard error of the regression coefficient also tends to be large increasing the probability of Type-II error. The Wald statistic also tends to be biased when data are sparse (Cohen, Cohen, West, & Aiken, 2002).

Case-control sampling

Suppose cases are rare (we mentioned this in Chapter 4). Then we might want to sample them more frequently than their prevalence in the population. For example, suppose there is a disease that affects 1 person in 10,000 and to collect our data we need to do a complete physical. It may be too expensive to do thousands of physicals of healthy people in order to get data on only a few diseased individuals. Thus, we may evaluate more diseased individuals. This is also called unbalanced data. As a rule of thumb, sampling controls at a rate of five times the number of cases is sufficient to get enough control data (Prentice & Pyke, 1979).

If we form a logistic model from such data, if the model is correct, the β_j parameters are all correct except for β_0. We can correct β_0 if we know the true prevalence as follows (Prentice & Pyke, 1979):

$$\hat{\beta}_0^* = \hat{\beta}_0 + \log\frac{\pi}{1-\pi}\log\frac{\hat{\pi}}{1-\hat{\pi}},$$

(8.4)

where π is the true prevalence and $\hat{\pi}$ is the prevalence in the sample.

As a two-way latent-variable model

Yet another formulation uses two separate latent variables:

$$Y_i^{0*} = \boldsymbol{\beta_0} \cdot \boldsymbol{X_i} + \varepsilon_0,$$

$$Y_i^{1*} = \boldsymbol{\beta_{01}} \cdot \boldsymbol{X_i} + \varepsilon_1, \qquad (8.5)$$

where

$$\varepsilon_0 \sim EV_1(0,1),$$

$$\varepsilon_1 \sim EV_1(0,1), \qquad (8.6)$$

where $EV_1(0,1)$ is a standard type-1 extreme value distribution: i.e.

$$Pr(\varepsilon_0 = x) = Pr(\varepsilon_1 = x) = e^{-x}e^{-e^{-x}}, \qquad (8.7)$$

Then

$$Y_i = \begin{cases} 1 & \text{if } Y_i^{1*} > Y_i^{0*} \\ 0 & \text{otherwise} \end{cases}. \qquad (8.8)$$

This model (8.8) has a separate latent variable and a separate set of regression coefficients for each possible outcome of the dependent variable. The reason for this separation is that it makes it easy to extend logistic regression to multi-outcome categorical variables, as in the multinomial logit model. In such a model, it is natural to model each possible outcome using a different set of regression coefficients. It is also possible to motivate each of the separate latent variables as the theoretical utility associated with making the associated choice, and thus motivate logistic regression in terms of utility theory. (In terms of utility theory, a rational actor always chooses the choice with the greatest associated utility.) This is the approach taken by economists when formulating discrete choice models, because it both provides a theoretically strong foundation and facilitates intuitions about the model, which in turn makes it easy to consider various sorts of extensions. (See the example below.)

The choice of the type-1 extreme value distribution (8.7) seems fairly arbitrary, but it makes the mathematics work out, and it may be possible to justify its use through *rational choice theory*.

It turns out that this model is equivalent to the previous model, although this does not seem obvious. Now there are now two sets of regression coefficients and error variables, and the error variables have a different distribution. In fact, this model reduces directly to the previous one with the following substitutions:

$$\beta = \beta_1 - \beta_0,$$

$$\varepsilon = \varepsilon_1 - \varepsilon_0.$$

An intuition for this comes from the fact that, since we choose based on the maximum of two values, only their difference matters, not the exact values — and this effectively removes one degree of freedom. Another critical fact is that the difference of two type-1 extreme value distributed variables is a logistic distribution, i.e. if

$$\varepsilon = \varepsilon_1 - \varepsilon_0 \sim \text{Logistic}(0,1). \tag{8.9}$$

We can demonstrate the equivalent as follows:

$$\Pr(Y_i = 1 | X_i) = \Pr\left(Y_i^{1*} > Y_i^{0*} | X_i\right)$$
$$= \Pr\left(Y_i^{1*} - Y_i^{0*} > 0 | X_i\right)$$
$$= \Pr(\boldsymbol{\beta_1} \cdot X_i + \varepsilon_1 - (\boldsymbol{\beta_0} \cdot X_i + \varepsilon_0) > 0)$$
$$= \Pr((\boldsymbol{\beta_1} \cdot X_i - \boldsymbol{\beta_0} \cdot X_i) + (\varepsilon_1 - \varepsilon_0) > 0)$$
$$= \Pr((\boldsymbol{\beta_1} - \boldsymbol{\beta_0}) \cdot X_i + (\varepsilon_1 - \varepsilon_0) > 0)$$
$$= \Pr((\boldsymbol{\beta_1} - \boldsymbol{\beta_0}) \cdot X_i + \varepsilon > 0)$$
$$= \Pr(\boldsymbol{\beta} \cdot X_i + \varepsilon > 0)$$
$$= \Pr(\varepsilon > -\boldsymbol{\beta} \cdot X_i)$$
$$= \Pr(\varepsilon < \boldsymbol{\beta} \cdot X_i)$$

$$= (\boldsymbol{\beta} \cdot \boldsymbol{X}_i)$$
$$= p_i.$$

Example

As an example, consider a state-level election where the choice is between a republican party, a democratic party, and a communist party. We would then use three latent variables, one for each choice. Then, in accordance with utility theory, we can then interpret the latent variables as expressing the utility that results from making each of the choices. We can also interpret the regression coefficients as indicating the strength that the associated factor (i.e. explanatory variable) has in contributing to the utility — or more correctly, the amount by which a unit change in an explanatory variable changes the utility of a given choice. A voter might expect that the republican party would lower taxes, especially on rich people. This would give low-income people no benefit, i.e. no change in utility (since they usually don't pay taxes); would cause moderate benefit (i.e. somewhat more money, or moderate utility increase) for middle-income people; and would cause significant benefits for high-income people. On the other hand, the democratic party might be expected to raise taxes and offset it with increased welfare and other assistance for the lower and middle classes. This would cause significant positive benefit to low-income people, perhaps weak benefit to middle-income people, and significant negative benefit to high-income people. Finally, the communist party would take direct actions on the economy by simply taking control of it. A low-income or middle-income voter might expect basically no clear utility gain or loss from this, but a high-income voter might expect negative utility, since he/she is likely to own companies, which will have a harder time doing business in such an environment and probably lose money.

These intuitions can be expressed as follows:

Table 8-1. Estimated strength of regression coefficient for different outcomes (party choices) and different values of explanatory variables

	Republican	Democrat	Communist
High-income	strong +	strong −	strong −
Middle-income	moderate +	weak +	none
Low-income	none	strong +	none

Table 8-1 illustrates the following:

1. Separate sets of regression coefficients need to exist for each choice. When phrased in terms of utility, this can be seen very easily. Different choices have different effects on net utility; furthermore, the effects vary in complex ways that depend on the characteristics of each individual, so there need to be separate sets of coefficients for each characteristic, not simply a single extra per-choice characteristic.

2. Even though income is a continuous variable, its effect on utility is too complex for it to be treated as a single variable. Either it needs to be directly split up into ranges, or higher powers of income need to be added so that polynomial regression on income is effectively done.

Model suitability

Our models' predictions cannot be expected to produce good forecasts if the logistic regression model we constructed was not stable over the sample period and will remain stable over the forecast period.

If the model's parameters are different during the forecast period than they were during the sample period, then the model we estimated will not be very useful, regardless of how well it was estimated. And, if the model's parameters were unstable over the sample period, then model was not even a good representation of the sample period.

A way to measure a model's suitability is to assess the model against a set of data that was not used to create the model (Mark & Goldberg,

2001). The class of techniques is called *cross-validation*. This holdout model assessment method is particularly valuable when data are collected in different settings (e.g., at different times or places) or when models are assumed to be generalizable.

To measure the suitability of a binary regression model, one can classify both the actual value and the predicted value of each observation as either 0 or 1 (Myers & Forgy, 1963). The predicted value of an observation can be set equal to 1 if the estimated probability that the observation equals 1 is above $1/2$, and set equal to 0 if the estimated probability is below $1/2$. Here logistic regression is being used as a binary classification model. There are four possible combined classifications defined below and shown in Table 8-1. Table 8-1 is often called a *classification table* or *confusion matrix*.

1. prediction of 0 when the holdout sample has a 0 (True Negative, the number of which is TN)
2. prediction of 0 when the holdout sample has a 1 (False Negative, the number of which is FN)
3. prediction of 1 when the holdout sample has a 0 (False Positives, the number of which is FP)
4. prediction of 1 when the holdout sample has a 1 (True Positives, the number of which is TP)

These classifications are used to calculate accuracy, precision (also called positive predictive value), recall (also called sensitivity), specificity and negative predictive value:

Definition 8.1. Accuracy in logistic regression is defined as the proportion of observations with correct classifications, and is given by:

$$\text{Accuracy} = \frac{TP + TN}{TP + FP + FN + TN}$$

(8.10)

Definition 8.2. Precision in logistic regression is defined as the proportion of predicted positives that are correct, and is given by:

$$Precision = Positive \ Predictive \ Value = \frac{TP}{TP + FP}$$

$$(8.11)$$

Definition 8.3. Negative Predictive Value in logistic regression is the proportion of predicted negatives that are correct, and is given by:

$$Negative \ Predictive \ Value = \frac{TN}{TN + FN}$$

$$(8.12)$$

Definition 8.4. Sensitivity in logistic regression is defined as the proportion of observations that are actually positive with a correct predicted classification, and is given by:

$$Sensitivity = True \ Positive \ Rate = \frac{TP}{TP + FN}$$

$$(8.13)$$

Definition 8.5. Specificity in logistic regression is defined as the proportion of observations that are actually negative with a correct predicted classification, and is given by:

$$Specificity = True \ Negative \ Rate = \frac{TN}{TN + FP}$$

$$(8.14)$$

Table 8-1. Classification Table

Prob Level	TN	FN	FP	TP	TPR= Sensitivity	TNR= Specificity	Accuracy
0.1	0.972	0.028	0.721	0.279	0.910	0.574	0.626
0.2	0.937	0.063	0.558	0.442	0.875	0.627	0.690
0.3	0.918	0.082	0.478	0.522	0.864	0.658	0.720
0.4	0.907	0.093	0.436	0.564	0.859	0.675	0.736
0.5	0.901	0.099	0.405	0.595	0.857	0.690	0.748
0.6	0.896	0.104	0.376	0.624	0.857	0.705	0.760
0.7	0.892	0.108	0.372	0.628	0.853	0.705	0.760
0.8	0.888	0.112	0.387	0.613	0.846	0.697	0.751
0.9	0.885	0.115	0.406	0.594	0.838	0.685	0.739
1	0.882	0.118			0.000	1.000	0.882

Another metric worth mention is *Cohen's Kappa*. It is essentially a measure of how well the classifier performed as compared to how well it would have performed simply by chance. In other words, a model will have a high Kappa score if there is a big difference between the accuracy and the null error rate.

The ROC Curve

The Receiver Operating Characteristic (ROC) curve is the most commonly used way to visualize the performance of a binary classifier, and Area Under the Curve (AUC) is one of the best ways to summarize its performance in a single number. As such, gaining a deep understanding of ROC curves and AUC is beneficial for data scientists, machine learning practitioners, and medical researchers (among others).

Let's pretend we built a classifier to predict whether a research paper will be admitted to a journal, based on a variety of factors. The features might be the length of the paper, the number of authors, the number of papers those authors have previously submitted to the journal, et cetera. The response (or "output variable") would be whether or not the paper was admitted.

144

Let's first take a look at Figure 8-1. The right portion of this diagram shows two distributions (I show normal distributions for convenience but they are probably not so). The red distribution contains all the "no" or negative responses, while the blue one contains all the "acceptance" or positive responses. We will say that every blue and red pixel represents a paper for which we want to predict the admission status. This is our validation (or "hold-out") set, we know the true admission status of each paper. The 250 red pixels are the papers that were not admitted, and the 250 blue pixels are the papers that were actually admitted. For now, we will ignore the pot to the left of Figure 8-1.

Since this is our validation set, we want to judge how well our model is doing by comparing your model's predictions to the true admission statuses of those 500 papers. We'll assume that we used logistic regression aa a classification method that can not only make a prediction for each paper, but can also output a predicted probability of admission for each paper. These blue and red distributions are one way to visualize how those predicted probabilities compare to the true statuses.

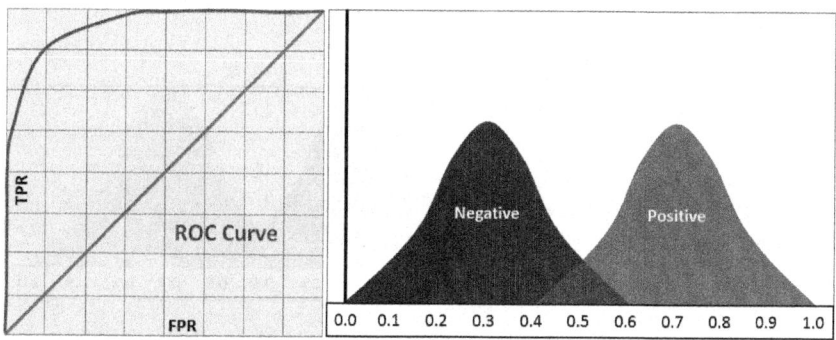

Figure 8-1. ROC plot with negative and positive response distributions

Let's examine this plot in detail. The x-axis represents our predicted probabilities, and the y-axis represents a count (we'll just estimate them) of observations, kind of like a histogram. Let's estimate that the height at 0.1 is 10 pixels in Figure 8-2. This plot tells you that there were 10 papers for which you predicted an admission probability of 0.1, and the true status for all 10 papers was negative (meaning not admitted).

This is good since the model gave them a very low probability for being admitted.

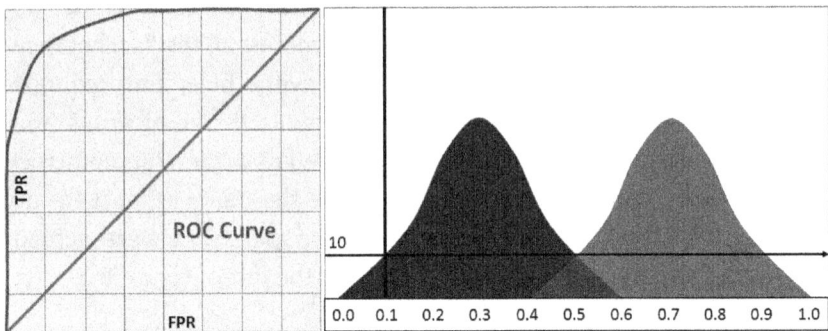

Figure 8-2. Ten papers were predicted to be accepted with probability 0.1 and were not accepted

Figure 8-3 shows there were about 50 papers for which we predicted an admittance probability of 0.3, and none of those 50 were admitted. This still good since the model gave the a low chance for acceptance.

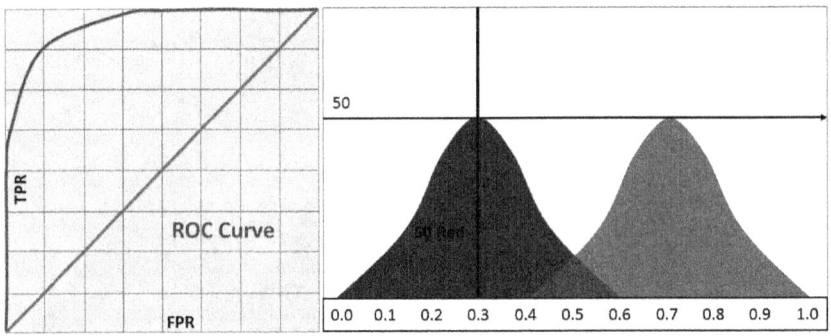

Figure 8-3. Fifty papers were predicted to be accepted with probability 0.3 and were not accepted

Figure 8-4 shows there were about 10 papers for which we predicted a probability of 0.5, and half of those were admitted and the other half were not. Here the model gave them a 50-50 chance for acceptance and that is what we got, so the model is still predicting very well.

146

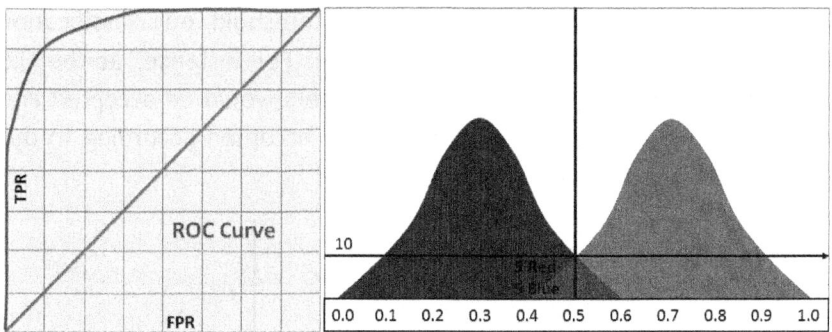

Figure 8-4. Ten papers were predicted to be accepted with probability 0.5 and half (5) were not accepted

Figure 8-5 shows there were 50 papers for which we predicted a probability of 0.7, and all of those were admitted, which is good. And so on.

Based on this plot, you might say that our classifier is doing quite well, since it did a good job of separating the classes. To actually make our class predictions, we might set our "threshold" at 0.5, and classify everything above 0.5 as admitted and everything below 0.5 as not admitted, which is what most classification methods will do by default. With that threshold, our accuracy rate would be above 90%, which is probably very good.

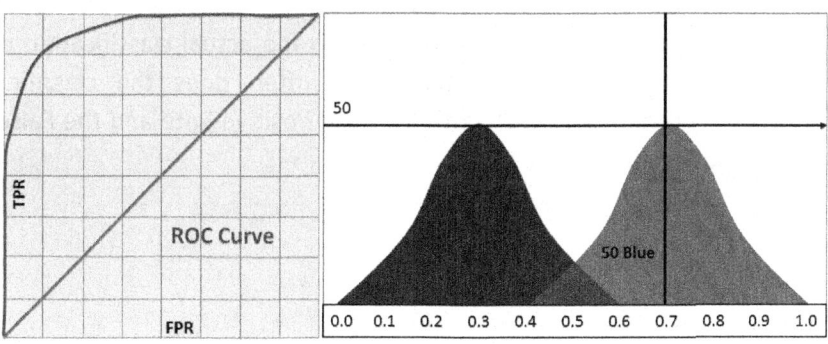

Figure 8-5. Fifty papers were predicted to be accepted with probability 0.7 and all 50 were accepted

Now let's say that our classifier didn't do nearly as well and move the red distribution. In Figure 8-6, we can see that there is a lot more overlap

147

here, and regardless of where we set our threshold, our classification accuracy will be much lower than before. For instance, at the 0.5 probability level, we projected that 50 papers would be accepted and half of all rejected papers (negative) were accepted according to our model (that number was 5 before).

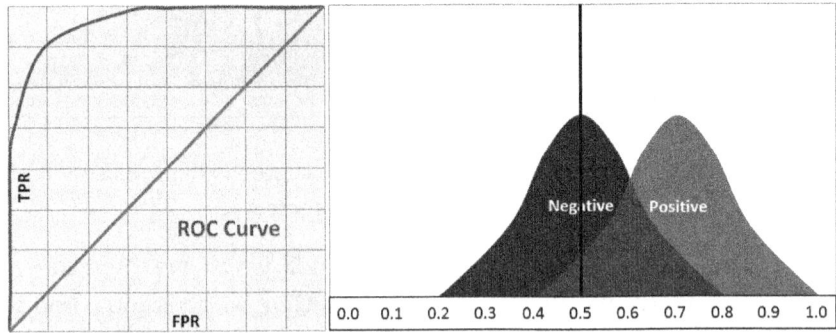

Figure 8-6. Fifty papers were predicted to be accepted with probability 0.5 and half of all the negative (not accepted) papers were accepted

Now let's talk about the ROC curve that you see in the left of Figure 8-7. So, what is an ROC curve? Its is a plot of the True Positive Rate (on the y-axis) versus the False Positive Rate (on the x-axis) for every possible classification threshold. As a reminder, the True Positive Rate answers the question, "When the actual classification is positive (meaning admitted), how often does the classifier predict positive?" The False Positive Rate answers the question, "When the actual classification is negative (meaning not admitted), how often does the classifier incorrectly predict positive?" Both the True Positive Rate and the False Positive Rate range from 0 to 1.

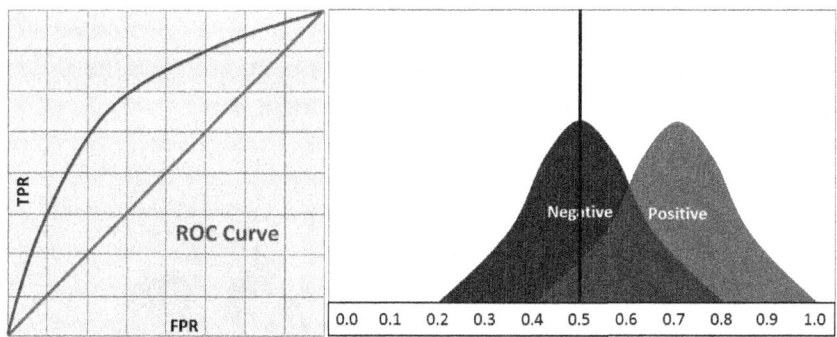

Figure 8-7. The ROC curve corresponding to the negate and positive distribution of papers

To see how the ROC curve is actually generated, let's set some example thresholds for classifying a paper as admitted.

A threshold of 0.8 would classify 50 papers as admitted, and 450 papers as not admitted as shown in Figure 8-8. The True Positive Rate would be the blue pixels to the right of the line divided by all blue pixels, or 50 divided by 250, which is 0.2. The False Positive Rate would be the red pixels to the right of the line divided by all red pixels, or 0 divided by 250, which is 0. Thus, we would plot a point at 0 on the x-axis, and 0.2 on the y-axis or (0, 0.2), which is right here (the ROC curve is approximate in the Figure so the red dot is not exactly at $x = 0$).

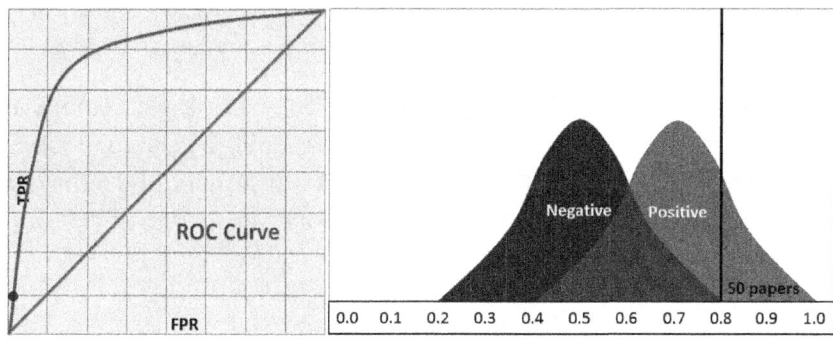

Figure 8-8. Fifty papers were predicted to be accepted with probability 0.8 and all of them were accepted

Let's set a different threshold of 0.5. That would classify 365 papers as admitted, and 135 papers as not admitted. The True Positive Rate would

149

be 240 divided by 250, or 0.96. The False Positive Rate would be 125 divided by 250, or 0.5. Thus, we would plot a point at 0.5 on the x-axis, and 0.96 on the y-axis in Figure 8-9, which is right here.

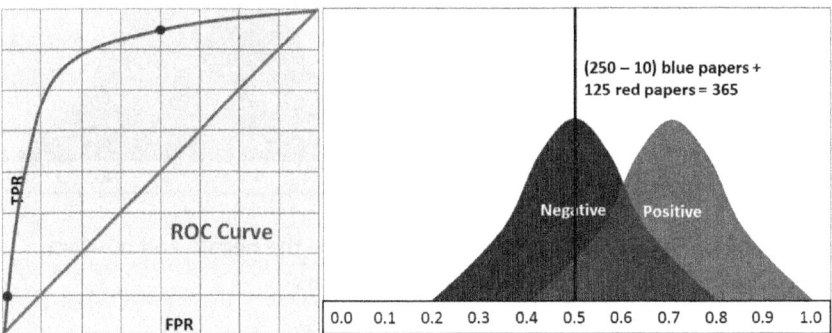

Figure 8-9. 365 papers were predicted to be accepted with probability 0.5 and 135 were predicted not to be accepted

We've plotted two points, but to generate the entire ROC curve, all we have to do is to plot the True Positive Rate versus the False Positive Rate for all possible classification thresholds which range from 0 to 1. That is a colossal benefit of using an ROC curve to evaluate a classifier instead of a simpler metric such as misclassification rate, in that a ROC curve visualizes all possible classification thresholds, whereas misclassification rate only represents our error rate for a single threshold. Note that we cannot actually see the thresholds used to generate the ROC curve anywhere on the curve itself.

Now, let's move the red distribution back to where it was before as shown in Figure 8-10. Because the classifier is doing a very good job of separating the blues and the reds, I can set a threshold of 0.6, have a True Positive Rate of 0.8, and still have a False Positive Rate of 0.

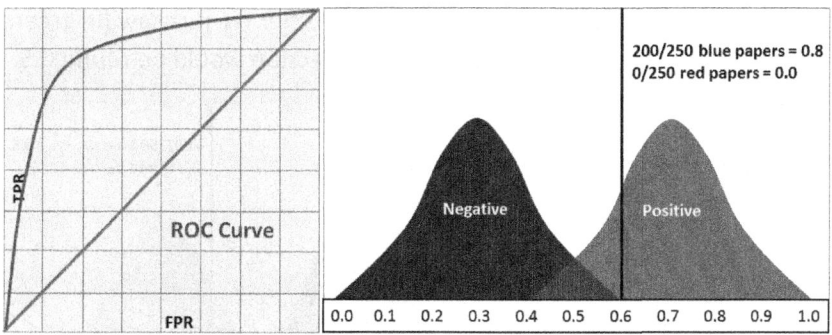

Figure 8-10. 200 blue papers were predicted to be accepted with probability 0.8 and were accepted, no red papers were accepted

Therefore, a classifier that does a very good job separating the classes will have an ROC curve that squeezes against the upper left corner of the plot area. Conversely, a classifier that does a very poor job separating the classes will have an ROC curve that is close to the black diagonal line as Shown in Figure 8-11. That line essentially represents a classifier that does no better than random guessing.

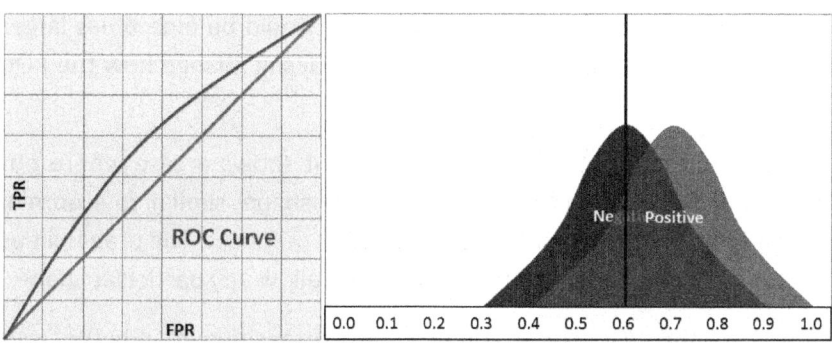

Figure 8-11. Here the crossover between positive and negative is so great, the model predicts more accepted than actually are accepted

Naturally, we might want to use the ROC curve to quantify the performance of a classifier, and give a higher score for this classifier than another classifier. That is the purpose of AUC, which stands for Area Under the Curve. AUC is literally just the percentage of the area that is under this curve. Figure 8-12 shows that our original classifier (in blue) has an AUC of around 0.8, the very poor classifier we just saw (in green) has an AUC of around 0.6, while random selection would be round 0.5.

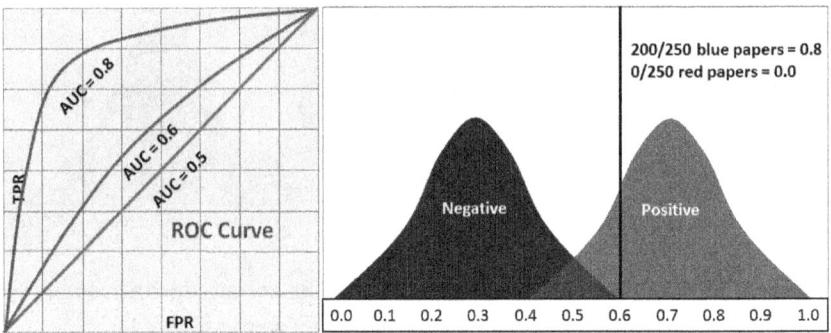

Figure 8.12. Comparison of a strong classifier (blue), a weak classifier (green), and a poor classifier (gray)

There are two things we want to mention about this diagram. First, this diagram shows a case where our classes are perfectly balanced, which is why the size of the blue and the red distributions are identical. In most real-world problems, this is not the case. For example, if only 10% of papers were admitted, the red distribution would be nine times larger than the blue distribution. However, that doesn't change how the ROC curve is generated.

A second note about this diagram is that it shows a case where our predicted probabilities have a very smooth shape, similar to a normal distribution. That was just for demonstration purposes. The probabilities output by our classifier will not necessarily follow any particular shape.

Note that the ROC curve and AUC are insensitive to whether our predicted probabilities are properly calibrated to actually represent probabilities of class membership. In other words, the ROC curve and the AUC would be identical even if our predicted probabilities ranged from 0.9 to 1 instead of 0 to 1, as long as the ordering of observations by predicted probability remained the same. All the AUC metric cares about is how well our classifier separated the two classes, and thus it is said to only be sensitive to rank ordering. We can think of AUC as representing the probability that a classifier will rank a randomly chosen positive observation higher than a randomly chosen negative observation, and so it is a useful metric even for datasets with highly unbalanced classes.

Summary

In this chapter we have studied tests for significance on coefficients, as well as the details of creating a ROC chart and finding the AUC. We have define such metrics as True Positive (TP), False Positive, Sensitivity, and so on. Understanding these concepts are prerequisites for scoring a model.

Exercises

1. Use the classification table below to create a ROC chart.

Incorrect		Percentages				
Event	Non-Event	Correct	Sensitivity	Specificity	False Pos.	False Neg.
10272	872	75.4	83.5	74.3	69.9	2.9
3910	2169	86.6	59	90.2	55.6	5.7
2012	3110	88.7	41.2	95	48	7.6
1211	3754	89	29	97	44.1	8.8
763	4167	89.1	21.2	98.1	40.5	9.6
515	4475	89	15.4	98.7	38.8	10.2
344	4713	88.8	10.9	99.1	37.4	10.6
225	4923	88.6	6.9	99.4	38.1	11
121	5095	88.5	3.7	99.7	38.4	11.3
0	5289	88.3	0	100	.	11.7

2. Find the AUC for Exercise 1.
3. When is the Wald Statistic inappropriate for measuring coefficient significance?

4. Complete the classification table below.

Classification Table									
	Correct		Incorrect		Percentages				
Prob	Event	Non-Event	Event	Non-Event	Cor-rect	Sensi-tivity	Speci-ficity	False POS	False NEG
0.1	4417	29650	10272	872					
0.2	3120	36012	3910	2169					
0.3	2179	37910	2012	3110					
0.4	1535	38711	1211	3754					
0.5	1122	39159	763	4167					
0.6	814	39407	515	4475					
0.7	576	39578	344	4713					
0.8	366	39697	225	4923					
0.9	194	39801	121	5095					
1	0	39922	0	5289					

9. Scoring and Model Performance

Scoring a Model

Scoring a data set, which is especially important for predictive modeling, means applying a previously fitted model to a new data set in order to compute the *posterior (conditional) probabilities* of each response category given the values of the predictive (explanatory) variables in each observation.

Scoring Code

Scoring code is comprised of a least four essential components (see Figure 9-1). Some software packages generate scoring code when called to do so—notably SAS Studio, SAS Enterprise Minor, SPSS Modeler, and certain R packages.

Date Macro (if applicable)
- Convert multiple date formats to one common scoring date format
- Convert multiple dates to one scoring input date variable

Predictor Variable Macro
- Pull independent variable
- Creat model effects
- Perform variable transformations
- Perform data imputations

Regression Macro
- Define model effect coeficients
- Define Posterior probabilities
- Define default posterior probabilities (for missing values if not imputed)

Score Ranking Macro
- Put score into increments (deciles, pentiles, etc.)
- Write scores and ranks to a file

Figure 9-1. Essential components of scoring code

Example Scoring Code from SAS Studio

SAS Studio generates model scoring code when prompted by the SCORE function in the PROC LOGISTICS code as follows:

```
SCORE /* plus options like out=score_file, FITSTAT*/
DATA=file_name; /*Input file, like TESTING*/
Code; /*generates scoring code}*/
```

The "Code" renders the scoring code in the log file, which I have wrapped in a macro called "SCOREPROG," as follows:

```
%MACRO SCOREPROG(INDATA,OUTDATA);
 DATA &OUTDATA;
 SET &INDATA;
 ****************************************************;
 ** SAS Scoring Code for PROC Logistic in log;
 ****************************************************;
 length I_RESP $ 12;
 label I_RESP = 'Into: RESP' ;
 label U_RESP = 'Unnormalized Into: RESP' ;
 format U_RESP BEST12.0;
 label P_RESP1 = 'Predicted: RESP=1' ;
 label P_RESP0 = 'Predicted: RESP=0' ;
 drop _LMR_BAD;
 _LMR_BAD=0;

 *** Check interval variables for missing values;
 if nmiss(age,balance,married,manual_labor) then do;
    _LMR_BAD=1;
    goto _SKIP_000;
 end;

 *** Compute Linear Predictors;
 drop _LP0;
 _LP0 = 0;

 *** Effect: age;
 _LP0 = _LP0 + (0.01231446050394) * age;
 *** Effect: balance;
 _LP0 = _LP0 + (0.00003739932928) * balance;
 *** Effect: married;
 _LP0 = _LP0 + (-0.39753987270199) * married;
 *** Effect: manual_labor;
 _LP0 = _LP0 + (-0.54646860891569) * manual_labor;

 *** Predicted values/posterior probabilities;
 drop _MAXP _IY _P0 _P1;
 _TEMP = -2.25567017967893  + _LP0; *** Intercept;
 if (_TEMP < 0) then do;
    _TEMP = exp(_TEMP);
    _P0 = _TEMP / (1 + _TEMP);
 end;
 else _P0 = 1 / (1 + exp(-_TEMP));
 _P1 = 1.0 - _P0;
 P_RESP1 = _P0;
 _MAXP = _P0;
 _IY = 1;
 P_RESP0 = _P1;
 if (_P1 > _MAXP + 1E-8) then do;
    _MAXP = _P1;
    _IY = 2;
```

```
   end;
select( _IY );
   when (1) do;
      I_RESP = '1' ;
      U_RESP = 1;
   end;
   when (2) do;
      I_RESP = '0' ;
      U_RESP = 0;
   end;
   otherwise do;
      I_RESP = '';
      U_RESP = .;
   end;
end;
_SKIP_000:
if _LMR_BAD = 1 then do;
I_RESP = '';
U_RESP = .;
P_RESP1 = .;
P_RESP0 = .;
end;
drop _TEMP;
*******************************************;
***    END SAS SCORING CODE  in log ***;
*******************************************;
%MEND SCOREPROG;
%SCOREPROG(WORK.TRAINING,WORK.BANK_TEMP);

*** Additional code generated by modeler;
%MACRO PUTDECILES(INDATA,SCORENAME,OUTDATA);
DATA GETPENT;
SET &INDATA(KEEP = RESP &SCORENAME);
RUN;
PROC SORT DATA=GETPENT; BY P_RESP1; RUN;
PROC RANK DATA=GETPENT GROUPS=10 OUT=HIGH3;
     VAR &SCORENAME;
     RANKS DECILE;
RUN;
DATA &OUTDATA;
SET HIGH3;
     RENAME &SCORENAME = SCORE;
     DECILE = 10 - DECILE;
RUN;
PROC FREQ DATA=&OUTDATA;
     TITLE 'FREQ - DECILES FOR RESP BANK MODEL';
     TABLES DECILE;
RUN;
%MEND;
%PUTDECILES(WORK.BANK_TEMP,P_RESP1,WORK.BANK_SCORE_OUT);

PROC TABULATE DATA= WORK.BANK_SCORE_OUT;
VAR SCORE RESP;
CLASS DECILE/ ORDER=UNFORMATTED MISSING;
TABLE DECILE, N SCORE*SUM RESP*SUM;
RUN;
```

157

Example Scoring Output

The last part of the scoring code, PROC TABULATE, generates Table 9-1 below, which contains the predicted and actual responses (apply for credit card, in the case of the Bank problem)

Table 9-1. PROC TABLULATE output for scoring code

FREQ - DECILES FOR RESP BIRTH WEIGHT MODEL

Rank for Variable P_RESP1	N	Predicted: RESP=1 Sum	RESP Sum
1	2255	1120	1112.16
2	2253	614	451.17
3	2254	393	303.88
4	2253	195	230.83
5	2253	115	181.8
6	2253	121	132.69
7	2253	48	100.32
8	2254	27	75.14
9	2253	16	47.32
10	2253	13	26.73

One of the other options for SCORE is "output=score_file." An example is shown in Figure 9-2.

marital	age	balance	homeowner				P_0	P_1
single	31	410	0	.	.	.	0.863126	0.136873
married	54	0	0	.	.	.	0.882802	0.117197
married	38	4297	0	.	.	.	0.884172	0.115827
married	41	1536	0	.	.	.	0.890873	0.109126
married	42	100	1	.	.	.	0.894771	0.105228
single	35	980	0	.	.	.	0.855650	0.144349
single	33	206	1	.	.	.	0.861520	0.138479

Figure 9-2. Excerpt from bank score file

The score file contains the posterior probabilities. P_0 and P_1, along with the final model effects and target variable. Sorting by posterior probabilities and dividing them into groups (like deciles) provides the information in Table 9-1.

Model Performance

There are a number of ways to measure model performance. Most (if not all, though I do not claim to know "all") methods of measuring performance depend directly on the output from the scoring code. Table 9-1 represents one of these.

Cumulative Percent Captured Response

We use the data in Table 9-1 to form a cumulative frequency distribution, and in turn a *receiver operating characteristic* (ROC) curve (introduced in Chapter 8). Technically (as we saw in Chapter 8), the ROC curve shows false positive rate (1-specificity) on X-axis, the probability of target=1 when its true value is 0, against true positive rate (sensitivity) on Y-axis, the probability of target=1 when its true value is 1 (we calculated these values in Chapter 8). However, the cumulative distribution can be used to construct the ROC curve. Table 9-2 shows the calculated cumulative frequency table and Figure 9-3 depicts the ROC curve.

Table 9-2. Cumulative Percent Captured Response Table

Decile	No Model	Model	Actual
0	0	0	0
1	0.10	0.420736	0.417785
2	0.20	0.651390	0.587268
3	0.30	0.799023	0.701421
4	0.40	0.872276	0.788132
5	0.50	0.915477	0.856426
6	0.60	0.960932	0.906271
7	0.70	0.978963	0.943957
8	0.80	0.989106	0.972183
9	0.90	0.995116	0.989959

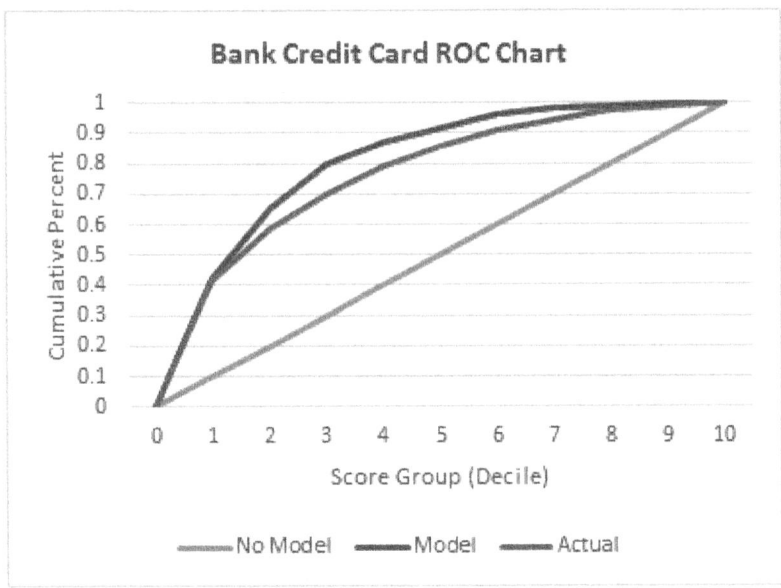

Figure 9-3. Bank Credit Card campaign ROC curve

The c-statistic (or concordance statistic) is associated with the ROC curve and is an indicator of goodness-of-fit in logistic regression. It is equal to the area under the ROC curve and ranges from 0.5 to 1.0. Some rules-of-thumb are given in Table 9-3.

Table 9-3. Rules-of-thumb for evaluating the c-statistic

0.5	the model is no better for predicting an outcome than random chance
over 0.7	indicate a good model
over 0.8	indicate a strong model
1.0	Indicate a perfect model (which I would be suspect of)

In our example, c is 0.855, indicating a strong model , at least in isolation of other measures. We should always examine multiple metrics for goodness-of-fit and performance before we decide on a model's usefulness. In light of the other measures we have looked at so far, our example appears to be a strong model.

Table 9-4. Association of predicted probabilities and observed responses

Percent Concordant	85.5	Somers' D	0.71
Percent Discordant	14.5	Gamma	0.71
Percent Tied	0	Tau-a	0.148
Pairs	52899264	c	0.855

Table 9-4 also shows *percent concordant, percent discordant* (some say "disconcordant" which is not a word and has no meaning), *percent tied*, and *pairs*.

Percent Concordant: Percentage of pairs where the observation with the desired outcome (event) has a higher predicted probability than the observation without the outcome (non-event).

Percent Discordant: Percentage of pairs where the observation with the desired outcome (event) has a lower predicted probability than the observation without the outcome (non-event).

Percent Tied: Percentage of pairs where the observation with the desired outcome (event) has same predicted probability than the observation without the outcome (non-event).

c-statistics (AUC) : c-statistics is also called area under curve (AUC). It is calculated by adding Concordance Percent and 0.5 times of Tied Percent

K-S Tests

The Kolmogorov-Smirnov (K-S) Test is a distribution independent measure of goodness-of-fit, and we use it here to measure the performance of our model.

A.N. Kolmogorov Dies at 84; Top Russian Mathematician

By JAMES GLEICK

Published: October 23, 1987

Andrei N. Kolmogorov, the founder of modern probability theory and one of the 20th century's most eminent mathematicians, died in Moscow on Tuesday, the Soviet press agency Tass reported yesterday. He was 84 years old. (Gleick, 1987)

Dr. Kolmogorov's contributions to mathematics in a career that spanned two generations were recognized by a host of honors both in the Soviet Union and internationally. An obituary signed by Mikhail S. Gorbachev, the Soviet leader, declared yesterday that his life "represented an incomparable feat for science."

Dr. Kolmogorov left his mark on many areas of mathematics. He developed an early theory for the flow of energy in turbulent fluids. He introduced the mathematical concept of entropy as a measure of disorder, an idea that now plays an important role in information theory.

But his greatest single achievement was in turning ideas of chance and probability into a rigorous mathematical system in the 1930's.

"He was one of the very greatest mathematicians," said Peter Lax of the Courant Institute of Mathematics at New York University. "He was to probability theory what Euclid was to geometry." Theory Is Still Central

As Euclid did in geometry, Dr. Kolmogorov built up a system of axioms, or fundamental principles, from which complex notions could be derived. His probability theory – described by a younger colleague as the "New Testament" of mathematics – remains central today.

Born in Tambov in central Russia in 1903, he attended Moscow University and became a professor there at the age of 28. He continue to serve in its administration and on its faculty until his death.

As a member of the Soviet Academy of Sciences and chairman of the Academy's committee on mathematical education, he played a central role in overhauling the teaching of mathematics in the Soviet Union in the 1960's.

Notions of randomness and predictability, order and disorder, ran as a constant current through Dr. Kolmogorov's work on a range of problems. As a result, his contributions to mathematics often spilled over into physics.

In the 1940's, he created a powerful technique for using probability to make predictions in the face of randomness, on the basis of a series of observations. The technique was applied to a wide range of systems, such as the problem of landing an airplane on an aircraft carrier bobbing in the sea, calculating ahead of time what its likely position would be. Instrumental in KAM Theorem

His legacy also includes the KAM theorem, or Kolmogorov-Arnold-Moser theorem, a pivotal idea in the study of stability in physical processes. KAM

Model versus No Model

The K-S test for model versus no model measures whether there is a statistically significant difference between the model and the data observed from having no model (sometimes called *random selection*). The null hypothesis is there the two curves are not statistically different and we want to reject the null hypothesis. Hence, we are looking for a large test statistic. The K-S statistic is the maximum of the differences between the two curves, calculated by groups (deciles in this example):

$$\text{K-S}_{\text{Statistic}} = \max\{ |x_1 - y_1|, |x_2 - y_2|, \ldots, |x_n - y_n| \} \quad (9.1)$$

In our example, the K-S Statistic is 0.498943 and the K-S Critical Value for alpha = 0.05 is

$$\text{K-S}_{\text{Critical}} = 1.36\sqrt{N} = 0.430$$

Since 0.499 > 0.430, we reject the null hypothesis and conclude the two curves are statistically different.

The K-S statistic also tell us where the maximum area under the ROC curve is. In this example, the K-S Statistic of 0.499 occurs at the 3rd decile which corresponds to the maximum of the green dotted line in Figure 9-4, and corresponds to the ROC curve where the area under the curve is 0.872 or 87.2%.

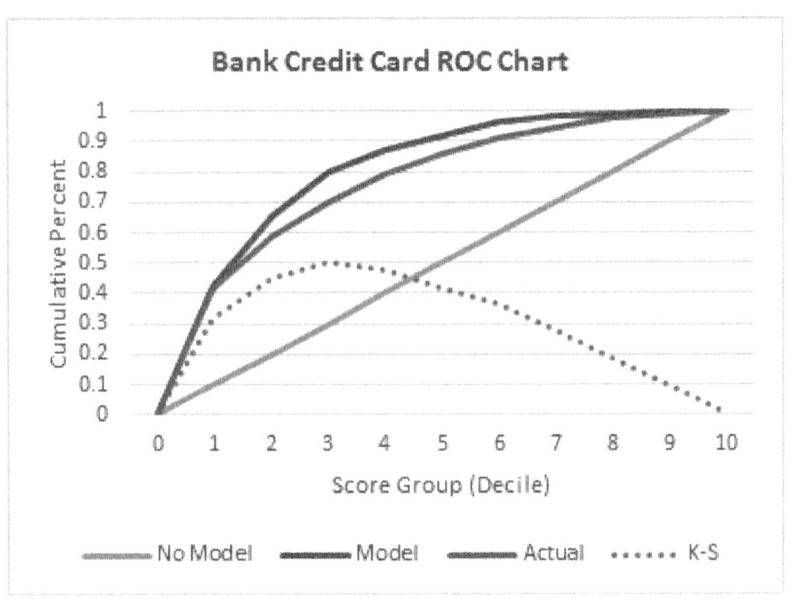

Figure 9-4. ROC Curve with the K-S test for model versus no model

Model Versus Actuals

The K-S test for model versus actuals is a goodness of fit test measuring model performance against the reference curve of actual responses. Again the K-S statistic is formed by the maximum of the distances between the two curves. In this case, the null hypothesis is that the two curves are the statistically the same and we want to not reject the null hypothesis (see Figure 9-5). The K-S Critical value at the alpha=0.05 level is 0.430. Since the K-S Statistic is 0.098, and since 0.098 < 0.430, were do not reject the null hypothesis and conclude that two curve are statistically the same.

Since the model in our example, is statistically different than random selection and not statistically different from the actuals, we can conclude that the model's performance is acceptable. However, when can we say that the model is more than acceptable?

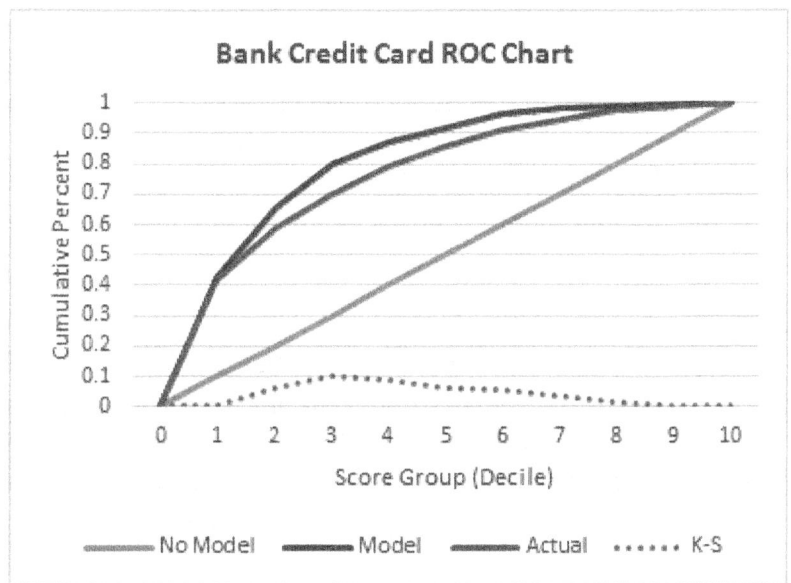

Figure 9-5. . ROC Curve with the K-S test for model versus actual

Incremental Response Rates

By incremental response rates, we mean the response rates for each group in the score data (deciles in our example). To illustrate this we will examine Figure 9.6.

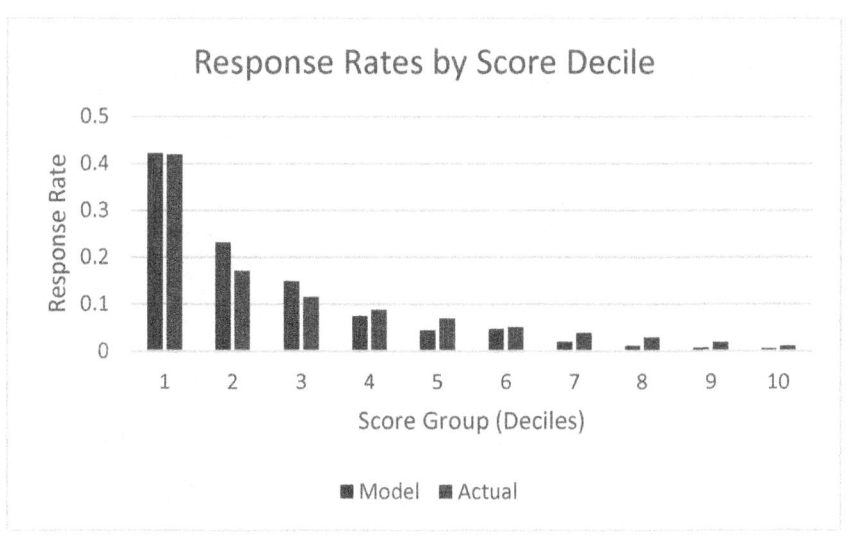

Figure 9.6. Response rated by score deciles

Note that the response rate in the first decile is about 42%. If we take the first two deciles, the response rate is 65%. Adding the third decile makes the response rate 80%. So if we market the credit card to the first three deciles in the model, we stand a chance to get an 80% response rate. As a rule of thumb, any predictive model that returns a response of 70% in the top four deciles is an useful model, and therefore a good model.

Summary

In this chapter we have examined the components of scoring code. We have also looked at examples of scoring code and learned how to prompt SAS Studio to print scoring code to the log file. Moreover, we have seen how to produce data from the score file to construct lift and gains charts, and perform K-S tests to measure a model performance.

Exercises

1. Provide the table below, construct a cumulative distribution for the predicted and actual values derived from a logistic regression model.

	N	Predicted Probability: RESP=1	RESP
		Sum	Sum
Rank for Variable P_1			
1	4521	2332.06	2318.00
2	4521	954.48	1307.00
3	4521	594.20	688.00
4	4521	419.41	379.00
5	4522	311.86	234.00
6	4521	235.38	164.00
7	4521	176.30	102.00
8	4521	129.46	60.00
9	4521	89.63	28.00
10	4521	46.22	9.00

2. Perform a K-S test for the actual versus predicted values using the table in Exercise 1.

10. Bayesian logistic regression

In a Bayesian statistics context, prior distributions are normally placed on the regression coefficients, usually in the form of Gaussian distributions. Unfortunately, the Gaussian distribution is not the conjugate prior of the likelihood function in logistic regression; in fact, the likelihood function is not an exponential family and thus does not have a conjugate prior at all. As a result, the posterior distributionis difficult to calculate, even using standard simulation algorithms (e.g. Gibbs sampling).

There are various possibilities:

- Don't do a proper Bayesian analysis, but simply compute a maximum *a posteriori* point estimate of the parameters. This is common, for example, in "maximum entropy" classifiers in machine learning.
- Use a more general approximation method such as the *Metropolis–Hastings* algorithm.
- Draw a *Markov chain Monte Carlo* sample from the exact posterior by using the Independent Metropolis–Hastings algorithm with heavy-tailed multivariate candidate distribution found by matching the mode and curvature at the mode of the normal approximation to the posterior and then using the Student's *t* shape with low degrees of freedom. This is shown to have excellent convergence properties.
- Use a *latent variable model* (we mentioned this in chapters 4 and 8) and approximate the logistic distribution using a more tractable distribution, e.g. a Student's *t*-distribution or a mixture of normal distributions.
- Do *probit regression* instead of logistic regression. This is actually a special case of the previous situation, using a normal distribution in place of a Student's *t*, mixture of normals, etc. This will be less accurate but has the advantage that probit regression is extremely common, and a ready-made Bayesian implementation may already be available (see Figure 17-2).
- Use the *Laplace approximation* of the posterior distribution. This

approximates the posterior with a Gaussian distribution. This is not a terribly good approximation, but it suffices if all that is desired is an estimate of the posterior mean and variance. In such a case, an approximation scheme such as variational Bayes can be used (Bishop, 2006).

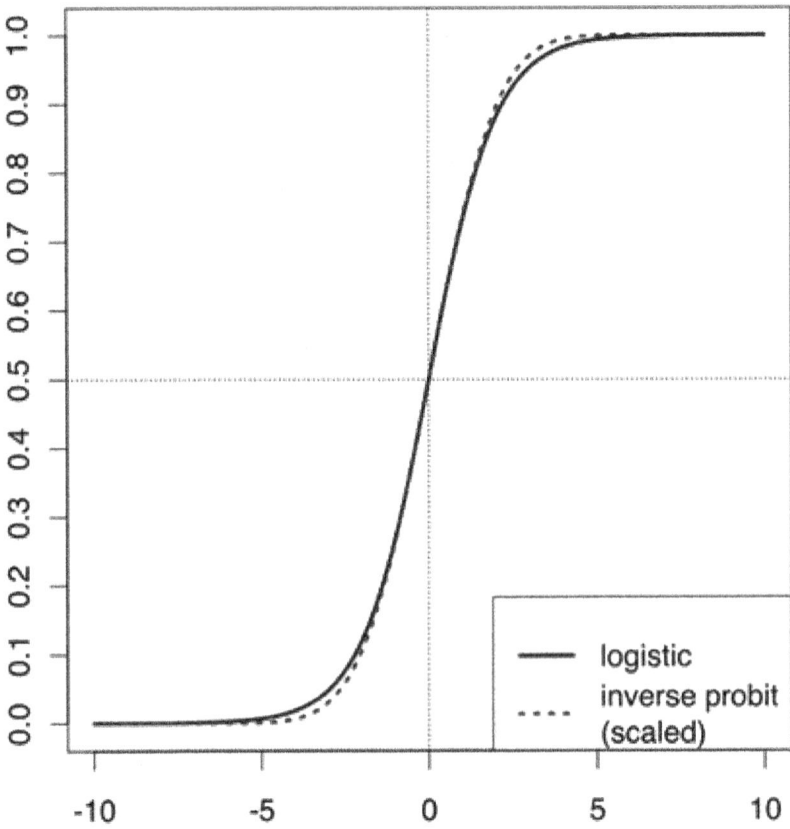

Figure 10-1. Comparison of logistic function with a scaled inverse probit function (i.e. the CDF of the normal distribution), comparing $\sigma(x)$ vs. $\Phi = \left(\sqrt{\frac{\pi}{8}} x \right)$, which makes the slopes the same at the origin. This shows the heavier tails of the logistic distribution.

Gibbs sampling with an approximating distribution

As shown in Figure 10-1, logistic regression is equivalent to a latent variable model with an error variable distributed according to a standard logistic distribution. The overall distribution of the latent variable Y_i^* is also a logistic distribution, with the mean equal to $\beta \cdot X_i$ (i.e. the fixed quantity added to the error variable). This model considerably simplifies the application of techniques such as Gibbs sampling (George & McCullochb, 1993). However, sampling the regression coefficients is still difficult, because of the lack of conjugacy between the normal and logistic distributions. Changing the prior distribution over the regression coefficients is of no help, because the logistic distribution is not in the exponential family and thus has no conjugate prior.

One possibility is to use a more general Markov chain Monte Carlo technique (Walsh, 2004), such as the Metropolis–Hastings algorithm (Chib & Greenberg, 1995), which can sample arbitrary distributions. Another possibility, however, is to replace the logistic distribution with a similar-shaped distribution that is easier to work with using Gibbs sampling. In fact, the logistic and normal distributions have a similar shape, and thus one possibility is simply to have normally distributed errors. Because the normal distribution is conjugate to itself, sampling the regression coefficients becomes easy. In fact, this model is exactly the model used in probit regression.

However, the normal and logistic distributions differ in that the logistic has heavier tails. As a result, it is more robust to inaccuracies in the underlying model (which are inevitable, in that the model is essentially always an approximation) or to errors in the data. Probit regression loses some of this robustness.

Another alternative is to use errors distributed as a Student's t-distribution. The Student's t-distribution has heavy tails, and is easy to sample from because it is the compound distribution of a normal distribution with variance distributed as an inverse gamma distribution. In other words, if a normal distribution is used for the error variable, and another latent variable, following an inverse gamma distribution, is added corresponding to the variance of this error variable, the marginal distribution of the error variable will follow a Student's t-distribution. Because of the various conjugacy relationships, all variables in this model are easy to sample from.

The Student's t-distribution that best approximates a standard logistic distribution can be determined by matching the moments of the two distributions. The Student's t-distribution has three parameters, and since the skewness of both distributions is always 0, the first four moments can all be matched, using the following equations:

$$\mu = 0$$

$$\frac{\nu}{\nu - 2}s^2 = \frac{\pi^2}{3}$$

$$\frac{6}{\nu - 4} = \frac{6}{5}.$$

This yields the following values:

$$\mu = 0$$

$$s = \sqrt{\frac{7}{9}\frac{\pi^2}{3}}$$

$$\nu = 9.$$

The following graphs compare the standard logistic distribution with the Student's t-distribution that matches the first four moments using the above-determined values, as well as the normal distribution that matches the first two moments. Note how much closer the Student's t-distribution agrees, especially in the tails. Beyond about two standard deviations from the mean, the logistic and normal distributions diverge rapidly, but the logistic and Student's t-distributions don't start diverging significantly until more than 5 standard deviations away (see Figure 10-2 through Figure 10-5).

(Another possibility, also amenable to Gibbs sampling, is to approximate the logistic distribution using a mixture density of normal distributions (Chen, Zhu, Wang, Zheng, & Zhang, 2013).)

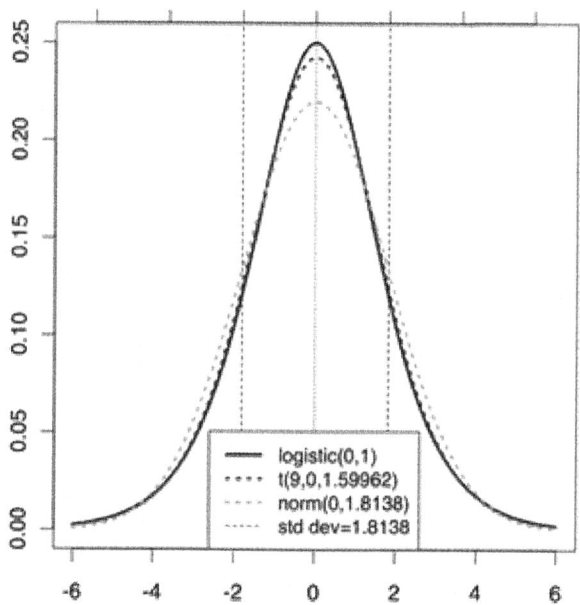

Figure 10-2. Comparison of logistic and approximating distributions (t, normal).

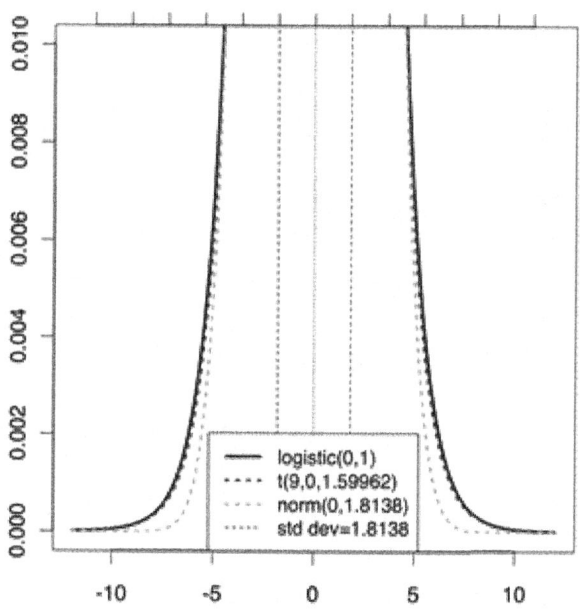

Figure 10-3. Tails of distributions.

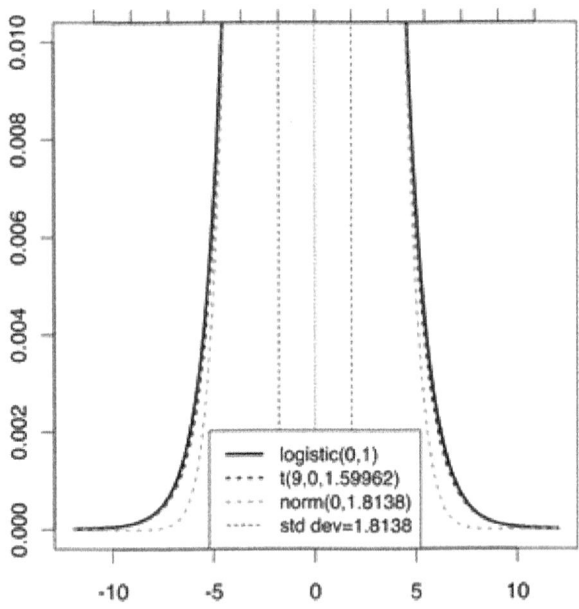

Figure 10-4. Further tails of distributions.

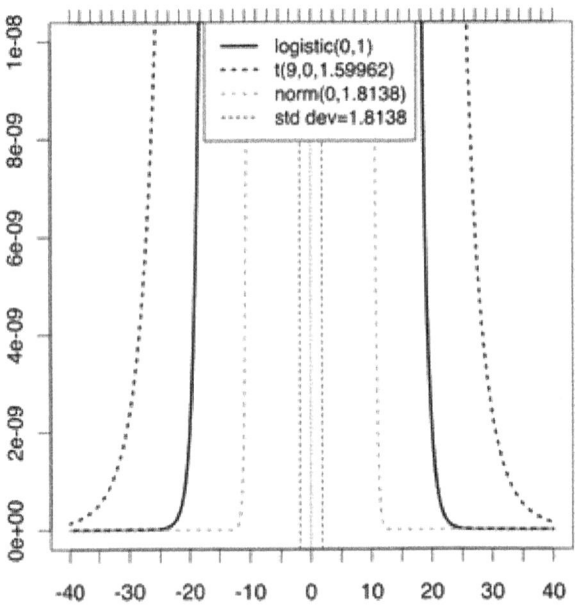

Figure 10-5. Extreme tails of distributions.

Extensions

There are large numbers of extensions:

- Multinomial logistic regression (or multinomial logit) handles the case of a multi-way categorical dependent variable (with unordered values, also called "classification"). Note that the general case of having dependent variables with more than two values is termed polytomous regression.
- Ordered logistic regression (or ordered logit) handles ordinal dependent variables (ordered values).
- Mixed logit is an extension of multinomial logit that allows for correlations among the choices of the dependent variable.
- An extension of the logistic model to sets of interdependent variables is the conditional random field.

Example

As an Example, let's say we want to estimate the probability that someone on the road is texting while driving. We will employ the binomial distribution to model this.

Our goal is to estimate a parameter θ, the probability of that a car's driver is texting. We take a random sample of ten cars while driving home, and note the following:

- As we passed three cars, the drivers' heads were staring at their laps.
- We note two cars that appear to be driving normally.
- Another two cars were swerving into other lanes.
- Two more cars appear to be driving normally.
- At a stoplight, one car wastes 10 seconds of everyone else's time before realizing the stoplight has turned green.

We can represent this in R as follows, as well as setup some other things for later.

```
drive = c('texting','texting','texting','not','not',
          'texting','texting','not','not','texting')
# convert to numeric, arbitrarily picking texting=1, not=0
driveNum = ifelse(drive=='texting', 1, 0)
N = length(drive)            # sample size
nTexting = sum(drive=='texting')# number of drivers texting
nNot = sum(drive=='not')     # number of those not
```

Recall the binomial distribution where we specify the number of trials for a particular observation and the probability of an event. Let's look at the distribution for a couple values for θ equal to 0.5 and 0.85 and N=10 observations. We will repeat this 1000 times (histograms not shown).

```
x1 = rbinom(1000, size=10, p=.5)
x2 = rbinom(1000, size=10, p=.85)

mean(x1); hist(x1)
mean(x2); hist(x2)
```

```
[1] 5.043
[1] 8.569
```

We can see the means are roughly around $N * p$ as we expect with the binomial.

Prior

Definition 10.1. The *prior probability* is the probability that an event will reflect established beliefs about the event before the arrival of new evidence or information. Prior probabilities are the original probabilities of an outcome, which be will updated with new information to create posterior probabilities.

For our current situation, we don't know θ and are trying to estimate it. We will start by supplying some possible values.

```
theta = seq(from=1/(N+1), to=N/(N+1), length=10)
```

For the Bayesian approach we must choose a *prior distribution* representing our initial beliefs about the estimate. I provide three possibilities and note that any one of them would work just fine for this situation. We'll go with a triangular distribution, which will put most of the weight toward values around 0.5. While we will talk more about this later, I will go ahead and mention that this is where some specifically have taken issue with Bayesian estimation in the past, because this part of the process is too subjective for their tastes. Setting aside the fact that subjectivity is an inherent part of the scientific process, and that ignoring prior information (if explicitly available from prior research) would be blatantly unscientific, the main point to make here is that this choice is not an arbitrary one. There are many distributions we might work with, but some will be better for us than others. Choose the prior that makes most sense to you.

```
### prior distribution
# uniform
# pTheta = dunif(theta)
# triangular as in Kruschke
pTheta = pmin(theta, 1-theta)
# beta prior with mean = .5
# pTheta = dbeta(theta, 10, 10)
pTheta = pTheta/sum(pTheta) # Normalize so sum to 1
```

So given some estimate of θ, we have a probability of that value based on our chosen prior.

Likelihood
Next we will compute the likelihood of the data given some value of θ. The likelihood function for the binomial can be expressed as:

$$p(y|\theta) = \binom{N}{k} \theta k (1-\theta)^{N-k}$$

where N is the total number of possible times in which the event of interest could occur, and k number of times the event of interest occurs. Our maximum likelihood estimate in this simple setting would simply be the proportion of events witnessed out of the total number of samples. We'll use the formula presented above Note that if we had covariates as in a regression model, we would have different estimates of theta for each observation, and thus would calculate each observation's likelihood and then take their product or sum their log values. Even here, if you turn this into binary logistic regression with 10 outcomes of texting vs. not, the "intercept only" model would be identical to our results here. Technically, the first term is not required, but it serves to normalize the likelihood as we did with the prior.

```
pDataGivenTheta = choose(N, nTexting) * theta^nTexting * (1
-theta)^nNot
```

Posterior

Definition 10.2. The *posterior probability* is the probability of event A occurring given that event B has occurred. It represents our uncertainty over theta after we have sampled the data.

Given the prior and likelihood, we can now compute the posterior distribution via Bayes theorem.

```
# first we calculate the denominator from Bayes theorem; th
is is the marginal
# probability of y
pData = sum(pDataGivenTheta*pTheta)
pThetaGivenData = pDataGivenTheta*pTheta/pData # Bayes theo
rem
```

Now lets examine what all we've got.

```
data.frame(theta, prior=pTheta, likelihood=pDataGivenTheta,
    posterior=pThetaGivenData)
```

theta	prior	likelihood	posterior
0.091	0.033	0.000	0.000
0.182	0.067	0.003	0.002
0.273	0.100	0.024	0.018
0.364	0.133	0.080	0.079
0.455	0.167	0.164	0.203
0.545	0.167	0.236	0.293
0.636	0.133	0.244	0.242
0.727	0.100	0.172	0.128
0.818	0.067	0.069	0.034
0.909	0.033	0.008	0.002

We can see that we've given most of our prior probability to the middle values with probability tapering off somewhat slowly towards either extreme. The likelihood suggests the data is most probable for θ values .55-.64, though as we know the specific maximum likelihood estimate for θ is the proportion for the sample, or .6. Our posterior will fall somewhere between the prior and likelihood estimates, and we can see it has shifted the bulk of the probability slightly away from center of the prior towards a θ value of .6.

Let's go ahead and see what the mean is:

```
posteriorMean = sum(pThetaGivenData*theta)
posteriorMean
```

```
[1] 0.5623611
```

So we start with a prior centered on a value of $\theta = 0.5$, add data whose ML estimate is $\theta = 0.6$, and our posterior distribution suggests we end up somewhere in between.

Perhaps we can understand this further via the figures below. In each of these the prior is represented by the blue density, the likelihood by the red, and the posterior by purple. Figure 10-6 is based on a different prior than just used in our example, and instead employs with the beta distribution noted among the possibilities in the code above. While the beta distribution is highly flexible, with shape parameters A and B set to 10 and 10 we get a symmetric distribution centered on $\theta = .5$. This would actually be a somewhat stronger prior than we might normally want to use, but serves to illustrate a point. The mean of the beta is $A/(A + B)$, and thus has a nice interpretation as a prior based on data with sample size equal to $A + B$. The posterior distribution that results would have a mean somewhere between the maximum likelihood value and that of the prior. With the stronger prior, the posterior is pulled closer to it.

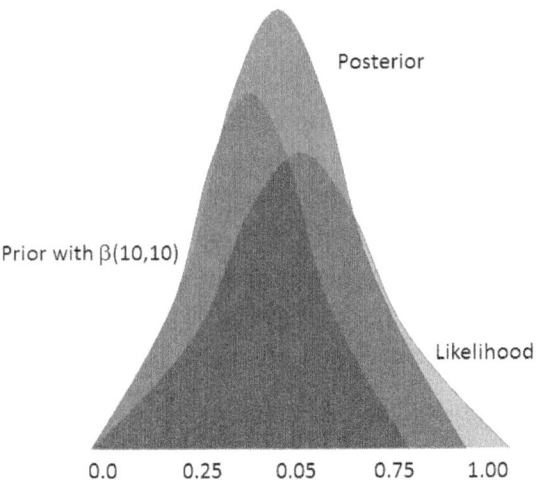

Figure 10-6. Prior with $\beta(10, 10)$, likelihood, and posterior probability distributions

Figure 10-7 utilizes a more diffuse prior of β(2,2) (β(1,1) is a uniform distribution). The result of using the vague prior is that the likelihood gets more weight with regard to the posterior. In fact, if we used a uniform distribution, we would be doing the equivalent of maximum likelihood estimation. As such most of the commonly used methods that implement maximum likelihood can be seen as a special case of a Bayesian approach.

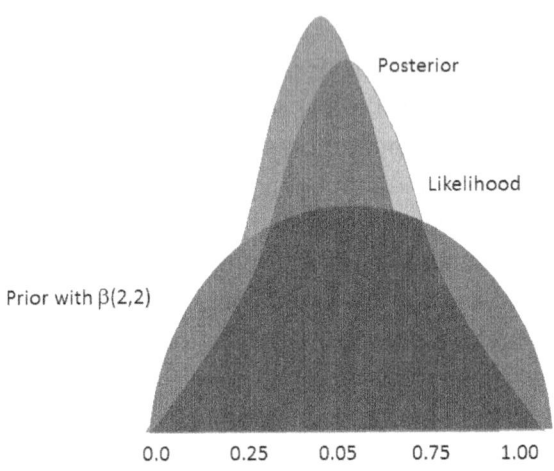

Figure 10-7. A more diffuse prior probability

Figure 10-8 employs the initial $\beta(10,10)$ prior again, but this time we add more observations to the data. Again this serves to give more weight to the likelihood, which is what we want. As scientists, we'd want the evidence, i.e. data, to eventually outweigh our prior beliefs about the state of things the more we have of it.

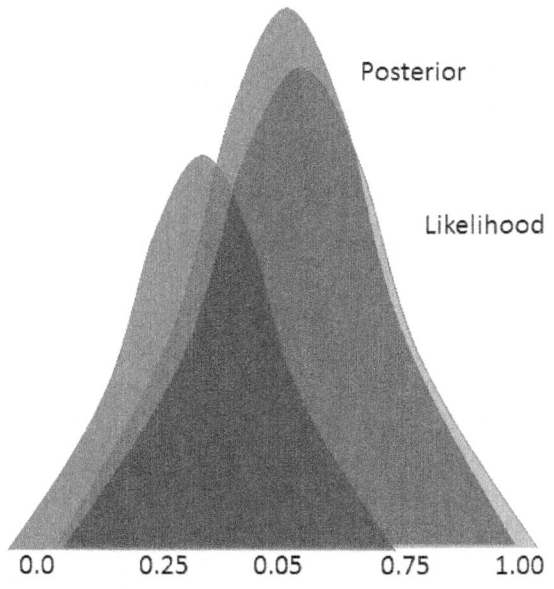

Figure 10-8. Same $\beta(10, 10)$ prior but with more observations

Example

R's MCMCpack (MCMC stands for *Markov Chain Monte Carlo*) package contains functions to perform Bayesian inference using posterior simulation for a number of statistical models. In this example, we will use MCMClogit. This function generates a sample from the posterior distribution of a logistic regression model using a random walk Metropolis algorithm. The user supplies data and priors, and a sample from the posterior distribution is returned as an MCMC object, which can be subsequently analyzed with functions provided in the coda package. Provides functions for summarizing and plotting the output from MCMC simulations. We first load the necessary R pakages.

```
library(lattice)
library(coda)
```

```
library(MASS)
library(MCMCpack)
```

Now we generate random values for x from a normal distribution and for y from a binomial distribution and then perform a logistic regression with y as the target variable.

```
x<-rnorm(1000)
y<-rbinom(1000,1,exp(1-x)/(1+exp(1-x)))
posterior <-MCMClogit(y~x, b0=0, B0=.001)
plot(posterior)
summary(posterior)
```

The output includes a summary of the regression and a plot of the posteriors.

```
Iterations = 1001:11000
Thinning interval = 1
Number of chains = 1
Sample size per chain = 10000

1. Empirical mean and standard deviation for each variable,
   plus standard error of the mean:

                Mean      SD  Naive SE Time-series SE
(Intercept)  1.001 0.07797 0.0007797       0.002343
x           -0.962 0.08930 0.0008930       0.002708

2. Quantiles for each variable:

                2.5%     25%     50%     75%   97.5%
(Intercept)  0.8488  0.9477  1.0011  1.0539  1.1549
x           -1.1357 -1.0214 -0.9618 -0.9014 -0.7871
```

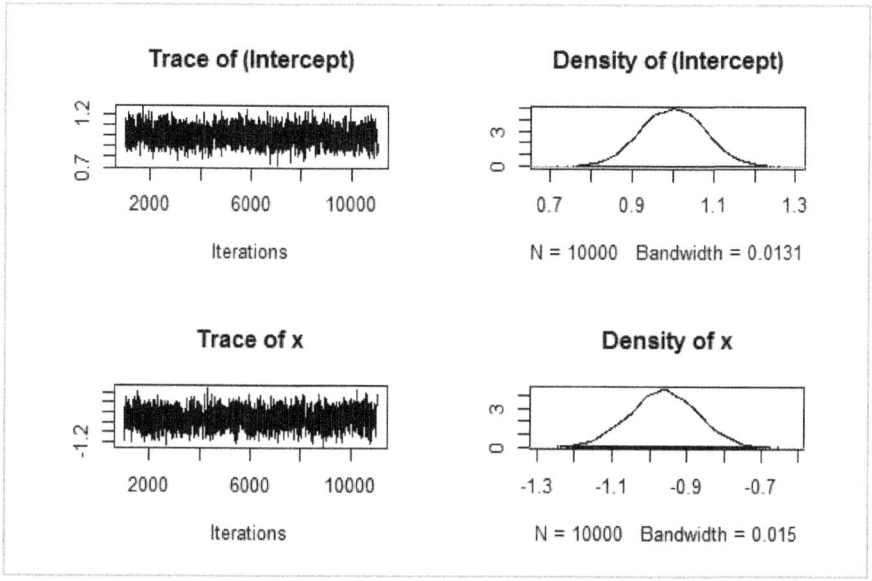

Summary

In this chapter we have studies Bayesian Logistic Regression. We also examine prior and posterior probabilities and looked at the role they play in logistic regression.

Exercises

1. Use the following inputs in R to run a MCMC logistic regression with y as the target variable. Print the summary and plot.

```
events.0=0    # for x = 0
events.1=5    # for x = 1
x = c(rep(0,100), rep(1,100))
y = c(rep(0,100-events.0), rep(1,events.0),
      rep(0, 100-events.1), rep(1, events.1))
```

2. Use the BayesLogit package and the spambase data set to construct the model:

    is.spam ~ word_freq_free + word_freq_1999

11.   A "log-linear" model

Yet another formulation combines the two-way latent variable formulation above with the original formulation higher up without latent variables, and in the process provides a link to one of the standard formulations of the multinomial logit (Greene, 2011).

Here, instead of writing the logit of the probabilities p_i as a linear predictor, we separate the linear predictor into two, one for each of the two outcomes:

$$\ln \Pr(Y_i = 0) = \boldsymbol{\beta_0} \cdot \boldsymbol{X}_i - \ln Z$$

$$\ln \Pr(Y_i = 0) = \boldsymbol{\beta_1} \cdot \boldsymbol{X}_i - \ln Z. \qquad (11.1)$$

Note that two separate sets of regression coefficients have been introduced, just as in the two-way latent variable model in Chapter 8, and the two equations (corresponding to Equation 8.5) appear a form that writes the logarithm of the associated probability as a linear predictor, with an extra term $- \ln Z$ at the end. This term, as it turns out, serves as the normalizing factor ensuring that the result is a distribution. This can be seen by exponentiating both sides:

$$\Pr(Y_i = 0) = \frac{1}{Z} e^{\boldsymbol{\beta_0} \cdot \boldsymbol{X}_i}$$

$$\Pr(Y_i = 1) = \frac{1}{Z} e^{\boldsymbol{\beta_1} \cdot \boldsymbol{X}_i}.$$

$$(11.2)$$

In this form it is clear that the purpose of Z is to ensure that the resulting distribution over Y_i is in fact a probability distribution, i.e. it sums to 1. This means that Z is simply the sum of all un-normalized probabilities, and by dividing each probability by Z, the probabilities become "normalized". That is:

$$Z = e^{\boldsymbol{\beta_0} \cdot \boldsymbol{X}_i} + e^{\boldsymbol{\beta_1} \cdot \boldsymbol{X}_i},$$

and the resulting equations are

$$\Pr(Y_i = 0) = \frac{e^{\beta_0 \cdot X_i}}{e^{\beta_0 \cdot X_i} + e^{\beta_1 \cdot X_i}}$$

$$\Pr(Y_i = 1) = \frac{e^{\beta_1 \cdot X_i}}{e^{\beta_0 \cdot X_i} + e^{\beta_1 \cdot X_i}}.$$

Or generally:

$$\Pr(Y_i = c) = \frac{e^{\beta_c \cdot X_i}}{\sum_h e^{\beta_h \cdot X_i}}.$$

This shows clearly how to generalize this formulation to more than two outcomes, as in multinomial logit (Greene, 2011).

In order to prove that this is equivalent to the previous model, note that the above model is over specified, in that $\Pr(Y_i = 0)$ and $\Pr(Y_i = 1)$ cannot be independently specified: $\Pr(Y_i = 0) + \Pr(Y_i = 1) = 1$ rather so knowing one automatically determines the other. As a result, the model is nonidentifiable, in that multiple combinations of β_0 and β_1 will produce the same probabilities for all possible explanatory variables. In fact, it can be seen that adding any constant vector to both of them will produce the same probabilities:

$$\Pr(Y_i = 1) = \frac{e^{(\beta_1 + C) \cdot X_i}}{e^{(\beta_0 + C) \cdot X_i} + e^{(\beta_1 + C) \cdot X_i}}$$

$$= \frac{e^{\beta_1 \cdot X_i} e^{C \cdot X_i}}{e^{\beta_0 \cdot X_i} e^{C \cdot X_i} + e^{\beta_1 \cdot X_i} e^{C \cdot X_i}}$$

$$= \frac{e^{\beta_1 \cdot X_i} e^{C \cdot X_i}}{e^{C \cdot X_i} (e^{\beta_0 \cdot X_i} + e^{\beta_1 \cdot X_i})}$$

$$= \frac{e^{\beta_1 \cdot X_i}}{(e^{\beta_0 \cdot X_i} + e^{\beta_1 \cdot X_i})}.$$

As a result, we can simplify matters, and restore identifiability, by picking an arbitrary value for one of the two vectors. We choose to set $\beta_0 = 0$. Then,

$$e^{\beta_0 \cdot X_i} = e^{0 \cdot X_i} = 1,$$

and so

$$\Pr(Y_i = 1) = \frac{e^{\beta_1 \cdot X_i}}{1 + e^{\beta_1 \cdot X_i}} = \frac{1}{1 + e^{-\beta_1 \cdot X_i}} = p_i,$$

which shows that this formulation is indeed equivalent to the previous formulation. (As in the two-way latent variable formulation, any settings where $\beta = \beta_1 - \beta_0$ will produce equivalent results.)

Note that most treatments of the multinomial logit model start out either by extending the "log-linear" formulation presented here or the two-way latent variable formulation presented above, since both clearly show the way that the model could be extended to multi-way outcomes (Greene, 2011). In general, the presentation with latent variables is more common in econometrics and political science, where discrete choice models and utility theory reign, while the "log-linear" formulation here is more common in computer science, e.g. machine learning and natural language processing.

As a single-layer perceptron
The model has an equivalent formulation

$$p_i = \frac{1}{1 + e^{-(\beta_{10} + \beta_1 \cdot X_{1,i} + \cdots + k \cdot X_{k,i})}}.$$

This functional form is commonly called a single-layer perceptron or single-layer artificial neural network (Da & Xiurun, 2005). A single-layer neural network computes a continuous output instead of a step function. The derivative of p_i with respect to $X = (x_1, \ldots, x_k)$ is computed from the general form:

$$y = \frac{1}{1 + e^{-f(x)}},$$

where $f(X)$ is an analytic function in X. With this choice, the single-layer neural network is identical to the logistic regression model. This function has a continuous derivative, which allows it to be used in backpropagation. This function is also preferred because its derivative is easily calculated:

$$\frac{dy}{dX} = y(1 - 4)\frac{df}{dX}.$$

187

In terms of binomial data

A closely related model assumes that each i is associated not with a single Bernoulli trial but with n_i independent identically distributed trials, where the observation Y_i is the number of successes observed (the sum of the individual Bernoulli-distributed random variables), and hence follows a binomial distribution:

$$Y_i \sim Bin(n_i, p_p), \text{ for } i = 1, \dots, n.$$

An example of this distribution is the fraction of seeds (p_i) that germinate after n_i are planted. In terms of expected values, this model is expressed as follows:

$$p_i = E\left[\frac{Y_i}{n_i} \middle| X_i\right],$$

so that

$$\text{logit}\left(E\left[\frac{Y_i}{n_i} \middle| X_i\right]\right) = \text{logit}(p_i) = \ln\left(\frac{p_i}{1-p_i}\right) = \boldsymbol{\beta} \cdot \boldsymbol{X_i},$$

Or equivalently:

$$\Pr(Y_i = y_i | X_i) = \binom{n_i}{k_i} p_i^{y_i} (1 - p_i)^{n_i - y_i}$$

$$= \binom{n_i}{k_i} \left(\frac{1}{1 + e^{-\boldsymbol{\beta} \cdot \boldsymbol{X_i}}}\right)^{y_i} \left(1 - \frac{1}{1 + e^{-\boldsymbol{\beta} \cdot \boldsymbol{X_i}}}\right)^{1 - y_i}.$$

This model can be fit using the same sorts of methods as the above more basic model.

Example

We will examine a data set called "Titanic", which is a built-in data set describing the outcome of the Titanic sinking in 1912. The data object is a four-dimensional table.

```
data(Titanic)
dimnames(Titanic)
```

```
$Class
[1] "1st"   "2nd"   "3rd"   "Crew"
```

```
$Sex
[1] "Male"    "Female"

$Age
[1] "Child" "Adult"

$Survived
[1] "No"   "Yes"
```

Log Linear Analysis

Our goal is to explain the observed frequencies in the "Titanic" table with as simple a model as possible. Here is what we have to work with.

EFFECTS	WHAT THEY MEAN
Class	there are more passengers in some classes than in others
Sex	there are more passengers of one sex than of the other
Age	there are more passengers of one age group than of the other
Survived	more passengers lived or died than the alternative
Class × Sex	Class and Sex are not independent
Class × Age	Class and Age are not independent
Class × Survived	Class and Survived are not independent
Sex × Age	Sex and Age are not independent
Sex × Survived	Sex and Survived are not independent
Age × Survived	Age and Survived are not independent
Class × Sex × Age	there is a three-way interaction between these factors
Class × Sex × Survived	there is a three-way interaction between these factors
Class × Age × Survived	there is a three-way interaction between these factors
Sex × Age × Survived	there is a three-way interaction between these factors
Class × Sex × Age × Survived	there is a four-way interaction between these factors

Notice we are not treating any of the factors differently, i.e., as response vs. explanatory variables. We could. We're just not, at this time. It's

189

crucial that you keep this in mind. There is a natural tendency here to see "Survived" as a response variable that we are trying to explain. We are NOT (at this time). We are trying to model (explain, predict, account for) the frequencies in the contingency table.

We begin like this.

```
summary(Titanic)
```

```
Number of cases in table: 2201
Number of factors: 4
Test for independence of all factors:
        Chisq = 1637.4, df = 25, p-value = 0
        Chi-squared approximation may be incorrect
```

You have just done a log linear analysis on the model that includes only the simple effects, i.e., the effects of the factors without any interactions between them, the first four lines of the above table. This model (null hypothesis) is rejected. Somewhere in these data, there are interactions we must find to explain the cell frequencies adequately. (The warning in the last line tells us we have EFs below 5. This is the only time you'll see this warning, so it's always a good idea to start off this way, in my opinion.)

Several functions in R can be used to fit log linear models. They include loglin() in the "stats" library (loaded by default), loglm() in the "MASS" library, and glm() in the "stats" library. Let's experiment a little.

```
library("MASS")    # load MASS so we can use loglm()
loglm ( ~ Sex + Survived, data=sex.survived)
```

```
Call:
loglm(formula = ~ Sex + Survived, data = sex.survived)
Statistics:
                      X^2 df P(> X^2)
Likelihood Ratio 434.4688  1        0
Pearson          456.8742  1        0
```

We are looking at the 2D table "Sex" by "Survived" that we created above, we are putting in only the simple effects of individual factors, and we are getting out the same result as we got when we used my `likelihood.test()` function. In other words, we've used log linear modeling to do a chi-square test of independence on this two-way contingency table. The model with just the simple effects is inadequate (null hypothesis rejected, p virtually 0). So, there must be an interaction between these two variables (we would propose).

Now let's do the same for the full data table.

```
loglm(~ Class + Sex + Age + Survived, data=Titanic)
```

```
Call:
loglm(formula = ~Class + Sex + Age + Survived, data = Titan
ic)

Statistics:
                      X^2 df P(> X^2)
Likelihood Ratio 1243.663 25        0
Pearson          1637.445 25        0
```

The result is the same one we got with the `summary(Titanic)` command. Essentially, we've done a four-way chi-square test of independence, and we reject the null hypothesis of independence. Somewhere in there are factors that are interacting with each other to produce the observed cell frequencies. The saturated model, on the other hand, produces nothing useful, as it always explains (predicts, models) the observed frequencies completely.

```
loglm (~ Class * Sex * Age * Survived, data=Titanic)
```

```
Call:
loglm(formula = ~Class * Sex * Age * Survived, data = Titan
ic)

Statistics:
                X^2 df P(> X^2)
Likelihood Ratio  0  0        1
Pearson         NaN  0        1
```

Null hypothesis (i.e., the saturated model) retained (p virtually 1). The "truth" (we hope) lies somewhere between these two extremes.

We will let you try it without the four-way interaction as an exercise.

Testing a Specific Hypothesis

Suppose we began with the hypothesis that gender was related to survival on the Titanic. From the two-way (bivariate) chi-square test we did above, this appears to be true. However, "Sex" is also related to "Class" (p virtually zero by chi-square test) and "Age" (p virtually zero), and both "Class" and "Age" are significantly related to "Survived". So "Class" and "Age" might be confounds in the relationship between "Sex" and "Survived". Like a multiple regression for numeric variables, log linear analysis will allow us to tease apart these effects.

If we remove all the interaction terms that involve both "Sex" and "Survived", and the model still fits the observed frequencies adequately, then we can conclude that gender and survival were unrelated.

```
sat.model = loglm (~ Class * Sex * Age * Survived, data=Tit
anic)
sat.model
```

```
Call:
loglm(formula = ~Class * Sex * Age * Survived, data = Titan
ic)

Statistics:
                   X^2 df P(> X^2)
Likelihood Ratio   0  0        1
Pearson          NaN  0        1
### already knew this...
```

```
model2 = update(sat.model, ~.-(Class:Sex:Age:Survived+
Sex:Age:Survived+Class:Sex:Survived+Sex:Survived))
model2
```

```
Call:
loglm(formula = ~Class + Sex + Age + Survived + Class:Sex +
Class:Age +  Sex:Age + Class:Survived + Age:Survived + Clas
s:Sex:Age +  Class:Age:Survived, data = Titanic)

Statistics:
                   X^2 df P(> X^2)
Likelihood Ratio 436.2715  8        0
```

The model does not adequately fit the observed frequencies unless we include some sort of "Sex" by "Survived" interaction. Notice the use of update here to get the new model. We could just have retyped the model formula with the factors we wanted to include into a new loglm() analysis, but update() is often a bit more convenient. The syntax reads "update sat.model by using all the same predictors (dot means "same") except subtract out (minus) the following terms." We leave it to you to do one with only the two-way interactions involving both "Sex" and "Survived," as an exercise.

Using glm()For Log Linear Modeling

We can also do log linear analysis using the glm() function, which is the function used for generalized linear models. For this we need a data frame rather than a contingency table, but this is easy enough to get.

```
ti = as.data.frame(Titanic)
ti    # it's a lot easier to look at the data this way too!
```

	Class	Sex	Age	Survived	Freq
1	1st	Male	Child	No	0
2	2nd	Male	Child	No	0
3	3rd	Male	Child	No	35
4	Crew	Male	Child	No	0
5	1st	Female	Child	No	0
6	2nd	Female	Child	No	0
7	3rd	Female	Child	No	17
8	Crew	Female	Child	No	0
9	1st	Male	Adult	No	118
10	2nd	Male	Adult	No	154
11	3rd	Male	Adult	No	387
12	Crew	Male	Adult	No	670
13	1st	Female	Adult	No	4
14	2nd	Female	Adult	No	13
15	3rd	Female	Adult	No	89
16	Crew	Female	Adult	No	3
17	1st	Male	Child	Yes	5
18	2nd	Male	Child	Yes	11
19	3rd	Male	Child	Yes	13
20	Crew	Male	Child	Yes	0
21	1st	Female	Child	Yes	1

```
22    2nd Female Child      Yes   13
23    3rd Female Child      Yes   14
24   Crew Female Child      Yes    0
25    1st   Male Adult      Yes   57
26    2nd   Male Adult      Yes   14
27    3rd   Male Adult      Yes   75
28   Crew   Male Adult      Yes  192
29    1st Female Adult       Yes  140
30    2nd Female Adult       Yes   80
31    3rd Female Adult       Yes   76
32   Crew Female Adult       Yes   20
```

The log linear analysis is then produced this way.

```
glm.model = glm(Freq ~ Class * Age * Sex * Survived, data=t
i, family=poisson)
```

This is the saturated model. The extractor function summary(glm.model) would produce a lot of puzzling output, so we'll use the extractor function anova().

```
anova(glm.model, test="Chisq")
Analysis of Deviance Table

Model: poisson, link: log

Response: Freq

Terms added sequentially (first to last)
```

	Df	Deviance	Resid.Df	Resid.Dev	P(>|Chi|)
NULL			31	4953.1	
Class	3	475.8	28	4477.3	8.326e-10
Age	1	2183.6	27	2293.8	0.0
Sex	1	768.3	26	1525.4	4.169e-17
Survived	1	148.3	22	1095.3	6.048e-32
Class:Sex	3	412.6	19	682.7	4.126e-89
Age:Sex	1	6.1	18	676.6	1.363e-02
Class:Survived	3	180.9	15	495.7	5.634e-39
Age:Survived	1	25.6	14	470.2	4.237e-07
Sex:Survived	1	353.6	13	116.6	7.053e-79
Class:Age:Sex	3	4.0	10	112.6	0.3
Class:Age:Survived	3	35.7	7	76.9	8.825e-08
Class:Sex:Survived	3	75.2	4	1.7	3.253e-16
Age:Sex:Survived	1	1.7	3	4.237e-10	0.2

Class:Age:Sex:Survived 3	0.0	0	4.463e-10	1.0

Deviance is a fancy term for the likelihood ratio chi-square value. The null model (all frequencies equal) is at the top. Clearly, the null model is not sufficient to describe this data set, as adding in subsequent terms produces significant reductions in deviance. At each step down the table, another predictor is added in, and this removes the amount of Deviance shown in that column, leaving the amount in the Resid.Dev. column. The p-value in the last column is based on the change in Deviance (column two) and the change in Df (column one) produced by adding that term into the model. Here we are looking for a significant reduction in deviance, indicating the new term helped in predicting cell (observed) frequencies.

This output suggests we might want to investigate three terms for possible elimination: the four-way interaction and two three-way interactions. Recall that step() retained the Class:Age:Sex interaction. We'll leave that as an exercise also.

Visualizing the Analysis
One of the better ways of trying to visualize the results of a log linear analysis is to use a mosaic plot.

```
mosaicplot(Titanic, shade=T)
```

Titanic

Standardized Residuals:

<-4 -4:-2 -2:0 0:2 2:4 >4

Summary

In this chapter we have looked at log-linear models. We calculate Log linear models using an iterative algorithm. We might consider this method as "computer intensive" in this respect. Different software packages may program the algorithm differently, or even use a different algorithm. Therefore, results from different software packages may not match up exactly. Hopefully, they will be close!

Exercises

1. Construct and analyze a log-linear model using the Titanic data with only the two-way interactions involving both "Sex" and "Survived."
2. Construct and analyze a log-linear model of the survival using the Titanic data, where it does not have the four-way interaction as it did in the example.
3. The output from the glm() model suggests we might want to investigate three terms for possible elimination: the four-way interaction and two three-way interactions. Perform this analysis.

12. Multinomial Logistic Regression

Preliminaries

We have thus far discussed binary logistic regression, where the response is a binary variable with "success" and "failure" being only two categories. But logistic regression can be extended to handle responses, Y, that are polytomous, i.e. taking $r > 2$ categories.

When $r = 2$, Y is dichotomous and we can model log of odds that an event occurs or does not occur. For binary logistic regression there is only 1 logit that we can form.

$$\log(\pi) = log\left(\frac{\pi}{1-\pi}\right)$$

When $r > 2$, we have a multi-category or polytomous response variable. There are $r\,(r-1)/2$ logits (odds) that we can form, but only $(r-1)$ are non-redundant. There are different ways to form a set of $(r-1)$ non-redundant logits, and these will lead to different polytomous (multinomial) logistic regression models.

Multinomial Logistic Regression models have multinomial response variable Y, which depends on a set of k explanatory variables, $X = (X_1, X_2, ... X_k)$. This is also a GLM where the random component assumes that the distribution of Y is Multinomial(n,π), where π is a vector with probabilities of "success" for each category. The systematic component are explanatory variables (can be continuous, discrete, or both) and are linear in the parameters, e.g., $\beta_0 + \beta_1 x_i + ... + \beta_0 + \beta x_k$. Again, transformation of the $X's$ themselves are allowed like in linear regression. The link function is the generalized Logit, that it the logit link for each pair of non-redundant logits as discussed above.

When analyzing a *polytomous response*, it is important to note whether the response is ordinal (consisting of ordered categories) or nominal (consisting of unordered categories). For binary logistic model this question does not arise.

Some types of models are appropriate only for ordinal responses; e.g., cumulative logit model, adjacent categories model, continuation ratios model Other models may be used whether the response is ordinal or nominal; e.g., baseline logit model, and conditional logit model.

If the response is ordinal, we do not necessarily have to take the ordering into account, but only very rarely this information is ignored. *Ordinality in the response is a vital information; neglecting it almost always will lead to sub-optimal models. Using the natural ordering can*

- lead to a simpler, more parsimonious model and
- increase power to detect relationships with other variables.

If the response variable is polytomous and all the potential predictors are discrete as well, we could describe the multi-way contingency table by a log-linear model. However, if you are analyzing a set of categorical variables, and one of them is clearly a "response" while the others are predictors, I recommend that you use logistic rather than log-linear models. Fitting a log-linear model in this setting could have two disadvantages:

1. It has many more parameters, and many of them are not of interest. The log-linear model, as we will learn later, describes the joint distribution of all the variables, whereas the logistic model describes only the conditional distribution of the response given the predictors.
2. The log-linear model is often more complicated to interpret. In the log-linear model, the effect of a predictor X on the response Y is described by the XY association. In a logit model, however, the effect of X on Y is a main effect.

Grouped versus ungrouped response

We have already pointed out in lessons on logistic regression, data can come in ungrouped (e.g., database form) or grouped format (e.g., tabular form).

Consider a study that investigates the cheese preference for four types of cheeses; for the detailed analysis see Cheese Tasting example below. The response variable Y is a Likert Scale response with nine categories:

$Y = 1$ for strong dislike ,

$Y = 2$ dislike,

.

.

.

$Y = 9$ for excellent taste.

The main predictor of interest is type of cheese (A, B, C and D). The data could arrive in ungrouped form, with one record per subject (as below) where the first column indicates the type of cheese and the second column the value of Y.

Example – Cheese Tasting

In this example (McCullagh & Nelder, 1989), subjects were randomly assigned to taste one of four different cheeses. Response categories are 1 = strong dislike to 9 = excellent taste.

Table 1.

Cheese	Response category								
	1	2	3	4	5	6	7	8	9
A	0	0	1	7	8	8	19	8	1
B	6	9	12	11	7	6	1	0	0
C	1	1	6	8	23	7	5	1	0
D	0	0	0	1	3	7	14	16	11

From the above table that records the number of individuals that rated a particular cheese with a particular score, we can easily see that D is the most preferable, and B is the worst; however between A and C the hierarchy of preference is not quite straight-forward. Let us model these data by a proportional-odds cumulative-logit model with three dummy variables to distinguish among the four cheeses. The model will have 8 intercepts (one for each of the logit equations) and 3 slopes, for a total of 11 free parameters. By comparison, the saturated model, which fits a separate 9-category multinomial distribution to each of the four cheeses, has $4 \times (9 - 1) = 32$ parameters to be estimated. Therefore, the overall goodness-of-fit test will have $32 - 11 = 21$ degrees of freedom.

SAS Program Code

This model can be fit in SAS using PROC LOGISTIC as follows in the SAS program cheese.sas:

```
options nocenter nodate nonumber linesize=72;
data cheese; input cheese $ response $ count; cards;
A 1 0
A 2 0
A 3 1
A 4 7
A 5 8
A 6 8
A 7 19
A 8 8
A 9 1
B 1 6
B 2 9
B 3 12
B 4 11
B 5 7
B 6 6
B 7 1
B 8 0
B 9 0
C 1 1
C 2 1
C 3 6
C 4 8
C 5 23
C 6 7
C 7 5
C 8 1
C 9 0
D 1 0
D 2 0
D 3 0
D 4 1
D 5 3
D 6 7
D 7 14
D 8 16
D 9 11
;
PROC LOGISTIC data=cheese; freq count;
class cheese / order=data param=ref ref=first;
model response (order=data descending) = cheese / link=logit
aggregate=(cheese) scale=none;
```

In PROC LOGISTIC, the order=data option tells SAS to arrange the response categories from lowest to highest in the order that they arise in the dataset. The option descending tells SAS to reverse the ordering of the categories, so that 9 becomes the lowest and 1 becomes the highest, and a positive β indicates that a higher value of X leads to greater liking.

Other procedures such as PROC GENMOD can be also used; this is left for your explorations.

The logit equations would then be

$$L_1 = \log\left(\frac{P(Y \le 1)}{P(Y > 1)}\right) = \alpha_1 + \beta_1 X_1 + \beta_2 X_2 + \beta_3 X_3$$

$$L_1 = \log\left(\frac{P(Y \le 2)}{P(Y > 2)}\right) = \alpha_2 + \beta_1 X_1 + \beta_2 X_2 + \beta_3 X_3$$

$$\vdots$$

$$L_8 = \log\left(\frac{P(Y \le 8)}{P(Y > 8)}\right) = \alpha_8 + \beta_1 X_1 + \beta_2 X_2 + \beta_3 X_3$$

where $X_1 = 1$ for cheese B and zero otherwise; $X_2 = 1$ for cheese C and zero otherwise; and $X_3 = 1$ for cheese D and zero otherwise. In this case, a positive coefficient β means that increasing the value of X tends to lower the response categories (i.e. produce greater dislike).

When we fit this model in SAS, we first see this output section after the model information:

The LOGISTIC Procedure

Score Test for the Proportional Odds Assumption		
Chi-Square	DF	Pr > ChiSq
17.2866	21	0.6936

This reports a test of the proportional-odds assumption, i.e. a test for whether the slopes of the X-variables are equal across logit equations. The null hypothesis is that the current model (fitting one slope for each dummy) is true, and the alternative is that different slopes ($8 \times 3 = 24$ in all) are needed. Therefore, this test has 21 degrees of freedom. The alternative model happens to be saturated, so this is also an overall goodness-of-fit test. The test does not indicate any serious lack of fit.

The overall fit statistics, shown below and can be evaluated as before, indicate a good fit. For example, all three statistics from the "Testing Global Null Hypothesis: BETA=0" indicate that at least one of the regression coefficients is different from zero and is statistically significant.

Deviance and Pearson Goodness-of-Fit Statistics				
Criterion	Value	DF	Value/DF	Pr > ChiSq
Deviance	20.3082	21	0.9671	0.5018
Pearson	20.9372	21	0.9970	0.4628

Number of unique profiles: 4

Model Fit Statistics		
Criterion	Intercept Only	Intercept and Covariates
AIC	875.802	733.348
SC	902.502	770.061
-2 Log L	859.802	711.348

Testing Global Null Hypothesis: BETA=0			
Test	Chi-Square	DF	Pr > ChiSq
Likelihood Ratio	148.4539	3	<.0001
Score	111.2670	3	<.0001
Wald	115.1504	3	<.0001

Type 3 Analysis of Effects			
Effect	DF	Wald Chi-Square	Pr > ChiSq
cheese	3	115.1504	<.0001

From the "Type 3 Analysis of Effects" table above, we can see that the effect of cheese is highly significant. Now let us look at the coefficients:

Analysis of Maximum Likelihood Estimates						
Parameter		DF	Estimate	Standard Error	Wald Chi-Square	Pr > ChiSq
Intercept	9	1	-3.1058	0.4044	58.9727	<.0001
Intercept	8	1	-1.5459	0.3042	25.8287	<.0001
Intercept	7	1	-0.0443	0.2598	0.0291	0.8646
Intercept	6	1	0.9077	0.2748	10.9125	0.0010
Intercept	5	1	2.2440	0.3262	47.3307	<.0001
Intercept	4	1	3.3126	0.3697	80.2992	<.0001
Intercept	3	1	4.4121	0.4247	107.9168	<.0001
Intercept	2	1	5.4673	0.5202	110.4514	<.0001
cheese	B	1	-3.3517	0.4235	62.6335	<.0001
cheese	C	1	-1.7098	0.3731	21.0072	<.0001
cheese	D	1	1.6128	0.3778	18.2265	<.0001

Odds Ratio Estimates			
Effect	Point Estimate	95% Wald Confidence Limits	
cheese B vs A	0.035	0.015	0.080
cheese C vs A	0.181	0.087	0.376
cheese D vs A	5.017	2.393	10.520

Association of Predicted Probabilities and Observed Responses			
Percent Concordant	67.6	Somers' D	0.578
Percent Discordant	9.8	Gamma	0.746
Percent Tied	22.6	Tau-a	0.500

Association of Predicted Probabilities and Observed Responses			
Pairs	18635	c	0.789

R Studio Code

This model can be fit in R using polr() function from the package MASS as follows in the R program cheese.R. This program reads in the data file xcheese.csv (http://www.humalytica.com/downloads.html).

```
file = "C:/Users/Strickland/Documents/Logistic Regression/c
heese.csv"
read.csv(file)<-cheese
summary(cheese)
```

```
cheese    X.response     X.count            Response
A:9    Min.   :1    Min.   : 0.000    1       : 4
B:9    1st Qu.:3    1st Qu.: 1.000    2       : 4
C:9    Median :5    Median : 6.000    3       : 4
D:9    Mean   :5    Mean   : 5.778    4       : 4
       3rd Qu.:7    3rd Qu.: 8.000    5       : 4
       Max.   :9    Max.   :23.000    6       : 4
                                      (Other):12
```

```
is.factor( cheese$Response )
```

```
[1] FALSE
```

```
cheese$Response <- factor( cheese$X.response, ordered=T )
#### load the MASS package

library(MASS)

#### fit the proportional-odds logistic regression model
result <- polr( Response ~ cheese, weights=X.count, data=ch
eese )
summary(result)
```

As always, you need change the working directory to where you save cheese.csv locally or change the path to access the data. The data has three columns, the first "cheese" indicating the type of cheese, the second column "X.response" indicating the level of the response and the third column labeled as "X.count" has the number of individuals giving the certain rating of the certain cheese.

Make sure that you treat the response as ordinal variable, which we do here by using the function factor(cheese$X.response, order=T); option order=T tells R to use the order of the levels of the response as entered in the dataset, which in this case is 1 < 2 < 3...< 8 < 9.

Then, fit the proportional–odds logistic regression model using polr() function. If weights=X.count are not specified, then R by default assumes that N=1 that is that data are ungrouped.

There are other procedures in R that could be used to fit this model; this is left for your exploration.

```
Re-fitting to get Hessian

Call:
polr(formula = Response ~ cheese, data = cheese, weights =
X.count)

Coefficients:
          Value Std. Error t value
cheeseB -3.352    0.4287  -7.819
cheeseC -1.710    0.3715  -4.603
cheeseD  1.613    0.3805   4.238

Intercepts:
      Value    Std. Error t value
1|2  -5.4674    0.5236   -10.4413
2|3  -4.4122    0.4278   -10.3148
3|4  -3.3126    0.3700    -8.9522
4|5  -2.2440    0.3267    -6.8680
5|6  -0.9078    0.2833    -3.2037
6|7   0.0443    0.2646     0.1673
7|8   1.5459    0.3017     5.1244
8|9   3.1058    0.4057     7.6547

Residual Deviance: 711.3479
AIC: 733.3479
```

The first part of the output is the coefficient estimates for the three dummy variables. The estimated slope for the first dummy variable, labeled cheese B, is -3.352. This indicates that cheese B does not taste as good as cheese A. If we were to bifurcate the response scale into "better" and "worse" groups—for example, taking

better = 7, 8, 9 and worse = 1, 2, 3, 4, 5, 6

or taking

better = 5, 6, 7, 8, 9 and worse=1, 2, 3, 4,

— and construct a 2 × 2 table comparing cheese A to cheese B,

	better	worse
cheese B		
cheese A		

the estimated odds ratio for this table would be $\exp(-3.352) = .035$. The standard error of 0.4287 and the t-value (t-statistic) of -7.819 with df=1, indicate that there is a significant difference between the preference for cheese A to B.

Looking at all three coefficients,

$$\hat{\beta}_1 = -3.352$$

$$\hat{\beta}_2 = -1.710$$

$$\hat{\beta}_3 = 1.613$$

and noting that cheese A is the reference category such that β_2 compares cheese C to A and β_3 cheese D to A, we see that the implied ordering of cheeses in terms of quality is $D > A > C > B$. Furthermore, D is significantly better preferred than A, but A is not significantly better than C.This can been also

```
exp(confint(result))
```

```
Waiting for profiling to be done...

Re-fitting to get Hessian

            2.5 %       97.5 %
cheeseB 0.01479494  0.07962504
cheeseC 0.08621686  0.37084182
cheeseD 2.40947358 10.74767430
```

The next part of the output is the table with estimated intercepts. The first parameter, labeled Intercept 1|2, is the estimated log-odds of falling into category 1 (excellent taste) versus all other categories when all X-variables are zero. Because $X_1 = X_2 = X_3 = 0$ when cheese=A, the estimated log-odds of worst taste for cheese A are exp(−5.4674). From the above output, the first estimated logit equation then is

$$L1 = \log\left(\frac{P(Y \leq 1)}{P(Y > 1)}\right) = -5.4674 - 3.352X_1 - 1.710X_2 + 1.613X_3$$

which is the estimated equation of the

$$L_1 = -\log\left(\frac{P(Y \leq 1)}{P(Y > 1)}\right) = -(\alpha_1 + \beta_1 X_1 + \beta_2 X_2 + \beta_3 X_3)$$

we stated earlier.

The next parameter, labeled Intercept 2|3, is the estimated log-odds of response 1 or 2 versus 3, . . . , 9 when cheese=A, and so on. Its estimated logit equation is

$$L_2 = \log\left(\frac{P(Y \leq 2)}{P(Y > 2)}\right) = -4.4122 - 3.352X_1 - 1.710X_2 + 1.613X_3$$

The last part of the output give you the fit statistics where the "residual deviance" equals to -2*loglikelihood* value for the current model. We can use this value to assess how well does this model fits in comparison to other models. For example, to compare it to the intercept only model ("nullmodel" in R code):

```
> deviance(nullmodel)- deviance(result)
```

```
[1] 148.4539
```

```
> df.residual(nullmodel)- df.residual(result)
```

```
[1] 3
```

We get the likelihood ratio value of about 148 with 3 df which is highly significant. Thus this model fits much better than the intercept only model, that is at least one of the regression coefficients is not equal to zero.

Data

Data sets used for multinomial logit estimation deals with some individuals, that make one or a sequential choice of one alternative among a set of several alternatives. The determinants of these choices are variables that can be alternative specific or purely individual specific.

Such data have therefore a specific structure that can be characterized by three indexes

- the alternative,
- the choice situation,
- the individual.

The last one being only relevant if we have repeated observations for the same individual.

Data sets can have two different shapes :

- **a wide shape** : in this case, there is one row for each choice situation,
- **a long shape** : in this case, there is one row for each alternative and, therefore, as many rows as there are alternatives for each choice situation.

This can be illustrated with three R package data sets.

Fishing is a data set included with the mlogit package and is a revealed preferences data sets that deals with the choice of a fishing mode,

TravelMode, from the AER package, is also a revealed preferences data sets which presents the choice of individuals for a transport mode for inter-urban trips in Australia,

Train, also from the mlogit package, is a stated preferences data sets for which individuals faces repeated virtual situations of choice for train tickets.

The mlogit package provides a mlogit.data function that take as first argument a data.frame and returns a data.frame in "long" format with some information about the structure of the data.

Summary

In this chapter, we looked at multinomial logistic regression where the dependent variable has three or more categories. In doing so, we looked at examples in R and SAS studio using the cheese tasting example.

Exercises

1. We will now use "fishing," for an exercise. Fishing has a "wide" format that is suitable to store individual specific variables. Otherwise, it is cumbersome for alternative specific variables because there are as many columns for such variables that there are alternatives.
   a. Use the mlogit.data function to change the format from "wide" to "long."
   b. Build a multinomial logistic regression model using this "long" format.
2. Return to Fishing's original "wide" format and build a multinomial logistic regression model. Perform a complete analysis.

13. Logistic Regression in SAS – Detailed

Up to this point, we have dealt with logistic regression by focusing on certain aspects as we examine different concepts and procedures. We now attempt to put all of this together with a few comprehensive examples. In this chapter we will work an example using SAS Studio. In Chapter 14, we will work an example using Python, and in Chapter 15 we will work an example using R.

This example illustrates the following:

1. The PROC LOGISTIC procedure in SAS Studio
2. Generating and using scoring model scoring code
3. Performing detailed diagnostics

The dataset I chose for this example in Longitudinal Low Birth Weight Study (CLSLOWBWT.DAT). (Hosmer & Lemeshow, 2000) These data are copyrighted by John Wiley & Sons Inc. and must be acknowledged and used accordingly.

Variable Description Codes/Values Name

1. Identification Code ID Number ID
2. Birth Number 1-4 BIRTH
3. Smoking Status 0 = No, 1 = Yes SMOKE During Pregnancy
4. Race 1 = White, 2 = Black RACE 3 = Other
5. Age of Mother Years AGE
6. Weight of Mother at Pounds LWT Last Menstrual Period
7. Birth Weight Grams BWT
8. Low Birth Weight 1 = BWT <=2500g, LOW 0 = BWT >2500g

PROBLEM STATEMENT: In this example, we want to predict Low Birth Weight using the remaining dataset variables. Low Birth Weight, the dependent variable, has two values: 1 = BWT <=2500g and 0 = BWT >2500g, making it a binary response.

```
ODS GRAPHICS ON
/*Import dataset CLSLOWBWT.CSV*/
%web_drop_table(WORK.IMPORT);

/*Here we name the file we will import by its url*/
FILENAME  REFFILE  "/home/jeff47/sasuser.v94/clslowbwt.csv"
TERMSTR=CR;

PROC IMPORT DATAFILE=REFFILE
      DBMS=CSV
      OUT=WORK.LOW_BIRTH_WEIGHT;
      GETNAMES=YES;
RUN;

/*View dataset CLSLOWBWT*/
PROC CONTENTS DATA=WORK. LOW_BIRTH_WEIGHT;
RUN;

%web_open_table(WORK. LOW_BIRTH_WEIGH);

PROC MEANS DATA = WORK. LOW_BIRTH_WEIGHT;
  VAR BIRTH  SMOKE  RACE  AGE  LWT;
RUN;
PROC FREQ data = WORK. LOW_BIRTH_WEIGHT;
  TABLES BIRTH LWT LWT*BIRTH;
RUN;

/*Perform Logistic Regression for target variable LOW*/
/*There ae 15 statement for PROC LOGISTIC but we only use
three here: PLOTS, */
/*MODEL and OUTPUT*/
PROC LOGISTIC DATA=WORK. LOW_BIRTH_WEIGHT
PLOTS(ONLY)=ALL
;
MODEL RESP(EVENT='1')= BIRTH SMOKE RACE AGE LWT /
SELECTION = STEPWISE
SLE=0.05 /* specifies significance level for entering
effects*/
SLS=0.05 /*specifies significance level for removing
effects*/
INCLUDE=0 /*specifies number of effects included in every
model*/
CORRB   /*Correlation matrix*/
COVB    /*Covariance matrix*/
LACKFIT /*specifies method to correct overdispersion*/
RSQUARE /*displays generalized R-squared*/
CTABLE /*displays classification table*/
PPROB=(0.1 0.2 0.3 0.4 0.5 0.6 0.7 0.8 0.9 1.0)
/*specifies probability cutpoints for classification*/
LINK=LOGIT /*specifies link function*/
CLPARM=WALD /*computes confidence intervals for
parameters*/
CLODDS=WALD /*computes confidence intervals for odds
ratios*/
ALPHA=0.05 /*specifies alpha for confidence intervals*/
```

```
      ;
OUTPUT out=WORK.Logistic_stats /*Names the output data
set*/
xbeta=xbeta_  /* Names the linear predictor*/
predicted=pred_ /*Names the predicted probabilities*/
lower=lcl_ /*Names the lower confidence limit*/
upper=ucl_ /*Names the upper confidence limit*/
reslik=reslik_ /*Names the likelihood residual*/
h=leverage_ /*Names the leverage*/
dfbetas=stdDfbeta_ /*Names the standardized deletion
parameter differences*/
/
alpha=0.05; /* Specifies α for the 100(1-α)% confidence
intervals*/
SCORE out=WORK.Logistic_scores; /*Names the SAS data set
containing predictions*/
code; /*soring code is recorded at end of log file*/

RUN;

ODS GRAPHICS OFF
```

For more information on PROC LOGISTIC see reference [2].

SAS Logistic Regression Scoring Code

```
%MACRO SCOREPROG(INDATA,OUTDATA);
DATA &OUTDATA;
SET &INDATA;
    **************************************************;
    ** SAS Scoring Code for PROC Logistic;
    **************************************************;

    length I_RESP $ 12;
    label I_RESP = 'Into: RESP' ;
    label U_RESP = 'Unnormalized Into: RESP' ;
    format U_RESP BEST12.0;

    label P_RESP1 = 'Predicted: RESP=1' ;
    label P_RESP0 = 'Predicted: RESP=0' ;

    drop _LMR_BAD;
    _LMR_BAD=0;

    *** Check interval variables for missing values;
    if nmiss(SMOKE,RACE,AGE) then do;
        _LMR_BAD=1;
        goto _SKIP_000;
    end;

    *** Compute Linear Predictors;
```

215

```
drop _LP0;
_LP0 = 0;

*** Effect: SMOKE;
_LP0 = _LP0 + (0.55511560456703) * SMOKE;
*** Effect: RACE;
_LP0 = _LP0 + (-0.29892228555342) * RACE;
*** Effect: AGE;
_LP0 = _LP0 + (0.03273258128386) * AGE;

*** Predicted values;
drop _MAXP _IY _P0 _P1;
_TEMP = -1.42125183052254  + _LP0;
if (_TEMP < 0) then do;
   _TEMP = exp(_TEMP);
   _P0 = _TEMP / (1 + _TEMP);
end;
else _P0 = 1 / (1 + exp(-_TEMP));
_P1 = 1.0 - _P0;
P_RESP1 = _P0;
_MAXP = _P0;
_IY = 1;
P_RESP0 = _P1;
if (_P1 > _MAXP + 1E-8) then do;
   _MAXP = _P1;
   _IY = 2;
end;
select( _IY );
   when (1) do;
      I_RESP = '1' ;
      U_RESP = 1;
   end;
   when (2) do;
      I_RESP = '0' ;
      U_RESP = 0;
   end;
   otherwise do;
      I_RESP = '';
      U_RESP = .;
   end;
end;
_SKIP_000:
if _LMR_BAD = 1 then do;
I_RESP = '';
U_RESP = .;
P_RESP1 = .; /*score variable for positive response*/
P_RESP0 = .; /*score variable for no response*/
end;
```

```
 drop _TEMP;
**********************************;
***    END SAS SCORING CODE    ***;
**********************************;
%MEND SCOREPROG; /*End macro*/
%SCOREPROG(WORK.LOW_BIRTH_WEIGHT,WORK.LBW_SCORE);
/*Execute macro*/

/*Macro to put variable into pentiles*/
%MACRO PUTPENTS(INDATA,SCORENAME,OUTDATA);
DATA GETPENT;
SET &INDATA(KEEP = ID RESP &SCORENAME);
RUN;
PROC SORT DATA=GETPENT NODUPKEY; BY ID; RUN;/*Sort
score data*/
PROC RANK DATA=GETPENT GROUPS=20 OUT=HIGH3; /*Rank
data by pentile & score*/
     VAR &SCORENAME;
     RANKS PENTILE;
RUN;
DATA &OUTDATA;
SET HIGH3;
     RENAME &SCORENAME = SCORE; /*Change PRESP_1 to
SCORE*/
     PENTILE = 20 - PENTILE;
RUN;
PROC FREQ DATA=&OUTDATA;
     TITLE 'FREQ - PENTILES FOR RESP BIRTH WEIGHT
MODEL';
     TABLES PENTILE;
RUN;
%MEND;/*End macro*/
%PUTPENTS(WORK.LBW_SCORE,P_RESP1,WORK.LBW_SCORE_OUT);
/*Execute macro*/
 DATA PER_FILE; /*build file for scores by pentile*/
 SET WORK.LBW_SCORE_OUT;
 WHERE SCORE NE .; /*exclude blank entries*/
 RUN;
 PROC TABULATE DATA=PER_FILE; /*generate score table
by pentile for performance*/
 VAR SCORE RESP;
 CLASS PENTILE/ ORDER=UNFORMATTED MISSING;
 TABLE PENTILE, N SCORE*SUM RESP*SUM; /*Calculate
modeled and actual responses*/
RUN;
PROC UNIVARIATE DATA=PER_FILE;/*generate histogram for
scores*/
 VAR SCORE;
```

```
HISTOGRAM;
TITLE "SCORE DISTRIBUTION FOR LOW BIRTH WEIGHT";
RUN;
```

SAS LOGISTIC REGRESSION OUTPUT

The following tables are output from running **PROC CONTENTS**.

Table 13-1. Host information provides the owner name and file name

Engine/Host Dependent Information	
Data Set Page Size	131072
Number of Data Set Pages	1
First Data Page	1
Max Obs per Page	2043
Obs in First Data Page	489
Number of Data Set Repairs	0
Filename	/saswork/SAS_work209D00008688_odaws02-prod-us/SAS_work641B00008688_odaws02-prod-us/low_birth_weight.sas7bdat
Release Created	9.0401M3
Host Created	Linux
Inode Number	28442641
Access Permission	rw-r--r--
Owner Name	jeff47
File Size	256KB
File Size (bytes)	262144

Table 13-2. Alphabetic list of the final model effects with attributes

Alphabetic List of Variables and Attributes					
#	Variable	Type	Len	Format	Informat
5	AGE	Num	8	BEST12.	BEST32.
2	BIRTH	Num	8	BEST12.	BEST32.
7	BWT	Num	8	BEST12.	BEST32.
1	ID	Char	2	$2.	$2.
8	LOW	Num	8	BEST12.	BEST32.
6	LWT	Num	8	BEST12.	BEST32.
4	RACE	Num	8	BEST12.	BEST32.
3	SMOKE	Num	8	BEST12.	BEST32.

Table 13-3 is produced by running **PROC MEANS** and contains descriptive statistics for the model effects. The statistics include measures of central tendency and measures of dispersion.

Table 13-3. Model effects descriptive statistics

Variable	N	Mean	Std Dev	Minimum	Maximum
BIRTH	488	1.8729508	0.8283019	1.0000000	4.0000000
SMOKE	488	0.3995902	0.4903167	0	1.0000000
RACE	488	1.8524590	0.9123576	1.0000000	3.0000000
AGE	488	26.4405738	5.8253635	14.0000000	48.0000000
LWT	488	142.7500000	32.4372558	80.0000000	272.0000000

Tables 13-4 and 13-5 are output resulting from running **PROC FREQ** and contain the frequency distribution for Birth and Low Weight (WLT).

Table 13-4. Frequency distribution for Birth

BIRTH	Frequency	Percent	Cumulative Frequency	Cumulative Percent
1	188	38.52	188	38.52
2	188	38.52	376	77.05
3	98	20.08	474	97.13
4	14	2.87	488	100.00

Table 13-5. Frequency distribution for Low Weight (LWT)

LWT	Frequency	Percent	Cumulative Frequency	Cumulative Percent
80	1	0.20	1	0.20
85	2	0.41	3	0.61
89	1	0.20	4	0.82
90	3	0.61	7	1.43
.				
.				
.				
254	1	0.20	485	99.39
262	1	0.20	486	99.59
267	1	0.20	487	99.80
272	1	0.20	488	100.00

Table 13-6 represents a cross tabulation for Birth and LWT. The table shows the frequency birth and LWT with row and column percentages. For instance, at LWT 85 (first column, second row), there were 2 women who experienced one birth.

Table 13-6. Cross tabulation of Birth and LWT

Table of LWT by BIRTH					
LWT	**BIRTH**				
Frequency Percent Row Pct Col Pct	**1**	**2**	**3**	**4**	**Total**
80	1 0.20 100.00 0.53	0 0.00 0.00 0.00	0 0.00 0.00 0.00	0 0.00 0.00 0.00	1 0.20
85	2 0.41 100.00 1.06	0 0.00 0.00 0.00	0 0.00 0.00 0.00	0 0.00 0.00 0.00	2 0.41
89	1 0.20 100.00 0.53	0 0.00 0.00 0.00	0 0.00 0.00 0.00	0 0.00 0.00 0.00	1 0.20
90	3 0.61 100.00 1.60	0 0.00 0.00 0.00	0 0.00 0.00 0.00	0 0.00 0.00 0.00	3 0.61
. . .					
272	0 0.00 0.00 0.00	0 0.00 0.00 0.00	1 0.20 100.00 1.02	0 0.00 0.00 0.00	1 0.20
Total	188 38.52	188 38.52	98 20.08	14 2.87	488 100.00
Frequency Missing = 1					

The rest of the output is a result of running **PROC LOGISTIC**. Table 13-7 provides model information including the data set that was used for modeling, the name of the response or target variable, number of response levels, type of model, and the method used for optimization. Table 13-8 contains the number of observations read and used, and Table 13-9 contains the frequency distribution for the response.

Table 13-7. Model information

Model Information	
Data Set	WORK.IMPORT
Response Variable	LOW
Number of Response Levels	2
Model	binary logit
Optimization Technique	Fisher's scoring

Table 13-8. Number of observations read and used

Number of Observations Read	489
Number of Observations Used	488

Table 13-9. Frequency distribution for the response, LOW

Response Profile		
Ordered Value	LOW	Total Frequency
1	0	337
2	1	151

Probability modeled is LOW='1'.

The first part of the above output tells us the file being analyzed (WORK.LOW_BIRTH_WEIGHT) and the number of observations used. We see that all 488 observations in our data set were used in the analysis. Note: one observation was deleted due to missing values for the response or explanatory variables. The output also shows the target variable and number of levels (two since it is binary).

221

This model used stepwise regression. The tables below are the results for each step up to when the model converged. The tables provide the model conversion status, the log likelihood, a residual Chi-Square test, a test for insignificant coefficients (i.e., $\beta = 0$), and model fits statistics.

Stepwise Selection Procedure

Step 0. Intercept entered:

Model Convergence Status
Convergence criterion (GCONV=1E-8) satisfied.

-2 Log L	=	603.793

Residual Chi-Square Test		
Chi-Square	DF	Pr > ChiSq
38.5095	5	<.0001

Step 1. Effect RACE entered:

Model Convergence Status
Convergence criterion (GCONV=1E-8) satisfied.

Model Fit Statistics		
Criterion	Intercept Only	Intercept and Covariates
AIC	605.793	587.065
SC	609.984	595.445
-2 Log L	603.793	583.065

R-Square	0.0416	Max-rescaled R-Square	0.0586

Testing Global Null Hypothesis: BETA=0			
Test	Chi-Square	DF	Pr > ChiSq
Likelihood Ratio	20.7286	1	<.0001
Score	20.0951	1	<.0001
Wald	19.4757	1	<.0001

Residual Chi-Square Test		
Chi-Square	DF	Pr > ChiSq
18.0354	4	0.0012

Note: No effects for the model in Step 1 are removed.

Step 2. Effect LWT entered:

Model Convergence Status
Convergence criterion (GCONV=1E-8) satisfied.

Model Fit Statistics		
Criterion	Intercept Only	Intercept and Covariates
AIC	605.793	581.536
SC	609.984	594.107
-2 Log L	603.793	575.536

R-Square	0.0563	Max-rescaled R-Square	0.0793

Testing Global Null Hypothesis: BETA=0			
Test	Chi-Square	DF	Pr > ChiSq
Likelihood Ratio	28.2575	2	<.0001
Score	27.3781	2	<.0001
Wald	26.2370	2	<.0001

Residual Chi-Square Test		
Chi-Square	DF	Pr > ChiSq
11.1477	3	0.0110

Note: No effects for the model in Step 2 are removed.

Step 3. Effect BIRTH entered:

Model Convergence Status
Convergence criterion (GCONV=1E-8) satisfied.

Model Fit Statistics		
Criterion	Intercept Only	Intercept and Covariates
AIC	605.793	577.926
SC	609.984	594.687
-2 Log L	603.793	569.926

R-Square	0.0670	Max-rescaled R-Square	0.0945

Testing Global Null Hypothesis: BETA=0			
Test	Chi-Square	DF	Pr > ChiSq
Likelihood Ratio	33.8673	3	<.0001
Score	32.5767	3	<.0001
Wald	30.8361	3	<.0001

Residual Chi-Square Test		
Chi-Square	DF	Pr > ChiSq
5.5932	2	0.0610

Note: No effects for the model in Step 3 are removed.

Step 4. Effect SMOKE entered:

Model Convergence Status
Convergence criterion (GCONV=1E-8) satisfied.

Model Fit Statistics

The portion of the output labeled Model Fit Statistics describes and tests the overall fit of the model. The -2LogL (565.509) can be used in comparisons of nested models, but we will not show an example of that here.

Table 13-10. Model fit statistics

Model Fit Statistics		
Criterion	Intercept Only	Intercept and Covariates
AIC	605.793	575.509
SC	609.984	596.461
-2 Log L	603.793	565.509

Table 13-11. R-Square Table

R-Square	0.0755	Max-rescaled R-Square	0.1063

Table 13-12. Test results for the null hypothesis

Testing Global Null Hypothesis: BETA=0			
Test	Chi-Square	DF	Pr > ChiSq
Likelihood Ratio	38.2842	4	<.0001
Score	37.4511	4	<.0001
Wald	35.1100	4	<.0001

Table 13-13. Chi-Square tests for the residuals

Residual Chi-Square Test		
Chi-Square	DF	Pr > ChiSq
1.1254	1	0.2888

Note: No effects for the model in Step 4 are removed.

Note: No (additional) effects met the 0.05 significance level for entry into the model.

In the next section of output, the likelihood ratio chi-square of 38.2842 with a p-value of < 0.0001 tells us that our model as a whole fits significantly better than an empty model. The Score and Wald tests are asymptotically equivalent tests of the same hypothesis tested by the likelihood ratio test, not surprisingly, these tests also indicate that the model is statistically significant.

Table 13-14. Summary of the stepwise regression showing which variable entered the model based on the Score Chi-Square. Had there been variables removed from the model, a Wald Chi-Square would have been provided.

Summary of Stepwise Selection						
	Effect			Number	Score	Wald	
Step	Entered	Removed	DF	In	Chi-Square	Chi-Square	Pr > ChiSq
1	RACE		1	1	20.0951		<.0001
2	LWT		1	2	7.1831		0.0074
3	BIRTH		1	3	5.6510		0.0174
4	SMOKE		1	4	4.4718		0.0345

Analysis of Maximum Likelihood Estimates

The section shows the hypothesis tests for each of the variables in the model individually. The chi-square test statistics and associated p-values shown in Table 13-15 indicate that each of the four variables in the model significantly improve the model fit.

Table 13-15. Analysis of the Maximum Likelihood Estimates including the significance of each component. Note that the intercept is not significant at the 0.05 level.

Analysis of Maximum Likelihood Estimates					
Parameter	DF	Estimate	Standard Error	Wald Chi-Square	Pr > ChiSq
Intercept	1	0.7346	0.6085	1.4573	0.2274
BIRTH	1	0.2788	0.1279	4.7543	0.0292
SMOKE	1	0.4641	0.2202	4.4441	0.0350
RACE	1	-0.4695	0.1262	13.8324	0.0002
LWT	1	-0.0101	0.00362	7.8257	0.0052

Table 13-15 shows the coefficients (labeled Estimate), their standard errors (error), the Wald Chi-Square statistic, and associated p-values. The coefficients for BIRTH, SMOKE, RACE, and LWT are statistically significant. The logistic regression coefficients give the change in the log odds of the outcome for a one unit increase in the predictor variable.

For every one unit change in BIRTH, the log odds of low birth weight (versus high birth weight) increases by 0.2788.

For a one unit increase in LWT, the log odds of having a low birth weight decreases by 0.0101.

Table 13-16. Confidence intervals for the parameter estimates

Parameter Estimates and Wald Confidence Intervals			
Parameter	Estimate	95% Confidence Limits	
Intercept	0.7346	-0.4581	1.9273
BIRTH	0.2788	0.0282	0.5294
SMOKE	0.4641	0.0326	0.8957
RACE	-0.4695	-0.7169	-0.2221
LWT	-0.0101	-0.0172	-0.00303

Association of Predicted Probabilities and Observed Responses

Percent Concordant refers to a pair of observations with different observed responses. An observation is said to be concordant if the observation with the lower ordered response value (LOW = 0) has a lower predicted mean score than the observation with the higher ordered response value (LOW = 1). Percent Discordant refers to the observation with the lower ordered response value, which has a higher predicted mean score than the observation with the higher ordered response value, then the pair is discordant.

Table 13-17. Association of predicted probabilities and observed responses

Association of Predicted Probabilities and Observed Responses			
Percent Concordant	67.1	Somers' D	0.343
Percent Discordant	32.8	Gamma	0.343
Percent Tied	0.1	Tau-a	0.147
Pairs	50887	c	0.671

In Table 13-17, Somers' delta (or Somers' D, for short), is a nonparametric measure of the strength and direction of association that exists between an ordinal dependent variable and an ordinal independent variable. It is defined as

$$\frac{n_c - n_d}{t}$$

where n_c is the number of pairs that are concordant, n_d the number of pairs that are discordant, and t is the number of total number of pairs with different responses While it is possible to analyze the association between two ordinal variables using Goodman and Kruskal's Gamma, Somers' D is appropriate when you want to distinguish between a dependent and independent variable. Since this model does not have ordinal variables, the Somers' D assumptions are violated.

Kendall's Tau-a is a modification of Somers' D that takes into the account the difference between the number of possible paired observations and the number of paired observations with a different response. It is defined to be the ratio of the difference between the number of concordant pairs and the number of discordant pairs to the number of possible pairs

$$\left(\frac{2(n_c - n_d)}{N(N - 1)}\right).$$

Usually Tau-a is much smaller than Somers' D since there would be many paired observations with the same response.

The discriminative-ability of a logistic regression model is frequently assessed using the concordance (or c) statistic, a unitless index denoting the probability that a randomly selected subject who experienced the outcome will have a higher predicted probability of having the outcome occur compared to a randomly selected subject who did not experience the event. One can calculate the c-statistic by taking all possible pairs of subjects consisting of one subject who experienced the event of interest and one subject who did not experience the event of interest. The c-statistic is the proportion of such pairs in which the subject who experienced the event had a higher predicted probability of experiencing the event than the subject who did not experience the event (Harrell F. E., 2001). For binary logistic regression, the c-statistic (equivalent to the area under the Receiver Operating Characteristic curve) is a standard measure of the predictive accuracy of a model (see Figures 13-2 and 13-3).

Odds Ratio Estimates and Wald Confidence Intervals

Table 13-18 gives the coefficients as odds ratios. An odds ratio is the exponentiated coefficient, and can be interpreted as the multiplicative change in the odds for a one unit change in the predictor variable. For example, for a one unit increase in BIRTH, the odds of having a low birth weight (versus a high birth weight) increase by a factor of 1.322 (se Figure 13-1).

Table 13-18. Odds Ratio Estimates with their associated Wald Confidence Intervals

Odds Ratio Estimates and Wald Confidence Intervals				
Effect	Unit	Estimate	95% Confidence Limits	
BIRTH	1.0000	1.322	1.029	1.698
SMOKE	1.0000	1.591	1.033	2.449
RACE	1.0000	0.625	0.488	0.801
LWT	1.0000	0.990	0.983	0.997

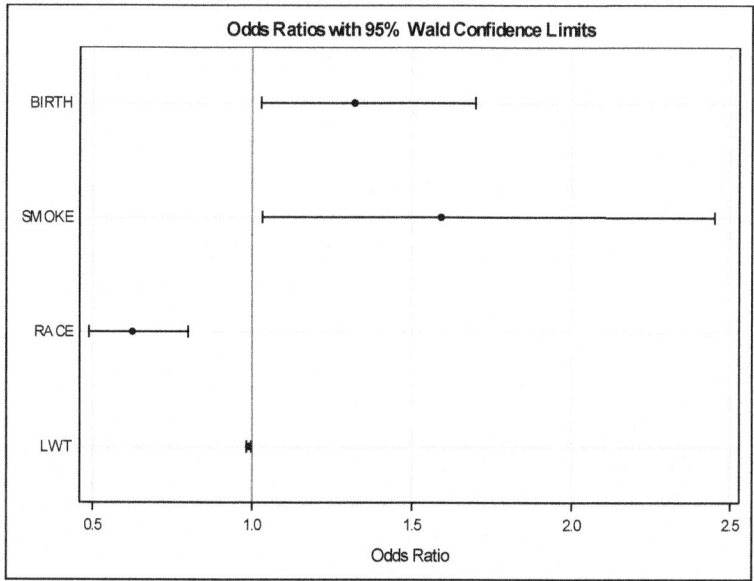

Figure 13-1. Wald Confidence Intervals of the Odds Ratios

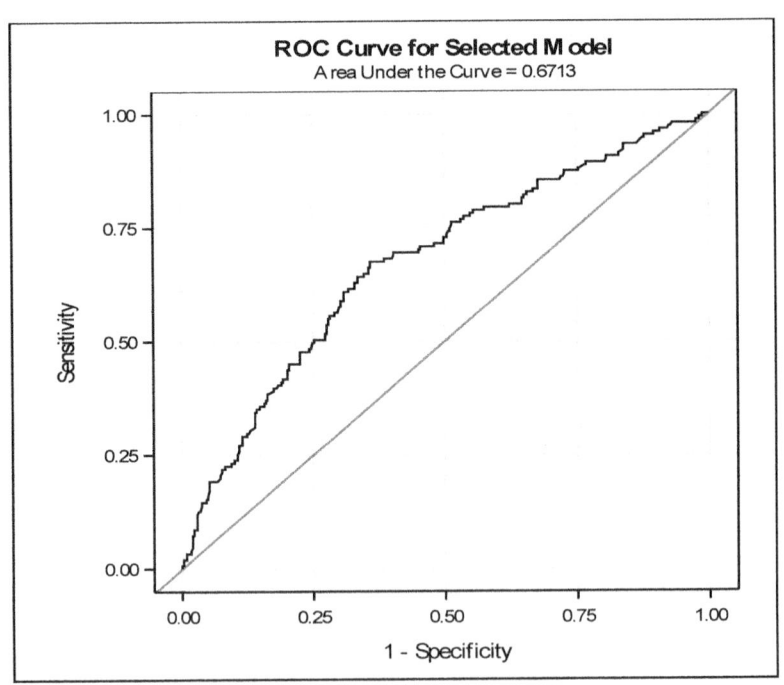

Figure 13-2. Selected Model ROC Curve

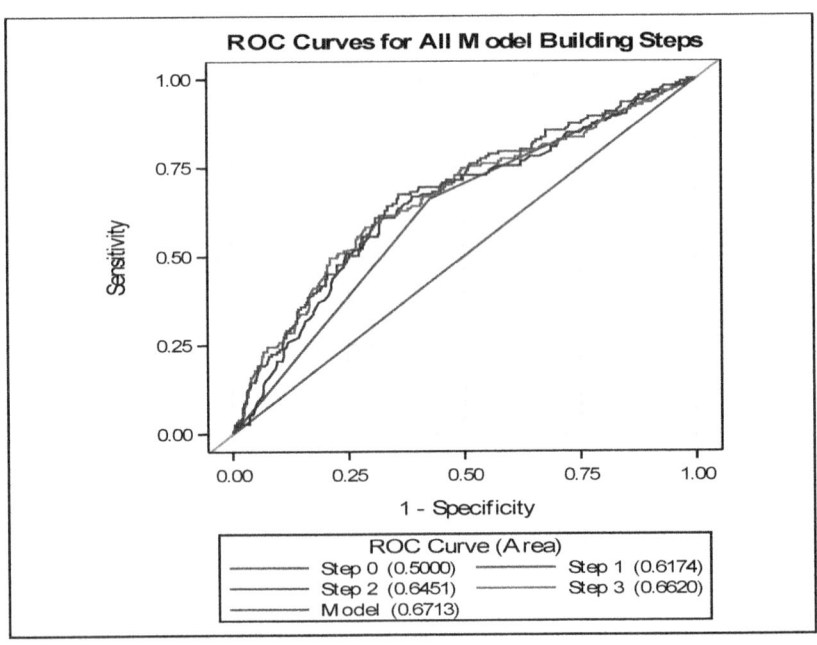

Figure 13-3.ROC Curves for all model building steps

We have seen that a Receiver Operating Characteristic Curve (ROC) is a standard technique for summarizing classifier performance over a range of trade-offs between true positive (TP) and false positive (FP) error rates. It is plotting the values of the cumulative percent of the captured responses.

Table 13-19. Covariance Matrix

Estimated Covariance Matrix					
Parameter	Intercept	BIRTH	SMOKE	RACE	LWT
Intercept	0.370317	-0.00738	-0.05322	-0.04181	-0.00178
BIRTH	-0.00738	0.016348	-0.00186	-0.00154	-0.00014
SMOKE	-0.05322	-0.00186	0.048474	0.010067	0.000122
RACE	-0.04181	-0.00154	0.010067	0.015934	0.000093
LWT	-0.00178	-0.00014	0.000122	0.000093	0.000013

Tables 13-19 and 13-20 contain the covariance and correlation matrices, respectively. Note that in Table 13-20, ignoring the insignificant intercept, the highest correlation is between SMOKE and RACE. We generally get concerned when correlation are higher that 0.40.

Table 13-20. Correlation matrix

Estimated Correlation Matrix					
Parameter	Intercept	BIRTH	SMOKE	RACE	LWT
Intercept	1.0000	-0.0948	-0.3972	-0.5443	-0.8079
BIRTH	-0.0948	1.0000	-0.0662	-0.0955	-0.3121
SMOKE	-0.3972	-0.0662	1.0000	0.3622	0.1528
RACE	-0.5443	-0.0955	0.3622	1.0000	0.2026
LWT	-0.8079	-0.3121	0.1528	0.2026	1.0000

Table 13-21. Hosmer and Lemeshow test showing the observed and expected values by group, used to calculate the Chi-Square goodness of fit statistic

Partition for the Hosmer and Lemeshow Test					
		LOW = 1		LOW = 0	
Group	Total	Observed	Expected	Observed	Expected
1	49	8	6.68	41	42.32
2	51	10	8.99	41	42.01
3	49	12	9.88	37	39.12
4	49	6	11.29	43	37.71
5	49	10	13.07	39	35.93
6	50	16	15.65	34	34.35
7	49	21	17.41	28	31.59
8	48	21	19.94	27	28.06
9	49	20	23.27	29	25.73
10	45	27	24.82	18	20.18

Table 13-22. Result of the Hosmer Lemeshow Chi-Square test showing the test is significant (Pr>Chi-Square = 0.4564), which verifies a good fit, i.e., at least one of the observed verses expected values is not true, probably group 4.

Hosmer and Lemeshow Goodness-of-Fit Test		
Chi-Square	DF	Pr > ChiSq
7.7688	8	0.4564

Table 13-23. Classification Table or Confusion Matrix

	Classification Table								
	Correct		Incorrect		Percentages				
Prob Level	Event	Non-Event	Event	Non-Event	Correct	Sensi-tivity	Speci-ficity	False POS	False NEG
0.100	150	4	333	1	31.6	99.3	1.2	68.9	20.0
0.200	126	95	242	25	45.3	83.4	28.2	65.8	20.8
0.300	100	202	135	51	61.9	66.2	59.9	57.4	20.2
0.400	61	269	68	90	67.6	40.4	79.8	52.7	25.1
0.500	27	316	21	124	70.3	17.9	93.8	43.8	28.2
0.600	3	334	3	148	69.1	2.0	99.1	50.0	30.7
0.700	0	337	0	151	69.1	0.0	100.0	.	30.9
0.800	0	337	0	151	69.1	0.0	100.0	.	30.9
0.900	0	337	0	151	69.1	0.0	100.0	.	30.9
1.000	0	337	0	151	69.1	0.0	100.0	.	30.9

The following diagnostic detect potential observations that have a significant impact on the model. There are several reasons that we need to detect influential observations.

1. We might have data entry errors
2. We might have influential observations of interest by themselves for us to study
3. We might have influential data points that badly skew the regression estimation

How large does each one have to be, to be considered influential? First of all, we always have to make our judgment based on our theory and our analysis. Secondly, there are some rule-of-thumb cutoffs when the sample size is large. These are shown below. When the sample size is large, the asymptotic distribution of some of the measures would follow some standard distribution. That is why we have these cutoff values, and why they only apply when the sample size is large enough. Usually, we would look at the relative magnitude of a statistic an observation has compared to others. That is, we look for data points that are farther away from most of the data points.

Table 13-24. Leverage and residual test results

Measure	Value
leverage (hat value)	>2 or 3 times of the average of leverage
abs(Pearson Residuals)	> 2
abs(Deviance Residuals)	> 2

In Table 13-24, *Pearson residuals* and its standardized version is one type of residual. Pearson residuals are defined to be the standardized difference between the observed frequency and the predicted frequency. They measure the relative deviations between the observed and fitted values. *Deviance residual* is another type of residual. It measures the disagreement between the maxima of the observed and the fitted log likelihood functions. Since logistic regression uses the maximal likelihood principle, the goal in logistic regression is to minimize the sum of the deviance residuals. Therefore, this residual is parallel to the raw residual in OLS regression, where the goal is to minimize the sum of squared residuals. Another statistic, sometimes called the hat diagonal since technically it is the diagonal of the hat matrix, measures the leverage of an observation. It is also sometimes called the *Pregibon leverage*. These three statistics, Pearson residual, deviance residual and Pregibon leverage are considered to be the three basic building blocks for logistic regression diagnostics. We always want to inspect these first, and this is worth highlighting:

Logistic Regression Goal

Since logistic regression uses the maximum likelihood principle, the goal is to minimize the sum of the deviance residuals by inspect three metrics:

- Pearson residuals

- Deviance residual

- Pregibon leverage

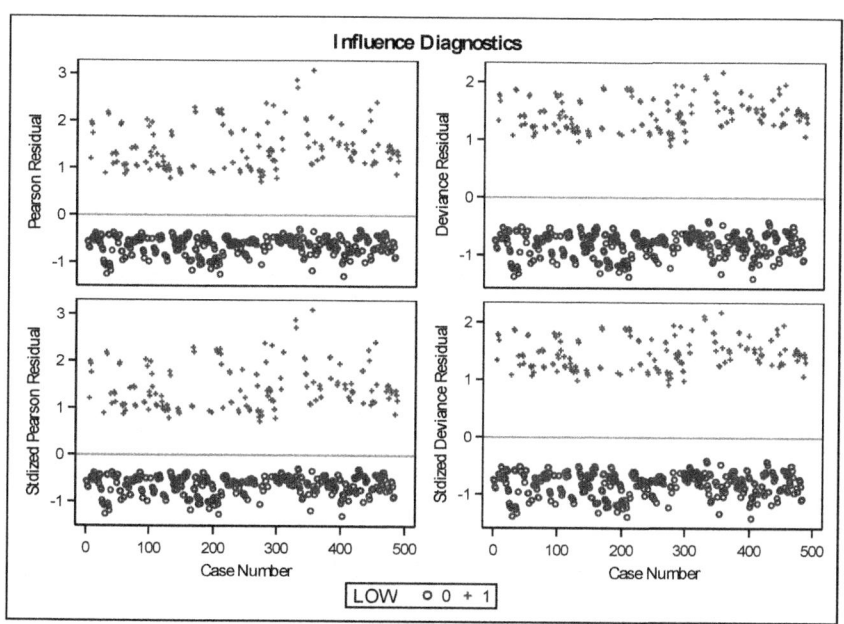

Figure 13-4. Influence Diagnostic plots

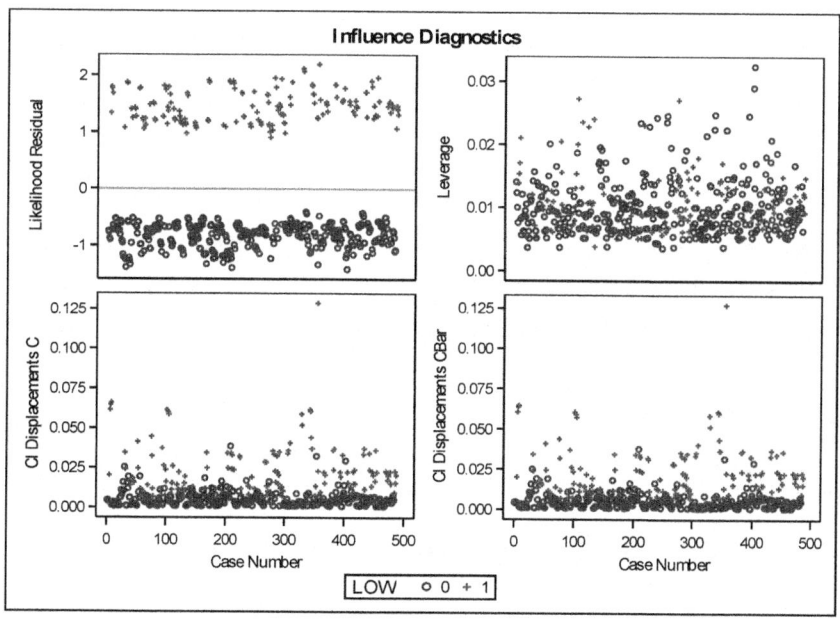

Figure 13-5. Influence Diagnostic plots

235

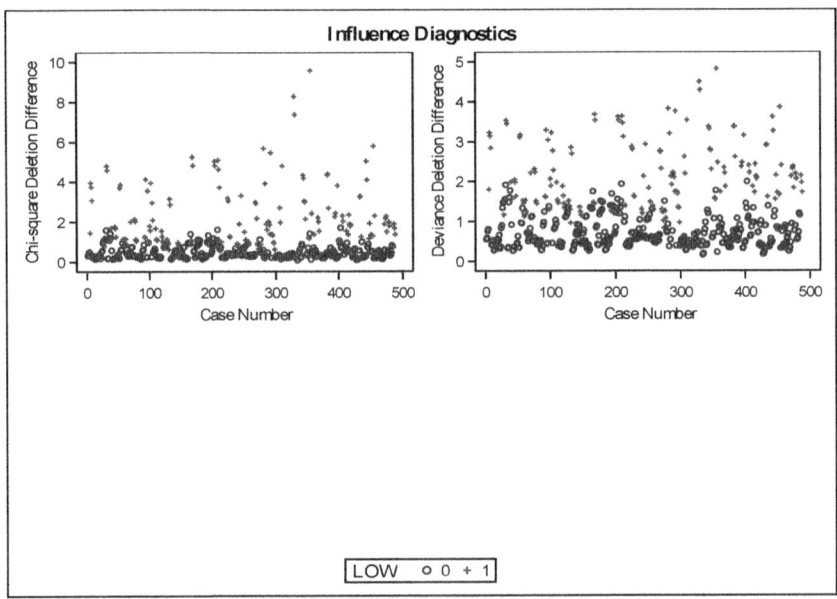

Figure 13-6. Influence Diagnostic plots

The last type of diagnostic statistics is related to coefficient sensitivity and is plotted for each predictor. Similar to OLS regression, logistic regression also has dfbeta's (see figures 13-7 and 13-8). They measure how much impact each observation has on each parameter estimate. As a rule-of-thumb, we take any observation outside ± 0.2 as suspect and should check them, unless there are very few among very many observations (say 1000), since the few would be hard to isolate and have little effect among the many.

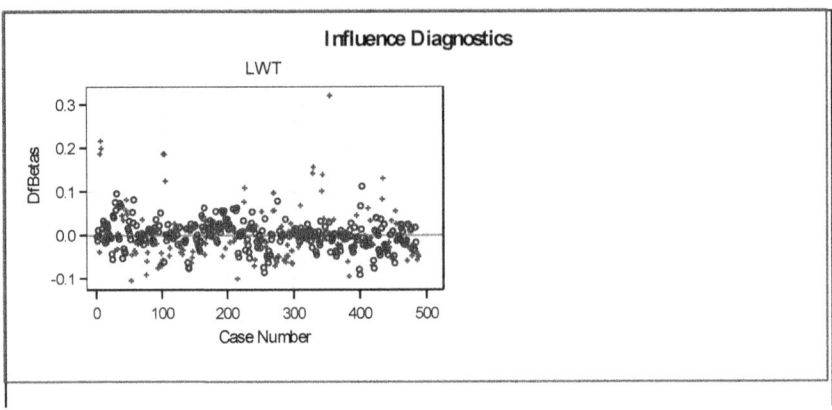

Figure 13-7. Influence Diagnostic plots

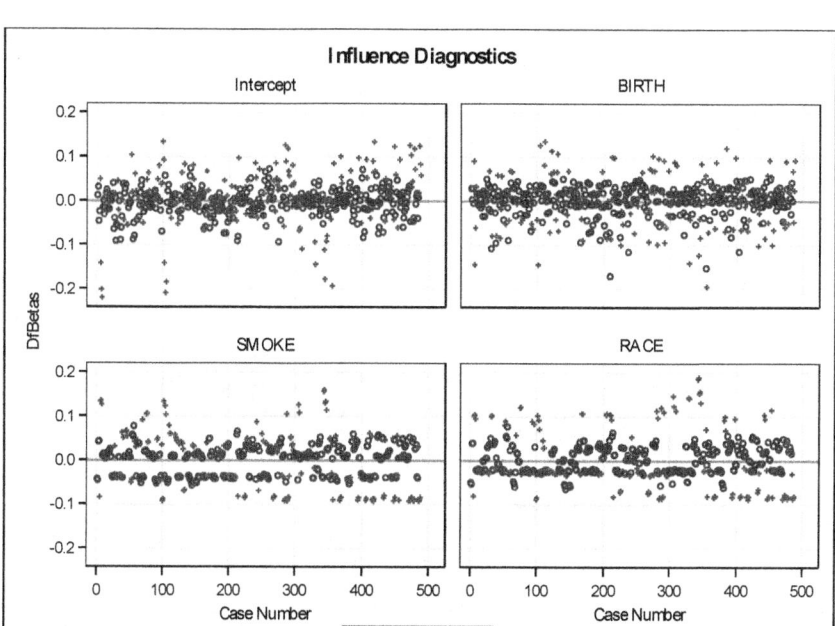

Figure 13-8. Influence Diagnostic plots

Figure 13-9 is generated from the PHAT option (I just chose to print all diagnostic plots with PLOTS(ONLY) = ALL.

The shapes of the plots are similar and show quadratic like curves. Points falling in the top left or top right corners of the plots are poorly fit. Assessment of this distance is partly based on numerical value and partly based on visual impression. Under n-asymptotic the value of upper ninety-fifth percentile of chi-square distribution with 1 degree of freedom is 3.84 and may provide some guidance as to whether an observation is an outlier or influential point. Thus the cases having numerical values larger than this cut-off point, which is based on $\chi2$ difference or deviance difference, can be considered as outlying observations.

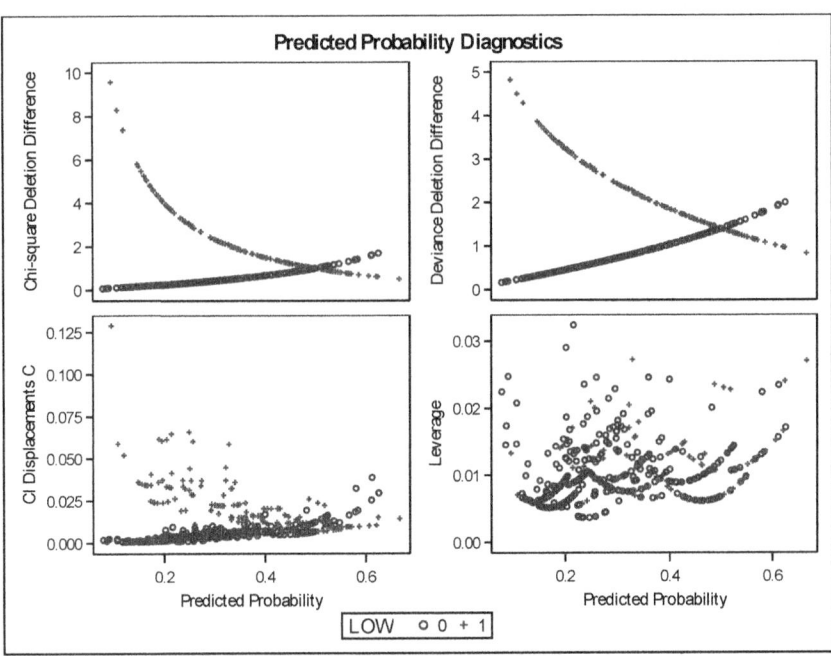

Figure 13-9. Predicted probability diagnostic plots

High-leverage points (see Figure 13-10) are those observations, if any, made at extreme or outlying values of the independent variables such that the lack of neighboring observations means that the fitted regression model will pass close to that particular observation (Everitt, Cambridge Dictionary of Statistics, 2002). Bad leverage points are outlying observations which do not lie in the pattern of the bulk of the data and they are highly influential. On the other hand, good leverage points are outlying observations which lie in the pattern of the bulk of the data but and in contrast, they contribute to the precision of the parameter estimation.

A well known fact about robust methods for dealing with leverage points is there is a risk of deleting or down-weighting good leverage points. Sanizah, et al, (Sanizah, Habshah, & Norazan, 2010)] proved that good leverage points are harmless to the maximum likelihood estimators and hence should not be unnecessarily down-weighted. It stated that the unnecessary down-weighting of good leverage points will lead to a loss of efficiency and the estimates of the parameters can give misleading

Interpretations. Venter and De la Rey (Venter & de la Rey, 2007) justified bad leverage points as being adversely affected to the maximum likelihood probability curve and may give an unduly effect on the parameter estimates whereas good leverage points can improve the fit.

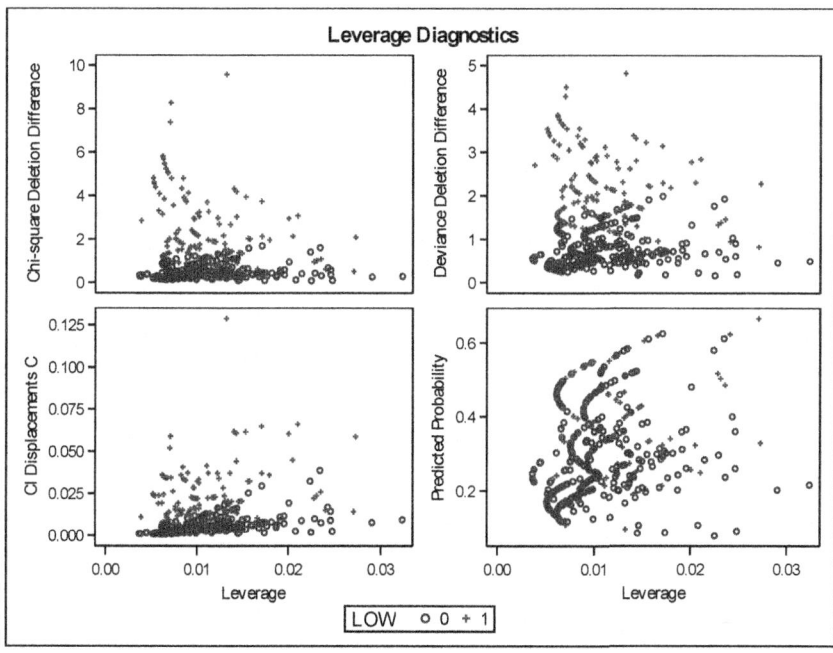

Figure 13-10. Leverage Diagnostic plots

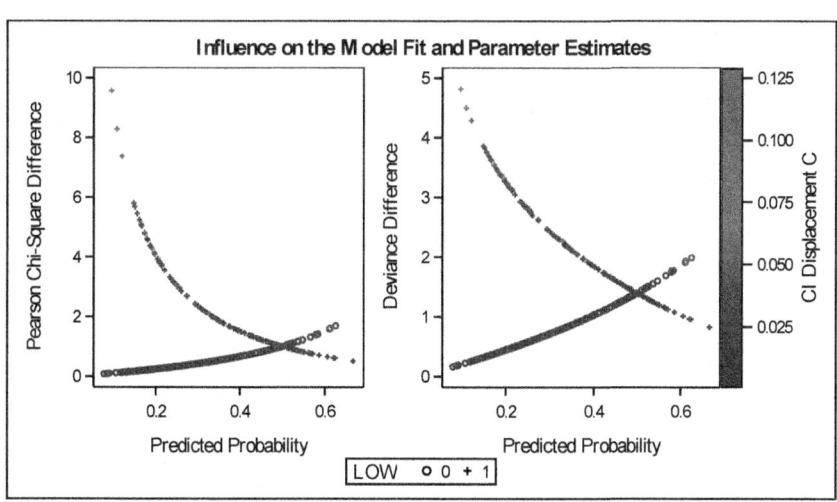

Figure 13.11. Influence on the Model Fir and Parameter Estimates

Figure 13-11 is generated from the DPC option (or PLOTS(ONLY) = ALL). If we have observations in the bottom "cup" in red then we need to scrutinize them more closely. These observations influence the parameter estimates to a relatively large extent but are not poorly fitted.

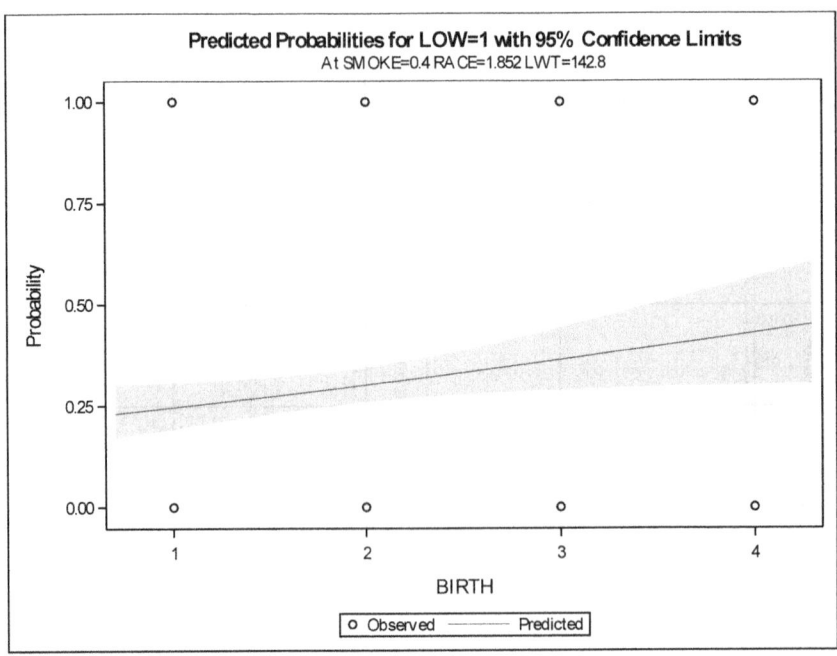

Figure 13-12. Predicted Probabilities for LOW = 1 with 95% confidence limits

SAS Score Output

Tables 13-25 and 13-26 are generated with the scoring code macro for grouping the scores. We use these to check the "quality" of our scoring distribution, and to build our performance plots. In this example we have used deciles (10 groups) that are evenly paced, with about 69 observation.

Table 13-25. FREQ - Deciles for RESP in the Low Birth Weight model

		Rank for Variable P_RESP1		
PENTILE	Frequency	Percent	Cumulative Frequency	Cumulative Percent
1	69	10.01	69	10.01
2	69	10.01	138	20.03
3	65	9.43	203	29.46
4	74	10.74	277	40.20
5	67	9.72	344	49.93
6	72	10.45	416	60.38
7	66	9.58	482	69.96
8	69	10.01	551	79.97
9	69	10.01	620	89.99
10	69	10.01	689	100.00

Table 13-26. FREQ – Deciles for the Model and the Actual positive counts

		Predicted: RESP=1	RESP
	N	Sum	Sum
Rank for Variable P_RESP1			
1	69	42.61	28.00
2	69	35.77	27.00
3	65	30.03	23.00
4	74	30.50	28.00
5	67	24.51	18.00
6	72	23.06	20.00
7	66	18.28	18.00
8	69	16.34	15.00
9	69	13.18	16.00
10	69	7.97	16.00

Moments			
N	689	Sum Weights	689
Mean	0.30220458	Sum Observations	208.218959
Std Deviation	0.10039431	Variance	0.01007902
Skewness	0.2557412	Kurtosis	-1.0445616
Uncorrected SS	69.8590883	Corrected SS	6.93436435
Coeff Variation	33.220645	Std Error Mean	0.00382472

Basic Statistical Measures			
Location		Variability	
Mean	0.302205	Std Deviation	0.10039
Median	0.300191	Variance	0.01008
Mode	0.172906	Range	0.40127
		Interquartile Range	0.16919

Note: The mode displayed is the smallest of 2 modes with a count of 18.

Tests for Location: Mu0=0				
Test	Statistic		p Value	
Student's t	t	79.01355	Pr > |t|	<.0001
Sign	M	344.5	Pr >= |M|	<.0001
Signed Rank	S	118852.5	Pr >= |S|	<.0001

Extreme Observations			
Lowest		Highest	
Value	Obs	Value	Obs
0.134731	563	0.511510	468
0.134731	452	0.511510	600
0.138592	526	0.527849	689
0.142547	222	0.535999	96
0.142547	125	0.535999	269

The scoring distribution in Figure 13-13 is not very good, but sometimes we cannot do any better. It may not be our modeling skills and could just be that the target is something not very predictable, or we just have bad data. A good scoring distribution would be skewed right.

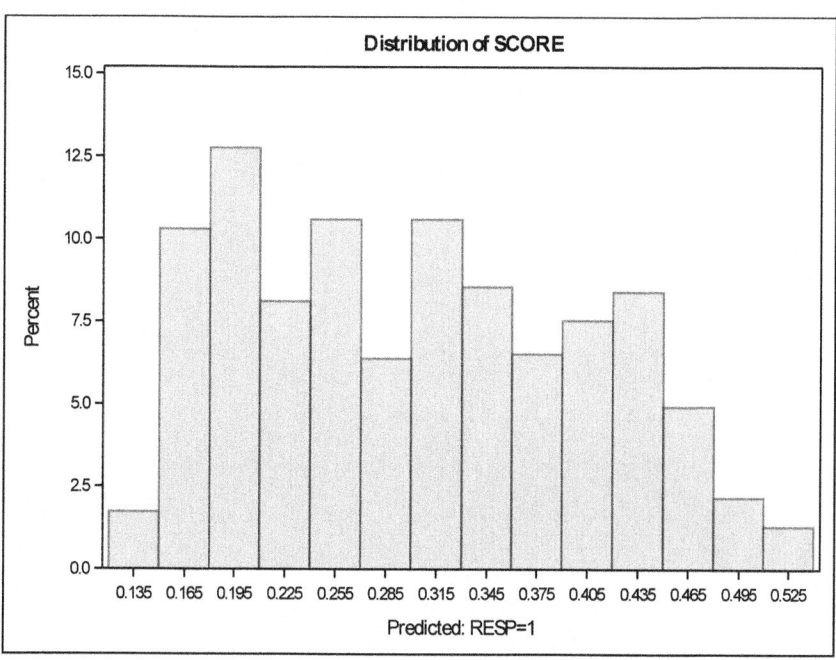

Figure 13-13. Score Distribution

Exercises

1. The first exercise suggested here is to duplicate this example in SAS Studio.

2. Using SAS Studio with the Polypharm dataset, construct a predictive model to project the likelihood that a member of the target audience will take drugs from more than three different classes.

3. Using SAS Studio and the Adolescent_Placement dataset, construct a multinomial logistic regression model with "Placement" as the target variable.

14. Examples Using R

Introduction to R and R-Studio

Download and install R from http://cran.us.r-project.org/. Select the appropriate version to install.

Download and Install R

Precompiled binary distributions of the base system and contributed packages, **Windows and Mac** users most likely want one of these versions of R:

- Download R for Linux
- Download R for (Mac) OS X
- Download R for Windows

R is part of many Linux distributions, you should check with your Linux package management system in addition to the link above.

Download and install R-Studio from https://www.rstudio.com/products/rstudio/download/.

Start R-Studio (R starts with it).

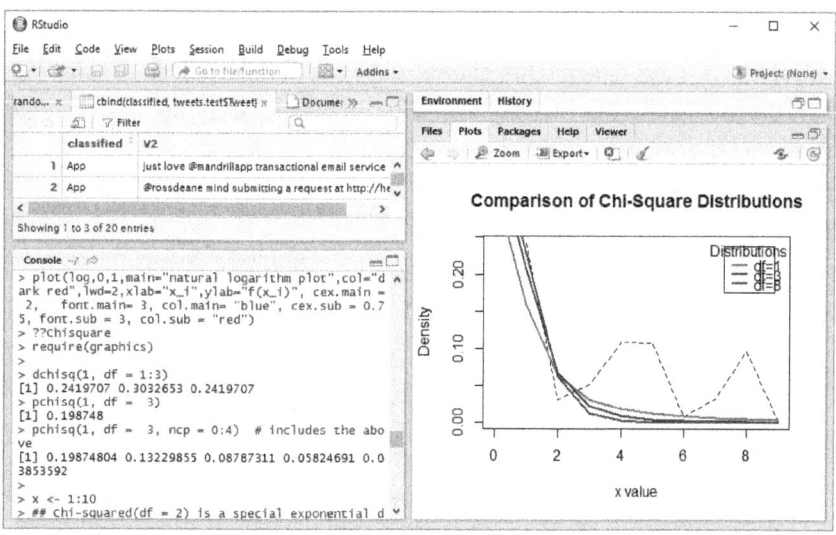

The Console pane (lower left) is where you enter R code and see R output. The right pain is for Plots, Available Packages, Help, etc. If you

245

enter the command, ??plot.gains, the help window will display the documentation for plot.gains.

Logistic Regression: Bank Marketing Campaign – Mixed Predictors

This data set was obtained from the UC Irvine Machine Learning Repository and contains information related to a direct marketing campaign of a Portuguese banking institution and its attempts to get its clients to subscribe for a term deposit.

Source

The path to this data set is https://archive.ics.uci.edu/ml/machine-learning-databases/00222/bank.zip. This data set was obtained by downloading the zip bank.zip, which includes bank-full.csv and bank.csv. The table contains 41,188 rows and 21 columns.

Input Variables (see below: Attribute Information)

There are 20 columns in the table that provide information about each client, such as age, marital status, and education level. A subset of these are related to the last contact of the current campaign, such as the month and day of the week the last contact was made as well as the number of days since the client was last contacted in a previous campaign. There are 10 columns in the table that are categorical, meaning that they contain textual values that correspond to a particular category for a given variable.

Citation Request

This dataset is public available for research. The details are described in [Moro et al., 2011]. Please include this citation if you plan to use this database:

Relevant Information

The data is related with direct marketing campaigns of a Portuguese banking institution. The marketing campaigns were based on phone calls. Often, more than one contact to the same client was required, in order to access if the product (bank term deposit) would be (or not) subscribed.

Model Goal: The classification goal is to predict if the client will subscribe a term deposit (variable y=RESP).

Number of Instances: 45211 for bank-full.csv (4521 for bank.csv)

Number of Attributes: 16 + output attributes.

Modification

I modified this data set by converting "Yes"/"No" variables to binary variables with 1 = yes and 0 = no.

In addition to the response variable for acquisition of a deposit account (RESP) there are 14 variables in the dataset.

1. AGE (numeric)
2. JOB : type of job (categorical: "admin.", "unknown", "unemployed", "management", "housemaid", "entrepreneur", "student", "blue-collar", "self-employed", "retired", "technician", "services")
3. MARITAL : marital status (categorical: "married", "divorced", "single"; note: "divorced" means divorced or widowed)
4. EDUCATION (categorical: "unknown", "secondary", "primary", "tertiary")
5. DEFAULT: has credit in default? (binary: "yes", "no")
6. BALANCE: average yearly balance, in euros (numeric)
7. HOMEOWNER: has housing loan? (binary: "yes", "no")
8. LOANS: has personal loan? (binary: "yes", "no")
   # related with the last contact of the current campaign:
9. CONTACT: contact communication type (categorical: "unknown", "telephone", "cellular")
10. LENGTH: length of most recent membership (numeric)
11. CAMPAIGN: number of contacts performed during this campaign and for this client (numeric, includes last contact)
12. PDAYS: number of days that passed by after the client was last contacted from a previous campaign (numeric, -1 means client was not previously contacted)
13. PREVIOUS: number of contacts performed before this campaign

and for this client (numeric)

14. POUTCOME: outcome of the previous marketing campaign (categorical: "unknown", "other", "failure", "success")
15. Output variable (desired target):
    RESP - has the client subscribed a term deposit? (binary: 1="yes", 0="no")

```
file = "C:/'your directory path'/Banking.csv"
```

Next, we read the .csv file into an R dataset called "lbw."

```
read.csv(file) -> bank
```

We can explore the data using the summary command.

```
summary(bank)
```

```
            job              marital              education
blue-collar:9732     divorced: 5207     primary  : 6851
management :9458     married :27214     secondary:23202
technician :7597     single  :12790     tertiary :13301
admin.     :5171                        unknown  : 1857
services   :4154
retired    :2264
(Other)    :6835
       age              balance              homeowner
Min.   :18.00     Min.   : -8019     Min.   :0.0000
1st Qu.:33.00     1st Qu.:    72     1st Qu.:0.0000
Median :39.00     Median :   448     Median :1.0000
Mean   :40.94     Mean   :  1362     Mean   :0.5558
3rd Qu.:48.00     3rd Qu.:  1428     3rd Qu.:1.0000
Max.   :95.00     Max.   :102127     Max.   :1.0000

      loans              default              contact
Min.   :0.0000     Min.   :0.00000     Min.   :0.000
1st Qu.:0.0000     1st Qu.:0.00000     1st Qu.:0.000
Median :0.0000     Median :0.00000     Median :2.000
Mean   :0.1602     Mean   :0.01803     Mean   :1.488
3rd Qu.:0.0000     3rd Qu.:0.00000     3rd Qu.:2.000
Max.   :1.0000     Max.   :1.00000     Max.   :3.000

      length              campaign              pdays
Min.   :   0.0     Min.   : 1.000     Min.   : -1.0
1st Qu.: 103.0     1st Qu.: 1.000     1st Qu.: -1.0
Median : 180.0     Median : 2.000     Median : -1.0
Mean   : 258.2     Mean   : 2.764     Mean   : 40.2
3rd Qu.: 319.0     3rd Qu.: 3.000     3rd Qu.: -1.0
Max.   :4918.0     Max.   :63.000     Max.   :871.0

     previous             poutcome              RESP
Min.   :  0.0000     Min.   :0.00     Min.   :0.000
1st Qu.:  0.0000     1st Qu.:2.00     1st Qu.:0.000
Median :  0.0000     Median :2.00     Median :0.000
Mean   :  0.5803     Mean   :1.75     Mean   :0.117
3rd Qu.:  0.0000     3rd Qu.:2.00     3rd Qu.:0.000
Max.   :275.0000     Max.   :2.00     Max.   :1.000
```

Now we divide the data into a training set and test set of equal length. We will use the training set to build a new logistic regression model and the test set to make predictions based on the model.

```
bank_train<-bank[2:22606,]
```

```
bank_test<-bank[22607:45211,]
```

We should form these as random samples from the base dataset, but I wanted to show you how to index arrays. In `bank_train[1:22606,]` we are calling records (rows) 1 to 22606 and by leaving a blank after the comma, we are calling all variables (columns). So we can think of the command as bank[rows,columns]. We could have also specified the columns as bank[1:22606, 1:6].

We can also plot the data. Here I will just plot variables 3 through 6. From the plot matrix it should be clear that EDUCATON is a categorical variable, while AGE and BALANCE are numeric variables. HOMEOWNER is a binary variable, for instance, it has two categories, Yes or No, represented by 1 and 0 respectively.

```
plot(bank_train[,3:6])
```

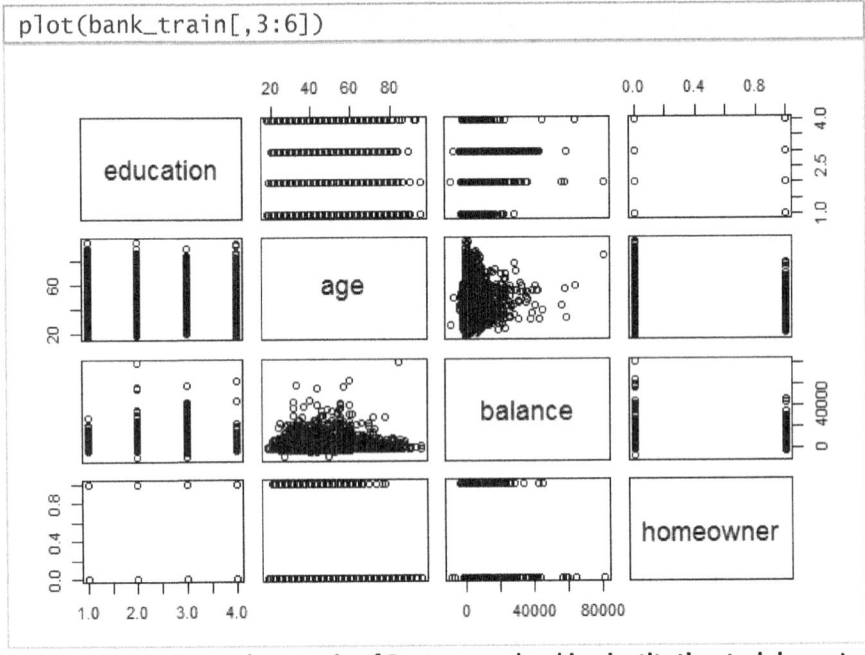

Figure 15-3. Scatterplot matrix of Portuguese banking institution training set

Now that we have the data in R, we can also print a correlation matrix and examine the results to see if there are any highly correlated variables. We can also plot the individual variables, for instance, AGE:

```
plot(bank_train[,"age"])
```

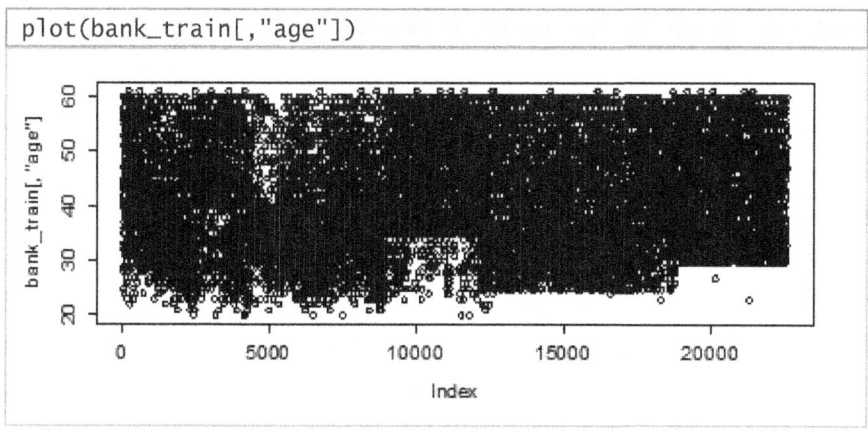

Figure 15-4. Scatterplot of Age from the training set

```
plot(bank_train[,"education"])
```

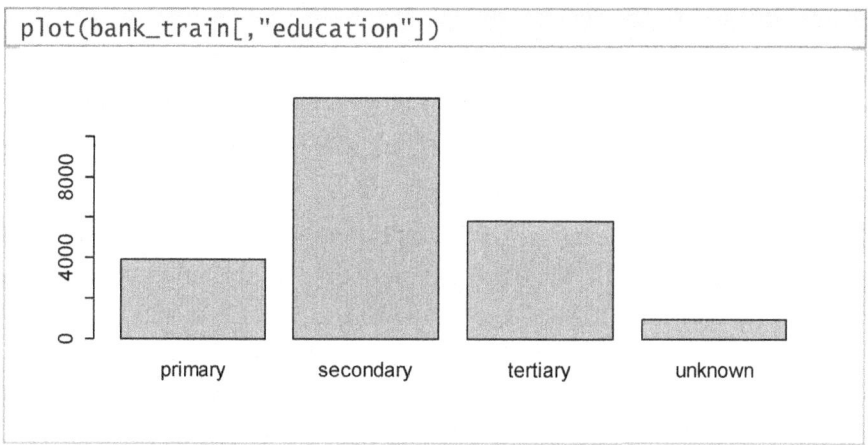

Figure 15-5. Plot of Education from the training set

```
cor(bank_train[,4:11])
```

	age	balance	homeowner
age	1.0000000000	0.080224168	-0.214549425
balance	0.0802241683	1.000000000	-0.053650626
homeowner	-0.2145494247	-0.053650626	1.000000000
loans	-0.0199884191	-0.085608194	-0.039299216
default	-0.0308172862	-0.079035629	-0.019621671
contact	0.0702207722	-0.016283046	-0.335629034
length	-0.0488567712	0.016637554	0.019384029
campaign	-0.0004657117	0.005620917	-0.004349685
	loans	default	contact
age	-0.0199884191	-0.030817286	0.070220772
balance	-0.0856081939	-0.079035629	-0.016283046

251

```
homeowner  -0.0392992163  -0.019621671  -0.335629034
loans       1.0000000000   0.083548500   0.101075921
default     0.0835484997   1.000000000   0.010899902
contact     0.1010759214   0.010899902   1.000000000
length     -0.0009396837  -0.006051515   0.001365633
campaign    0.0046629738   0.004675987   0.115804459
                   length      campaign
age        -0.0488567712  -0.0004657117
balance     0.0166375539   0.0056209170
homeowner   0.0193840290  -0.0043496853
loans      -0.0009396837   0.0046629738
default    -0.0060515155   0.0046759871
contact     0.0013656332   0.1158044593
length      1.0000000000  -0.0714542068
campaign   -0.0714542068   1.0000000000
```

It appears that of all our variables, AGE and BIRTH are highly correlated. We can include both for the initial modeling, but we have to ensure the less significant variable is removed afterward if one or poth prove to be significant.

Now, we fit a logistic regression model using a general linear model in R (glm is part of base R). RESP is the dependent variable and we use JOB, MARITAL, EDUCATION, AGE, BALANCE, HOMEOWNER, LOANS, DEFAULT, CONTACT, LENGTH, CAMPAIGN, PDAYS, PREVIOUS, and POUTCOME as possible predictors. Recall that our response variable, RESP, is binomial. Since we are performing a logistic regression, we use a logit link function.

```
bank.model <- glm( RESP ~ job+marital+education+age+balance
+homeowner+loans+default+contact+length+campaign+pdays+prev
ious+poutcome , data = bank_train, family=binomial(logit))
```

Print a summary of the fitted model

```
summary(bank.model)
```

```
Call:
glm(formula = RESP ~ job + marital + education + age + bala
nce +
    homeowner + loans + default + contact + length + campai
gn +
```

```
     pdays + previous + poutcome, family = binomial(logit),
data = bank_train)

Deviance Residuals:
    Min       1Q    Median       3Q      Max
-5.1945   -0.1982   -0.1414   -0.1066   3.2080

Coefficients: (3 not defined because of singularities)
                     Estimate Std. Error z value
(Intercept)         -4.682e+00  3.210e-01  -14.585
jobblue-collar      -2.164e-02  1.508e-01   -0.143
jobentrepreneur      1.198e-01  2.407e-01    0.498
jobhousemaid        -9.775e-01  3.005e-01   -3.253
jobmanagement       -2.320e-01  1.758e-01   -1.319
jobretired          -1.325e-01  2.490e-01   -0.532
jobself-employed    -1.611e-01  2.541e-01   -0.634
jobservices         -2.266e-01  1.796e-01   -1.262
jobstudent           2.950e-01  4.694e-01    0.628
jobtechnician       -6.867e-02  1.529e-01   -0.449
jobunemployed        1.587e-01  2.648e-01    0.599
jobunknown          -9.036e-01  7.610e-01   -1.187
maritalmarried      -6.651e-01  1.142e-01   -5.824
maritalsingle       -3.288e-01  1.327e-01   -2.477
educationsecondary   2.445e-02  1.285e-01    0.190
educationtertiary    8.051e-03  1.635e-01    0.049
educationunknown    -3.372e-01  2.455e-01   -1.374
age                 -8.115e-03  5.018e-03   -1.617
balance             -1.054e-05  1.593e-05   -0.662
homeowner           -2.429e-01  8.783e-02   -2.766
loans               -2.800e-01  1.065e-01   -2.630
default              4.963e-01  2.233e-01    2.223
contact              3.147e-01  4.150e-02    7.583
length               5.496e-03  1.179e-04   46.623
campaign            -1.220e-03  1.287e-02   -0.095
pdays                      NA         NA       NA
previous                   NA         NA       NA
poutcome                   NA         NA       NA
                     Pr(>|z|)
(Intercept)          < 2e-16 ***
jobblue-collar       0.88594
jobentrepreneur      0.61870
jobhousemaid         0.00114 **
jobmanagement        0.18710
jobretired           0.59451
jobself-employed     0.52613
jobservices          0.20695
```

```
jobstudent           0.52973
jobtechnician        0.65345
jobunemployed        0.54889
jobunknown           0.23505
maritalmarried       5.74e-09 ***
maritalsingle        0.01324  *
educationsecondary   0.84905
educationtertiary    0.96073
educationunknown     0.16946
age                  0.10584
balance              0.50804
homeowner            0.00567  **
loans                0.00855  **
default              0.02622  *
contact              3.38e-14 ***
length               < 2e-16  ***
campaign             0.92446
pdays                     NA
previous                  NA
poutcome                  NA
---
Signif. codes:
0 '***' 0.001 '**' 0.01 '*' 0.05 '.' 0.1 ' ' 1

(Dispersion parameter for binomial family taken to be 1)

    Null deviance: 8724.4  on 22604  degrees of freedom
Residual deviance: 5046.9  on 22580  degrees of freedom
AIC: 5096.9

Number of Fisher Scoring iterations: 7
Jobhousemaid, maritalmarried, maritalsingle, homeowner, loa
ns, default, contact, length
```

The conclusion we make here is Response to a Marketing Campaign is predictable using JOB, MARITAL, HOMEOWNER, LOANS, DEFAULT, CONTACT and LENGTH.

Previously, we divided the data into a training set and test set of equal length. We will use the training set to build a new logistic regression model and the test set to make predictions based on the model.

The next step is to fit a logistic regression model to the training set.

```
bank.model2 <- glm( RESP ~ job+marital+homeowner+loans+defa
ult+contact+length , data = bank_train, family=binomial(log
it))
```

Now perform an analysis of variance (ANOVA)

```
anova(bank.model2, test="Chisq")
```

```
Analysis of Deviance Table

Model: binomial, link: logit

Response: RESP

Terms added sequentially (first to last)


            Df Deviance Resid. Df Resid. Dev  Pr(>Chi)
NULL                        22604     8724.4
job         11     14.7      22593     8709.6 0.1947876
marital      2     53.8      22591     8655.8 2.055e-12
homeowner    1     13.3      22590     8642.6 0.0002695
loans        1      1.6      22589     8640.9 0.2031058
default      1      0.5      22588     8640.5 0.4898255
contact      1     62.4      22587     8578.0 2.743e-15
length       1   3524.5      22586     5053.5 < 2.2e-16

NULL
job
marital   ***
homeowner ***
loans
default
contact   ***
length    ***
---
Signif. codes:
0 '***' 0.001 '**' 0.01 '*' 0.05 '.' 0.1 ' ' 1
```

The ANOVA gives us what amounts to regression coefficients with standard errors and a z-test. Three of the coefficients are significantly different from zero, SMOKE, RACE, and LWT, which supports our model analysis above. The deviance was reduced by 3670.9 points (8724.4 − 5053.5) on 18 degrees of freedom, for a p-value of:

```
pval<-1 - pchisq(5053.5, df=18)
pval
```

```
[1] 0
```

Now, we construct a frequency distribution to use for constructing a plot of the fitted data.

```
with(bank_train(RESP))
```

```
RESP
   0     1
21517 1088
```

This tells us that the percent of deposit accounts acquired is about 1088/21517 = 5%.

Finally, we plot the fitted data

```
plot(bank.model$fitted)
abline(v=11303,col="red",lwd=2)
abline(h=.25,col="green",lwd=2)
abline(h=.5,col="green",lwd=2)
abline(h=.75,col="green",lwd=2)
text(15,.6,"RESP = 0")
text(400,.1,"RESP = 1")
```

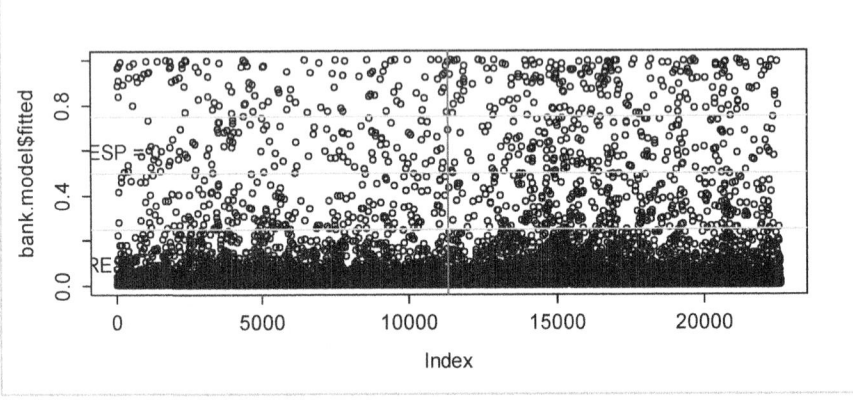

Figure 15-6. Plot of the Bank model with fitted values

For our next task, we need to load the library "gains". Here we will partition our data and build a new logistic regression using a training set and then use the fitted model to make a prediction using a test set. After we have the predicted values, we will use gains to construct a gains table and plot.gains to plot several outcomes of the gains function.

```
require(gains)
```

```
Loading required package: gains
Warning message:
package 'gains' was built under R version 3.1.3
```

Now we predict values using the fitted model.

```
bank.pred<-predict(bank.model2, newdata = bank_test, type="
response")
```

Note the command, predict(fitted model, test set, type of prediction), fits the test dated using the logistic regression model that we constructed from the training set.

Now we use our fitted values from the logistic regression and the values we just predicted to calculate the gains table.

```
bank.gains<-gains(actual=bank.model$fitted.values,predicted
=bank.pred,optimal=TRUE)
bank.gains
```

Depth of File	N	Cume N	Mean Resp	Cume Mean Resp	Cume Pct of Total
10	2260	2260	0.04	0.04	9.00%
20	2261	4521	0.05	0.05	19.60%
30	2260	6781	0.04	0.05	29.00%
40	2261	9042	0.05	0.05	39.60%
50	2260	11302	0.05	0.05	49.50%
60	2262	13564	0.05	0.05	60.10%
70	2259	15823	0.04	0.05	69.30%
80	2261	18084	0.05	0.05	79.60%
90	2266	20350	0.05	0.05	89.90%
100	2255	22605	0.05	0.05	100.00%

Depth			Optimal	Optimal	Mean

of	Lift	Cume	Lift	Cume	Model
File	Index	Lift	Index	Lift	Score
10	90	90	720	720	0.38
20	106	98	102	411	0.07
30	93	97	50	291	0.04
40	107	99	34	226	0.03
50	99	99	26	186	0.02
60	106	100	21	159	0.02
70	92	99	17	138	0.01
80	103	99	14	123	0.01
90	103	100	10	110	0.01
100	101	100	7	100	0.01

Now we plot the "Mean Response", "Cumulative Mean Response", and "Mean Predicted Response" using the gains output.

```
plot(with(subset(bank,bank_train==0), bank.gains), main="Ba
nk Gains Table Plot")
```

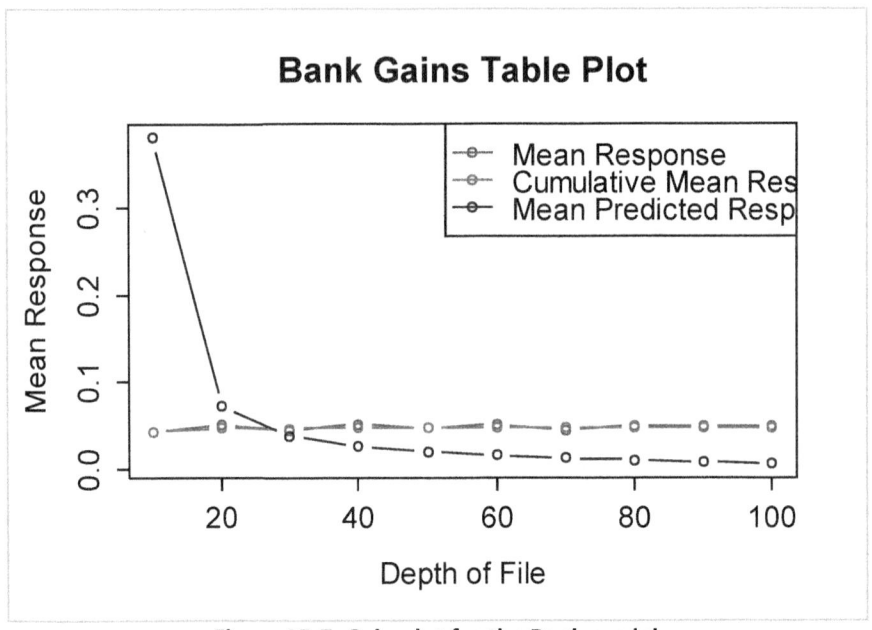

Figure 15-7. Gain plot for the Bank model

Create the following individual plots: Cumulative Percent of Total, Cumulative Mean Response, cumulative Lift, Optimal Cumulative Lift, and Mean Prediction.

```
plot(bank.gains$cume.mean.resp,type="l",main="Mean Response
",,lwd=2)
```

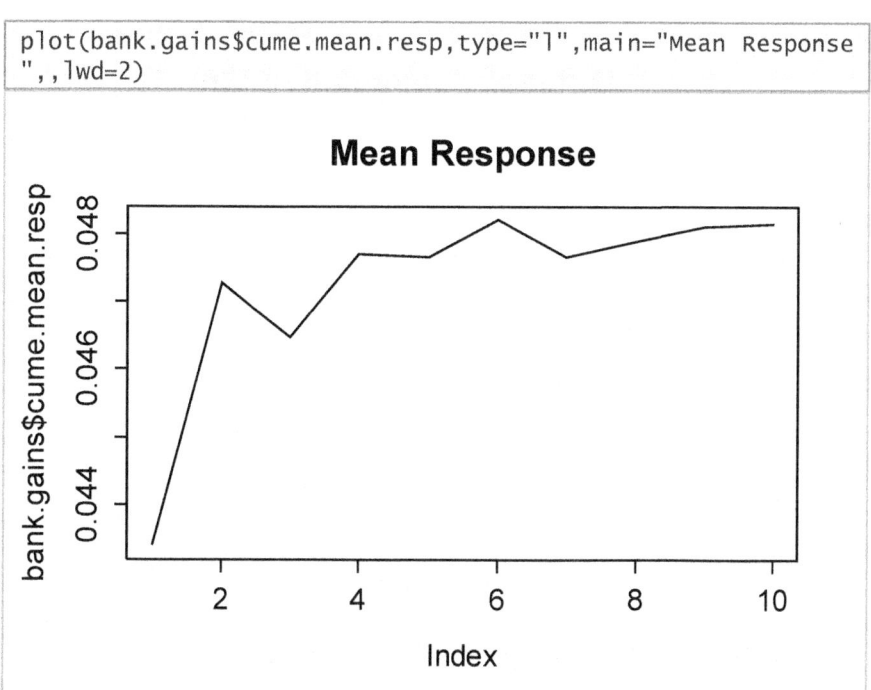

Figure 15-8. Plot of the Mean Response from the Gains Table

```
plot(bank.gains$opt.cume.lift,type="l",main="Optimal Cummul
ative Lift",,lwd=2)
```

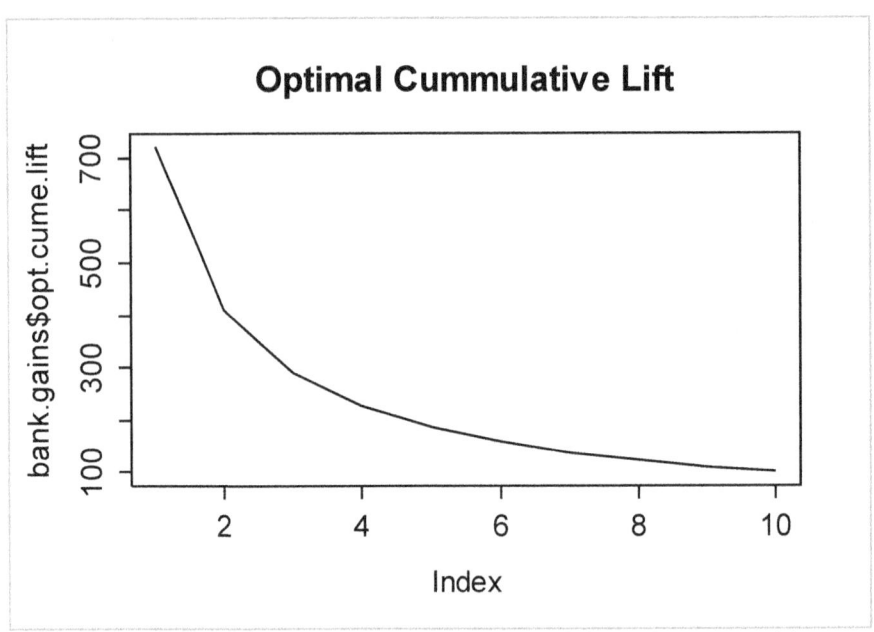

Figure 15-9. Plot of the Optimal Cumulative Lift from the Gains Table

```
plot(bank.gains$mean.prediction,type="l", lwd=2, main="Mean
Predicted")
```

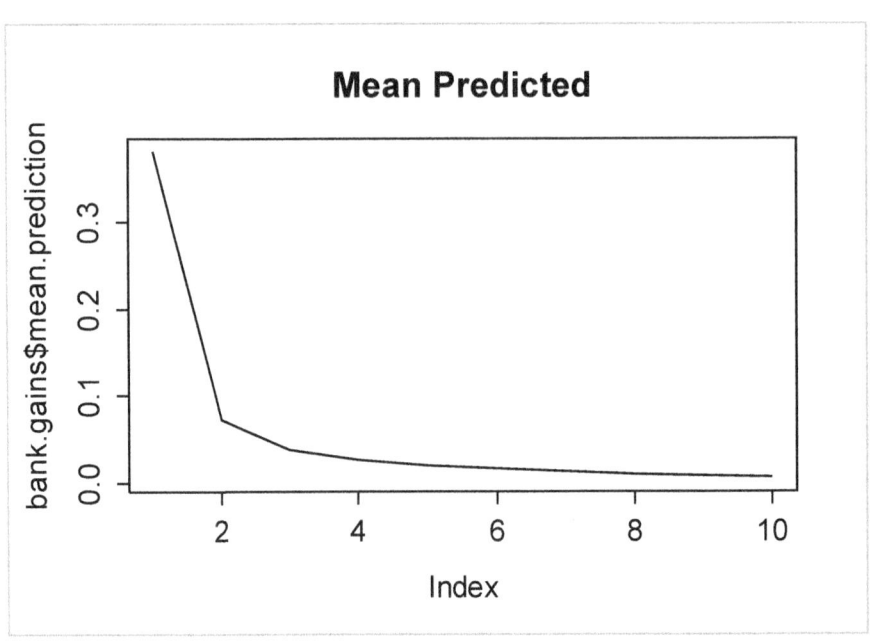

Figure 15-10. Plot of the Mean Predicted Response from the Gains Table

Logistic Regression: Multiple Numerical Predictors

Inattentional Blindness (IB) refers to situations in which a person fails to see an obvious stimulus right in front of his eyes. It is hypothesized that IB could be predicted from performance on the Stroop Color Word test. This test produces three scores: "W" (word alone, i.e., a score derived from reading a list of color words such as red, green, black), "C" (color alone, in which a score is derived from naming the color in which a series of Xs are printed), and "CW" (the Stroop task, in which a score is derived from the subject's attempt to name the color in which a color word is printed when the word and the color do not agree). The data are in the following table, in which the response, "seen", is coded as 0=no and 1=yes...

	seen	W	C	CW
1	0	126	86	64
2	0	118	76	54
3	0	61	66	44
4	0	69	48	32
5	0	57	59	42
6	0	78	64	53
7	0	114	61	41
8	0	81	85	47
9	0	73	57	33
10	0	93	50	45
11	0	116	92	49
12	0	156	70	45
13	0	90	66	48
14	0	120	73	49
15	0	99	68	44
16	0	113	110	47
17	0	103	78	52
18	0	123	61	28
19	0	86	65	42
20	0	99	77	51
21	0	102	77	54
22	0	120	74	53
23	0	128	100	56
24	0	100	89	56
25	0	95	61	37
26	0	80	55	36

```
27     0  98   92 51
28     0 111   90 52
29     0 101   85 45
30     0 102   78 51
31     1 100   66 48
32     1 112   78 55
33     1  82   84 37
34     1  72   63 46
35     1  72   65 47
36     1  89   71 49
37     1 108   46 29
38     1  88   70 49
39     1 116   83 67
40     1 100   69 39
41     1  99   70 43
42     1  93   63 36
43     1 100   93 62
44     1 110   76 56
45     1 100   83 36
46     1 106   71 49
47     1 115  112 66
48     1 120   87 54
49     1  97   82 41
```

To get them into R, try this first...

```
file = "http://ww2.coastal.edu/kingw/statistics/R-tutorials
/text/gorilla.csv"
read.csv(file) -> gorilla
str(gorilla)
```

```
'data.frame':   49 obs. of  4 variables:
 $ seen: int  0 0 0 0 0 0 0 0 0 0 ...
 $ W   : int  126 118 61 69 57 78 114 81 73 93 ...
 $ C   : int  86 76 66 48 59 64 61 85 57 50 ...
 $ CW  : int  64 54 44 32 42 53 41 47 33 45 ...
```

If that doesn't work (and it should), try copying and pasting this script into R at the command prompt...

```
### Begin copying here.
gorilla = data.frame(rep(c(0,1),c(30,19)),
        c(126,118,61,69,57,78,114,81,73,93,116,156,90,120,
99,113,103,123,86,99,102,120,128,100,95,80,98,111,101,102,1
```

```
00,112,82,72,72,89,108,88,116,100,99,93,100,110,100,106,115
,120,97),
        c(86,76,66,48,59,64,61,85,57,50,92,70,66,73,68,110
,78,61,65,77,77,74,100,89,61,55,92,90,85,78,66,78,84,63,65,
71,46,70,83,69,70,63,93,76,83,71,112,87,82),
        c(64,54,44,32,42,53,41,47,33,45,49,45,48,49,44,47,
52,28,42,51,54,53,56,56,37,36,51,52,45,51,48,55,37,46,47,49
,29,49,67,39,43,36,62,56,36,49,66,54,41))
colnames(gorilla) = c("seen","W","C","CW")
str(gorilla)
### End copying here.
```

And if that does not work, well, you know what you have to do! We might begin like this...

```
> cor(gorilla)              ### a correlation matrix
            seen          W          C         CW
seen   1.00000000 -0.03922667 0.05437115 0.06300865
W     -0.03922667  1.00000000 0.43044418 0.35943580
C      0.05437115  0.43044418 1.00000000 0.64463361
CW     0.06300865  0.35943580 0.64463361 1.00000000
```

...or like this...

```
with(gorilla, tapply(W, seen, mean))
```

```
        0         1
100.40000  98.89474
```

```
with(gorilla, tapply(C, seen, mean))
```

```
        0         1
73.76667 75.36842
```

```
with(gorilla, tapply(CW, seen, mean))
```

```
        0         1
46.70000 47.84211
```

The Stroop scale scores are moderately positively correlated with each other, but none of them appears to be related to the "seen" response variable, at least not to any impressive extent. There doesn't appear to be much here to look at. Let's have a go at it anyway.

Since the response is a binomial variable, a logistic regression can be done as follows...

```
glm.out = glm(seen ~ W * C * CW, family=binomial(logit),
    data=gorilla)
summary(glm.out)
```

```
Call:
glm(formula = seen ~ W * C * CW, family = binomial(logit),
data = gorilla)

Deviance Residuals:
    Min       1Q   Median       3Q      Max
-1.8073  -0.9897  -0.5740   1.2368   1.7362

Coefficients:
              Estimate Std. Error z value Pr(>|z|)
(Intercept) -1.323e+02  8.037e+01  -1.646   0.0998 .
W            1.316e+00  7.514e-01   1.751   0.0799 .
C            2.129e+00  1.215e+00   1.753   0.0797 .
CW           2.206e+00  1.659e+00   1.329   0.1837
W:C         -2.128e-02  1.140e-02  -1.866   0.0621 .
W:CW        -2.201e-02  1.530e-02  -1.439   0.1502
C:CW        -3.582e-02  2.413e-02  -1.485   0.1376
W:C:CW       3.579e-04  2.225e-04   1.608   0.1078
---
Signif.codes:0 '***' 0.001 '**' 0.01 '*' 0.05 '.' 0.1 ' ' 1

(Dispersion parameter for binomial family taken to be 1)

    Null deviance: 65.438  on 48  degrees of freedom
Residual deviance: 57.281  on 41  degrees of freedom
AIC: 73.281

Number of Fisher Scoring iterations: 5
```

```
anova (glm.out, test="Chisq")
```

```
Analysis of Deviance Table

Model: binomial, link: logit
```

```
Response: seen

Terms added sequentially (first to last)

         Df Deviance Resid. Df Resid. Dev Pr(>Chi)
NULL                     48      65.438
W         1   0.0755     47      65.362  0.78351
C         1   0.3099     46      65.052  0.57775
CW        1   0.1061     45      64.946  0.74467
W:C       1   2.3632     44      62.583  0.12423
W:CW      1   0.5681     43      62.015  0.45103
C:CW      1   1.4290     42      60.586  0.23193
W:C:CW    1   3.3053     41      57.281  0.06906 .
---
Signif.codes:0 '***' 0.001 '**' 0.01 '*' 0.05 '.' 0.1 ' ' 1
```

Two different extractor functions have been used to see the results of our analysis. What do they mean?

The first gives us what amount to regression coefficients with standard errors and a z-test, as we saw in the single variable example above. None of the coefficients are significantly different from zero (but a few are close). The deviance was reduced by 8.157 points on 7 degrees of freedom, for a p-value of...

```
1 - pchisq(8.157, df=7)
```

```
[1] 0.3189537
```

Overall, the model appears to have performed poorly, showing no significant reduction in deviance (no significant difference from the null model).

The second print out shows the same overall reduction in deviance, from 65.438 to 57.281 on 7 degrees of freedom. In this print out, however, the reduction in deviance is shown for each term, added sequentially first to last. Of note is the three-way interaction term, which produced a nearly significant reduction in deviance of 3.305 on 1 degree of freedom (p = 0.069).

In the event you are encouraged by any of this, the following graph might be revealing...

```
plot(glm.out$fitted)
abline(v=30.5,col="red")
abline(h=.3,col="green")
abline(h=.5,col="green")
text(15,.9,"seen = 0")
text(40,.9,"seen = 1")
```

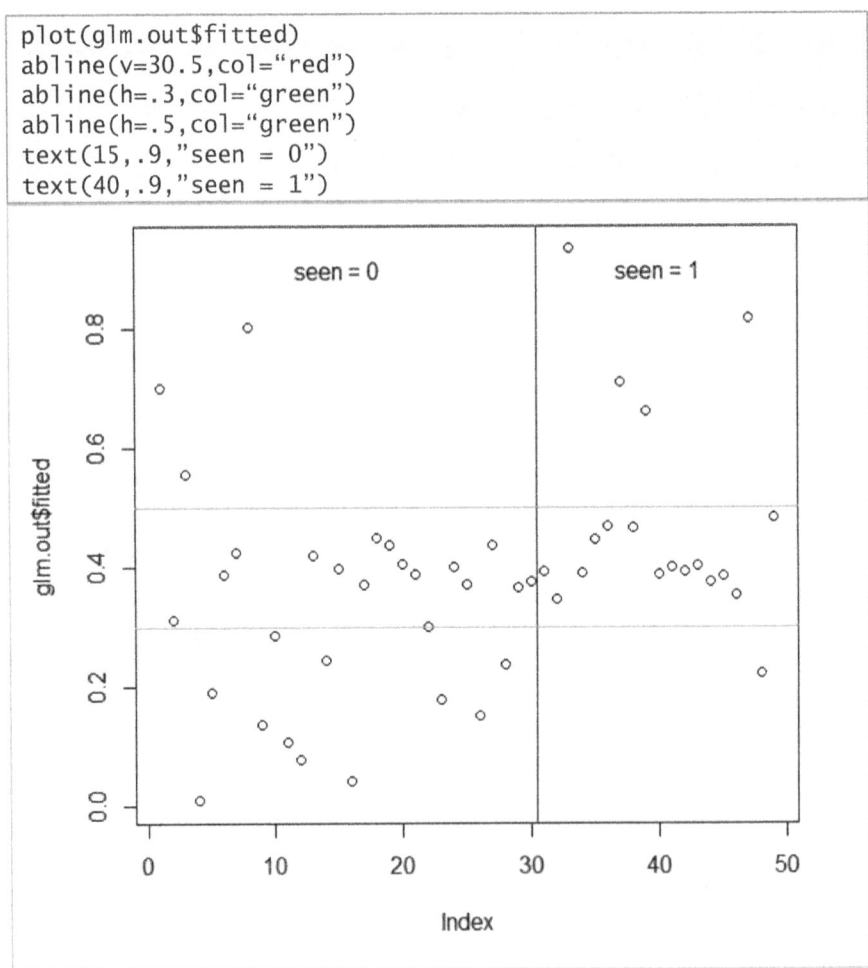

Figure 15-11. Plot of the model with fitted values

We leave it up to you to interpret this.

Logistic Regression: Categorical Predictors

Categorical data are commonly encountered in three forms: a frequency table or cross-tabulation, a flat table, or a case-by-case data frame. Let's begin with the last of these. Copy and paste the following lines ALL AT ONCE into R. That is, highlight these lines with your mouse, hit Ctrl-C on your keyboard, click at a command prompt in R, and hit Ctrl-V on your keyboard, and hit Enter if necessary, i.e., if R hasn't returned to a command prompt. On the Mac, use Command-C and Command-V. This will execute these lines as a script and create a data frame called "ucb" in your workspace. WARNING: Your workspace will also be cleared, so save anything you don't want to lose first.

```
# Begin copying here.
rm(list=ls())
gender = rep(c("female","male"),c(1835,2691))
admitted = rep(c("yes","no","yes","no"),c(557,1278,1198,149
    3))
dept = rep(c("A","B","C","D","E","F","A","B","C","D","E","F
    "), c(89,17,202,131,94,24,19,8,391,244,299,317))
dept2 = rep(c("A","B","C","D","E","F","A","B","C","D","E","
    F"), c(512,353,120,138,53,22,313,207,205,279,138,351))
department = c(dept,dept2)
ucb = data.frame(gender,admitted,department)
rm(gender,admitted,dept,dept2,department)
ls()
# End copying here.
[1] "ucb"
```

Data sets that are purely categorical are not economically represented in case-by-case data frames, and so the built-in data sets that are purely categorical come in the form of tables (contingency tables or crosstabulations). We have just taken the data from one of these (the "UCBAdmissions" built-in data set) and turned it into a case-by-case data frame. It's the classic University of California, Berkeley, admissions data from 1973 describing admissions into six different graduate programs broken down by gender. Let's examine the "UCBAdmissions" data set.

```
ftable(UCBAdmissions, col.vars="Admit")
```

		Admit	Admitted	Rejected
Gender	Dept			
Male	A		512	313
	B		353	207
	C		120	205
	D		138	279
	E		53	138

	F	22	351
Female	A	89	19
	B	17	8
	C	202	391
	D	131	244
	E	94	299
	F	24	317

The data are from 1973 and show admissions by gender to the top six grad programs at the University of California, Berkeley. Looked at as a two-way table, there appears to be a bias against admitting women…

```
dimnames(UCBAdmissions)
```

```
$Admit
[1] "Admitted" "Rejected"

$Gender
[1] "Male"    "Female"

$Dept
[1] "A" "B" "C" "D" "E" "F"
```

```
margin.table(UCBAdmissions, c(2,1))
```

```
         Admit
Gender    Admitted Rejected
  Male        1198     1493
  Female       557     1278
```

However, there are also relationships between "Gender" and "Dept" as well as between "Dept" and "Admit", which means the above relationship may be confounded by "Dept" (or "Dept" might be a lurking variable, in the language of traditional regression analysis). Perhaps a logistic regression with the binomial variable "Admit" as the response can tease these variables apart.

If there is a way to conveniently get that flat table into a data frame (without splitting an infinitive), I do not know it. So I had to do this…

```
ucb.df = data.frame(gender=rep(c("Male","Female"),c(6,6)),
    dept=rep(LETTERS[1:6],2), yes=c(512,353,120,138,53,22,8
```

```
     9,17,202,131,94,24), no=c(313,207,205,279,138,351,19,8,
     391,244,299,317))
ucb.df
```

```
     gender dept yes   no
1     Male    A  512  313
2     Male    B  353  207
3     Male    C  120  205
4     Male    D  138  279
5     Male    E   53  138
6     Male    F   22  351
7   Female    A   89   19
8   Female    B   17    8
9   Female    C  202  391
10  Female    D  131  244
11  Female    E   94  299
12  Female    F   24  317
```

Once again, we do not have a binary coded response variable, so the last two columns of this data frame will have to be bound into the columns of a table to serve as the response in the model formula...

```
mod.form = "cbind(yes,no) ~ gender * dept"
glm.out = glm(mod.form,family=binomial(logit),data=ucb.df)
```

We used a trick here of storing the model formula in a data object, and then entering the name of this object into the glm( ) function. That way, if we made a mistake in the model formula (or want to run an alternative model), we have only to edit the "mod.form" object to do it.

Let's see what we have found...

```
options(show.signif.stars=F)  # turn off significance
                              # stars (optional)
anova(glm.out, test="Chisq")
```

```
Analysis of Deviance Table

Model: binomial, link: logit

Response: cbind(yes, no)

Terms added sequentially (first to last)
```

	Df	Deviance	Resid. Df	Resid. Dev	Pr(>Chi)
NULL			11	877.06	
gender	1	93.45	10	783.61	< 2.2e-16
dept	5	763.40	5	20.20	< 2.2e-16
gender:dept	5	20.20	0	0.00	0.001144

This is a saturated model, meaning we have used up all our degrees of freedom, and there is no residual deviance left over at the end. Saturated models always fit the data perfectly. In this case, it appears the saturated model is required to explain the data adequately. If we leave off the interaction term, for example, we will be left with a residual deviance of 20.2 on 5 degrees of freedom, and the model will be rejected ($p = 0.001144$). It appears all three terms are making a significant contribution to the model.

How they are contributing appears if we use the other extractor...

```
summary(glm.out)
```

```
Call:
glm(formula = mod.form, family = binomial(logit), data = uc
b.df)

Deviance Residuals:
 [1]  0  0  0  0  0  0  0  0  0  0  0  0

Coefficients:
                   Estimate Std. Error  z value Pr(>|z|)
(Intercept)          1.5442     0.2527    6.110 9.94e-10
genderMale          -1.0521     0.2627   -4.005 6.21e-05
deptB               -0.7904     0.4977   -1.588  0.11224
deptC               -2.2046     0.2672   -8.252  < 2e-16
deptD               -2.1662     0.2750   -7.878 3.32e-15
deptE               -2.7013     0.2790   -9.682  < 2e-16
deptF               -4.1250     0.3297  -12.512  < 2e-16
genderMale:deptB     0.8321     0.5104    1.630  0.10306
genderMale:deptC     1.1770     0.2996    3.929 8.53e-05
genderMale:deptD     0.9701     0.3026    3.206  0.00135
genderMale:deptE     1.2523     0.3303    3.791  0.00015
genderMale:deptF     0.8632     0.4027    2.144  0.03206

(Dispersion parameter for binomial family taken to be 1)
```

```
    Null deviance:  8.7706e+02  on 11  degrees of freedom
Residual deviance: -1.6676e-13  on  0  degrees of freedom
AIC: 92.94

Number of Fisher Scoring iterations: 3
```

These are the regression coefficients for each predictor in the model, with the base level of each factor being suppressed. Remember, we are predicting log odd"...

```
exp(-1.0521)         # antilog of the genderMale coefficient
```

```
[1] 0.3492037
```

```
1/exp(-1.0521)
```

```
[1] 2.863658
```

This shows that men were actually at a significant *disadvantage* when department and the interaction are controlled. The odds of a male being admitted were only 0.35 times the odds of a female being admitted. The reciprocal of this turns it on its head. All else being equal, the odds of female being admitted were 2.86 times the odds of a male being admitted.

Each coefficient compares the corresponding predictor to the base level. So...

```
exp(-2.2046)
```

```
[1] 0.1102946
```

...the odds of being admitted to department C were only about 1/9th the odds of being admitted to department A, all else being equal. If you want to compare, for example, department C to department D, do this...

```
exp(-2.2046) / exp(-2.1662)        # C:A / D:A leaves C:D
```

```
[1] 0.9623279
```

All else equal, the odds of being admitted to department C were 0.96 times the odds of being admitted to department D. (To be honest, I am not sure I am comfortable with the interaction in this model. You might want to examine the interaction, and if you think it doesn't merit inclusion, run the model again without it. Statistics are nice, but in the end it's what makes sense that should rule the day.)

Exercises

1. Using the R-Studio with the Polypharm dataset, construct a predictive model to project the likelihood that a member of the target audience will take drugs from more than three different classes.

2. Using SAS Studio and the Adolescent_Placement dataset, construct a multinomial logistic regression model with "Placement" as the target variable.

Works Cited

Aldrich, J. (2005). Fisher and Regression. *Statistical Science, 20*(4), 401–417. doi:10.1214/088342305000000331

Bhalla, D. (2016). *Weight of Evidence (WOE) and Information Value Explained.* Retrieved 03 09, 2017, from Listen Data: http://www.listendata.com/2015/03/weight-of-evidence-woe-and-information.html

Bhandari, M., & Joensson, A. (2008). *Clinical Research for Surgeons.* Thieme.

Bishop, C. (2006). *Pattern Recognition and Machine Learning.* New York: Springer. Retrieved from http://www.hua.edu.vn/khoa/fita/wp-content/uploads/2013/08/Pattern-Recognition-and-Machine-Learning-Christophe-M-Bishop.pdf

Boyd, C. R., Tolson, M. A., & Copes, W. S. (1987). Evaluating trauma care: The TRISS method. Trauma Score and the Injury Severity Score. *The Journal of trauma, 27*(4), 370–378.

Chen, J., Zhu, J., Wang, Z., Zheng, X., & Zhang, B. (2013). Scalable Inference for Logistic-Normal Topic Models. In *Advances in Neural Information Processing Systems* (p. 2445{2453).

Chib, S., & Greenberg, E. (1995). Understanding the metropolis-hastings algorithm. *The American Statistician, 49*(4). doi:10.1080/00031305.1995.10476177

Cohen, J., Cohen, P., West, S., & Aiken, L. (2002). *Applied Multiple Regression/Correlation Analysis for the Behavioral Sciences* (3rd ed.). Routledge.

Da, Y., & Xiurun, G. (2005). An improved PSO-based ANN with simulated annealing technique. In T. e. Villmann, *New Aspects in Neurocomputing: 11th European Symposium on Artificial Neural*

Networks. New York: Elsevier. doi:10.1016/j.neucom.2004.07.002

Edgeworth, F. Y. (1908, Dec). On the probable errors of frequency-constants. *Journal of the Royal Statistical Society, 71*(4), 651–678. doi:doi:10.2307/2339378

Everitt, B. S. (2002). *Cambridge Dictionary of Statistics.* Cambridge University Press.

Fisher, R. (1922). The goodness of fit of regression formulae, and the distribution of regression coefficients. *Journal of the Royal Statistical Society, 85*(4), pp. 597–612. doi:10.2307/2341124

Fisher, R. A. (1954). *Statistical Methods for Research Workers* (12th ed.). Edinburgh: Oliver and Boyd.

Galton, F. (1877). Typical laws of heredity. *Nature, 15,* pp. 492–495, 512–514, 532–533.

Galton, F. (1885). Presidential address, Section H, Anthropology.

Galton, F. (1989). Kinship and Correlation (reprinted 1989). *Statistical Science, 4*(2), pp. 80-86. doi:10.1214/ss/1177012581

Gauss, C. (1823). Theoria combinationis observationum erroribus minimis obnoxiae. Retrieved 11 20, 2106

Gauss, C. F. (1809). Theoria Motus Corporum Coelestium in Sectionibus Conicis Solem Ambientum. Retrieved 12 29, 2016

Generalized Linear Models, J. A., & Wedderburn, R. M. (1972). Generalized Linear Models. *Journal of the Royal Statistical Society. Series A (General), 135*(3), 370-384. doi:10.2307/2344614

George, E., & McCullochb, R. (1993). Variable Selection via Gibbs Sampling. *Journal of the American Statistical Association,*

88(423). doi:10.1080/01621459.1993.10476353

Gleick, J. (1987, October 23). A.N. Kolmogorov Dies at 84; Top Russian Mathematician. *The Wall Street Journal*. New York. Retrieved 2 27, 2017, from http://www.nytimes.com/1987/10/23/obituaries/an-kolmogorov-dies-at-84-top-russian-mathematician.html

Gopalan, P., Hofman, J. M., & Blei, D. (2014). Scalable Recommendation with Poisson Factorization. arXiv.org.

Greene, W. (2011). *Econometric Analysis* (7th ed.). New York: Prentice Hall.

Greenfield B, H. M., Dougherty, G., Zhang, X., Fombonne, E., Lis, E., Lapalme-Remis, & Harnden, B. (2008). Previously suicidal adolescents: Predictors of six-month outcome. *Journal of the Canadian Association of Child and Adolescent Psychiatry, 17*(4), 197–201. Retrieved from https://www.ncbi.nlm.nih.gov/pmc/articles/PMC2583916/

Hale, G., & Hale, G. (2006). *Uneasy Partnership: The Politics of Business and Government in Canada.* Toronto: University of Toronto Press.

Harrell, F. (2010). *Regression Modeling Strategies: With Applications to Linear Models, Logistic Regression, and Survival Analysis.* New York: Springer-Verlag.

Harrell, F. E. (2001). *Regression modeling strategies.* New York: Springer.

Hogg, R. V., & Craig, A. T. (1978). *Introduction to Mathematical Statistics* (4th ed.). New York: Macmillan.

Hosmer, D. W., & Lemeshow, S. (2000). *Applied Logistic Regression* (2nd ed.). New York: Wiley-Interscience Publication.

James, G., Witten, D., Hastie, T., & Tibshirani, R. (2013). *An Introduction* to *Statistical Learning.* New York: Springer.

Kutcher, S., & Szumilas, M. (2009). *Suicide Risk Management BMJ Point of Care [Internet].* London: BMJ Publishing Group; 2009.

Lahman, S. (2015). The Lahman Baseball Database. Retrieved 4 21, 2016, from http://www.baseball1.com

Legendre, A. M. (1805). Nouvelles méthodes pour la détermination des orbites des comètes. Paris. Retrieved 01 15, 2017

Lin, A. Z., & Hsieh, T. (2014). Expanding the Use of Weight of Evidence and Information Value to Continuous Dependent Variables for Variable Reduction and Scorecard Development. *SESUG 2014,* (pp. 1-23).

Mark, J., & Goldberg, M. (2001). Multiple Regression Analysis and Mass Assessment: A Review of the Issues. *The Appraisal Journal,* 89– 109.

McCullagh, P., & Nelder, J. (1989). *Generalized Linear Models* (2nd ed.). Boca Raton: Chapman and Hall/CRC.

Menard, S. (2002). *Applied Logistic Regression* (2nd ed.). SAGE.

Mogull, R. G. (2004). *Second-Semester Applied Statistics.* Kendall/Hunt Publishing Company.

Moro, S., Laureano, R., & Cortez, p. (2011). Using Data Mining for Bank Direct Marketing: An Application of the CRISP-DM Methodology. In e. a. P. Novais (Ed.), *Proceedings of the European Simulation and Modelling Conference - ESM'2011,* (pp. 117-121). Guimaraes, Portugal.

Myers, J. H., & Forgy, E. W. (1963). The Development of Numerical Credit Evaluation Systems. *J. Amer. Statist. Assoc., 49*(12), 799–806. doi:10.1080/01621459.1963.10500889

Nelder, J., & Wedderburn, R. (1989). Generalized Linear Models. *Journal of the Royal Statistical Society. Series A (General), 135*(3), 370–384. doi:10.2307/2344614

Owen, A. B. (2001). *Empirical Likelihood.* Boca Raton, FL: CRC Press.

Palei, S. K., & Das, S. K. (2009). Logistic regression model for prediction of roof fall risks in bord and pillar workings in coal mines: An approach. *Safety Science, 47*, 88. doi:10.1016/j.ssci.2008.01.002

Park, S. Y., & Bera, A. K. (2009). Maximum entropy autoregressive conditional heteroskedasticity model. *Journal of Econometrics,* 219–230. doi:10.1016/j.jeconom.2008.12.014

Pearson, K., Yule, G., Blanchard, N., & Lee, A. (1903). (1903). "The Law of Ancestral Heredity". . . 2 (2): . doi:10.1093/biomet/2.2.211. *Biometrika, 2*(2), pp. 211–236. doi:10.1093/biomet/2.2.211

Peduzzi, P., Concato, J., Kemper, E., Holford, T., & Feinstein, A. (1996). A simulation study of the number of events per variable in logistic regression analysis. *Journal of Clinical Epidemiology, 49*(12), 1373–9. doi:10.1016/s0895-4356(96)00236-3

Prentice, R., & Pyke, R. (1979). Logistic disease incidence models and case-control studies. *Biometrika, 66*(3), 403-411. doi:10.1093/biomet/66.3.403

Ramcharan, R. (2006, March). Regressions: Why Are Economists Obessessed with Them? Retrieved 12 11, 2016

Rational Choice Theory. (n.d.). *Invetopedia.* Retrieved from http://www.investopedia.com/terms/r/rational-choice-theory.asp#ixzz4a8XfUnwz

Sanizah, A., Habshah, M., & Norazan, M. R. (2010). Robust Estimators in Logistic regression: A Comparative Simulation Study. *Journal of Modern Applied Statistical Methods, 9*(2), 502-511.

Strano, M., & Colosimo, B. (2006). Logistic regression analysis for experimental determination of forming limit diagrams. *International Journal of Machine Tools and Manufacture, 46*(6). doi:10.1016/j.ijmachtools.2005.07.005

Szklo, M., & Nieto, F. J. (2997). *Epidemiology: Beyond the basics* (2nd ed.). Sudbury, MA: Jones and Bartlett Publishers.

Venter, J. H., & de la Rey, T. (2007). Detecting outliers using weights. *South African Satistical Journal, 41*, 127-160.

Walsh, B. (2004, April 26). *Markov Chain Monte Carlo and Gibbs Sampling.* Retrieved from Lecture Notes for EEB 581: http://web.mit.edu/~wingated/www/introductions/mcmc-gibbs-intro.pdf

Wilks, S. S. (1938). The Large-Sample Distribution of the Likelihood Ratio for Testing Composite Hypotheses. *Annals of Mathematical Statistics, 9*, 60–62. doi:doi:10.1214/aoms/1177732360

Wilks, S. S. (1938). Weighting systems for linear functions of correlated variables when there is no dependent variable. *Psychometrika, 3*(1), 23-40. doi:10.1007/BF02287917

Wilks, S. S. (1962). *Mathematical Statistics.* New York: John Wiley & Sons.

Yule, G. U. (1897). On the Theory of Correlation. *Journal of the Royal Statistical Society, 60*(4), pp. 812–54. doi:10.2307/2979746

Index

CPSIA information can be obtained
at www.ICGtesting.com
Printed in the USA
BVOW06*0138250118

506205BV00004B/4/P